1999

√B

PODHORETZ N

D0499997

NORMAN PODHORETZ

EX-FRIENDS

*Falling Out with Allen Ginsberg,
Lionel & Diana Trilling, Lillian Hellman,
Hannah Arendt, and Norman Mailer*

THE FREE PRESS

THE FREE PRESS
A Division of Simon & Schuster Inc.
1230 Avenue of the Americas
New York, NY 10020

THE FREE PRESS and colophon are trademarks
of Simon & Schuster Inc.

Designed by Carla Bolte

Manufactured in the United States of America

10 9 8 7 6 5 4 3 2 1

Library of Congress Cataloging-in-Publication Data

Podhoretz, Norman.
    Ex-friends : Falling out with Allen Ginsberg, Lionel and Diana Trilling,
    Lillian Hellman, Hannah Arendt, and Norman Mailer/ Norman Podhoretz.
        p.   cm.
    Includes index.
    ISBN 0-684-85594-1
    1. Podhoretz, Norman—Friends and associates.   2. Politics and
    literature—United States—History—20th century.   3. United States
    —Intellectual life—20th century.   4. Authors, American—20th
    century—Biography.   5. Intellectuals—United States—Biography.
    6. Critics—United States—Biography.   I. Title.
    PS29.P63A3   1999
    818'.543—dc21
    [b]   98-26687
                                                            CIP

In 1982 I had two infant grandsons, Jacob Abrams and Samuel Munson, to whom I dedicated a book. Since then, eight more grandchildren have been granted to me, and it is to these wondrous and beloved creatures (listed in the order in which they came into the world) that I wish to dedicate this book: Sarah Abrams, Noam Blum, Zachary Munson, Joseph Abrams, Alon Blum, Leah Munson, and the twins Boaz and Avital Blum.

CONTENTS

HOW OUR "FAMILY"
BROKE UP

I HAVE OFTEN SAID THAT IF I WISH TO NAME-DROP, I have only to list my ex-friends. The remark always gets a laugh, but, in addition to being funny, it has the advantage of being true.

Of course, the main subjects on whom I concentrate here represent only a small sample of the ex-friends I have made whose names are famous enough to be worth dropping. The reason I have decided to focus on these half-dozen in particular is that all of them were once, and for a considerable period of time, very close to me. This was true even of Allen Ginsberg, whose closeness consisted not in a genuine friendship but in the many years we went back and the recurrent visions and dreams he had about me. As it happens, these special ex-friends were all Jewish in one way or another, perhaps because the literary-intellectual milieu in which I lived was predominantly Jewish, or perhaps because some tribalistic instinct of which we were loftily unaware drew us together.

Nevertheless, I can claim with all due deference to current law and fashion that I am an equal-opportunity maker of famous ex-friends, as will become clear from the many eminently droppable non-Jewish names that crop up throughout the chapters that follow. I was closer to some of these people than to others, but to none was I as close as to the ones I focus on in this book, and my friendly relations with most of them lasted a much shorter time. A few of these latter make cameo appearances whenever their presence is required by the stories of the leading characters. Still others—some of them still well known and some (*sic transit*) with names once considered worth dropping but now almost entirely forgotten—are also mentioned in passing. But even adding all these to the main characters does not begin to exhaust the list of famous people whose friendship I have managed to lose or throw away in the past thirty years.

Thirty years. That means from the late 1960s, when I was approaching forty, to the present. Before the late 1960s, I was much better at making friends of strangers than at making enemies of friends. Strange as it may seem to those who have come to know me in my rather reclusive dotage, as a young man I was very outgoing and gregarious and curious about other people—what they were like, what they did, and how they did it. It will seem even stranger to my more recent acquaintances that in my younger years I was also full of fun, as Norman Mailer confirmed when he said that I was "merrier" in the "old days." The same word was once used by Max Lerner, the historian and columnist (now among the almost forgotten), who after spending a few days in my company at a conference described me (to general agreement) as the "merry madcap" of the group.

Obviously, not everyone I met liked me; nor did I like all of them. Indeed, not all of the people who I thought liked me actually did. There were also always those I rubbed the wrong way (sometimes to the point of outright enmity) by being too brash or too arrogant or too ambitious or too precociously successful—or by not being inhibited or tactful enough to refrain from writing about my career, especially in *Making It*, which came out in the late 1960s. But all that being said, the fact remains that I was more popular than not in the circles I frequented and that I always had many close friends and many more friendly acquaintances.

An interesting measure of the personal standing I enjoyed is what happened when I began—as I would call the process in the title of a book published about ten years after *Making It*—"breaking ranks" with the dogmas and orthodoxies of the world in which I lived. What happened was that it did not occur to anyone to invoke the classical leftist explanation that I was "selling out" for money and/or power.* In my case, because I seemed to be destroying rather than advancing my career, the theory circulated that I had gone mad. One of my best friends at the time even tried to persuade my wife to have me committed to a mental institution before my clearly self-destructive actions had a chance to reach their consummation in literal self-destruction—that is, suicide. He did this not out of hostility or spite but out of love: it was his way of excusing and forgiving what would, if I were sane enough to be held responsible, have had to be deemed inexcusable and unforgivable.

The problem was that not only had I not gone mad, but that I was saner than ever, having finally come to my senses after more than a decade of experimenting with radical ideas that were proving dangerous to me and destructive to America, not to mention the threat they posed to my own children, and everyone else's as well. No sooner did it become clear that this was how I really felt, and that I fully intended to carry on with the war I had started against those ideas, than the exculpatory explanation for my apostasy was dropped, and in its place came shock and a deep sense of betrayal. Some of my friends simply cut me off, or perhaps it would be metaphorically more apt to say that they excommunicated me. Others made a brave but ultimately futile effort to remain in touch—futile because getting together led either to unpleasant arguments or to the equally unpleasant biting of tongues and the avoiding of precisely those subjects that we all most burned to talk about.

But this was by no means a one-way street; I did my own share of cutting off old friends and letting others drift away, because continuing to see them became so awkward and uncomfortable. Nor was this process confined to the private sphere. I attacked them in print, at first

---

*It was only much later, when I acquired the (mostly exaggerated) reputation of having great influence with the Reagan administration, that this explanation was brought into play. According to my critics, I had evidently possessed the ability to foresee the coming to power of the conservatives a decade later and, far from being self-destructive, had sold out preemptively for the rewards that would eventually come my way.

mostly in articles in *Commentary,* of which I was the editor, and then later in *Breaking Ranks: A Political Memoir,* and they attacked me back or else tried to pretend, by ignoring my work, that I did not exist.

Yet all this is much too general. As I hope to show, each ex-friendship was marked by its own wrinkles, particularities, and complexities, as well as its own special mix of feelings and personal involvements. I also hope that the stories I am about to tell will provide at least indirect answers to the two questions I have been asked over and over again by puzzled people to whom such experiences are completely foreign.

The first of these questions is why it is so hard for friends who disagree about large and apparently impersonal subjects like politics or literature to remain friends. To this my answer is that they can— but only provided the things they disagree about are not all that important to them. Such, I think, is the situation with most people. They go from day to day, trying to earn a living and to raise their kids as best they can in accordance with the morals, customs, and traditions they have inherited from their own parents or have absorbed almost unknowingly from the culture around them. The ideas that underlie their way of life are mostly taken for granted and remain unexamined—luckily for them, since the biggest lie ever propagated by a philosopher was Socrates' self-aggrandizing assertion that the unexamined life is not worth living.

Another big lie is that the "apathy" toward politics that so many Americans feel, at least judging by their persistently low turnouts in elections, is a sign of dissatisfaction with our system. In reality, it is just the opposite. Rightly or wrongly, and more often the former than the latter, very large numbers of Americans are content with their lot and do not believe that it will make much difference to their lives if this Republican or that Democrat wins or loses this or that campaign. Why then should their friendships be helped or hurt by whether they are members of one or the other party, any more than they are helped or hurt by their rooting for rival football or baseball or basketball teams, whose fortunes, if truth be told, most Americans are more passionate about than they are about politics or perhaps anything else besides their own families?

More power, I say (and I say it, believe me, without a trace of condescension) to such people. But I only wish that *their* greatest wish, which is to be left alone by outside forces so that they can tend to their own affairs as they see fit, were as easy to grant as they seem to imagine. How hard this actually is I learned from Robert Warshow, a dear old friend who edited the first pieces I wrote for *Commentary* when I was starting out in the early 1950s and who did not live long enough to become an ex-friend, though it would break my heart to think that I might ever have split even with him. Writing about the wish to be left alone, as it was expressed by the characters in a movie he was reviewing, Warshow remarked, "One could almost weep at the innocence that makes them think this is a small thing to ask."*

The innocence at which Warshow nearly wept in the 1950s is still with us in the 1990s, but it is being lost by the day (or even by the hour). Forty and fifty years ago it was still possible for communities to quarantine themselves with local ordinances and social sanctions against outside influences they considered undesirable and did not even want to know about. But thanks to the "imperial judiciary," the ubiquity of the mass media, and now the Internet, quarantines are no longer possible to declare, and anyone who tries soon discovers that they cannot be maintained. This came home to me with unusual force when it was discovered that a convicted pedophile serving time in a Minnesota prison had access on the inside to a state-of-the-art computer and was using it to collect and disseminate information to his fellow pedophiles on the outside about local potential victims, who ranged in age from two or three to twelve. Apart from the intrinsic horror of the story itself, the reason it made such a large impression on me was that the ring of pedophiles being supplied by this prisoner was operating only a stone's throw away from St. Paul, where my mother-in-law was born

---

*Bob Warshow died of a heart attack in 1955 at the age of age of thirty-seven and is by now even more completely forgotten than some of the other intellectuals who appear in this book. Yet he was in my opinion the best film critic and one of the most elegant essayists this country has ever seen. Never very prolific, he was granted only enough time to produce a small body of work, most of which can now be found only in back issues of *Commentary* and *Partisan Review* and in a collection, long out of print, entitled *The Immediate Experience*, which was brought out in a paperback edition some years after his death.

and raised and where she lived until her death in 1972. "Such things don't happen in our part of the country," she used to assure me whenever anything involving any departure from conventional sexual morality would come to light in New York. And though she was undoubtedly wrong in making so categorical an assertion, she was not wrong in believing that a place like St. Paul, Minnesota, was, thanks to its local laws and mores, much more inhospitable to such "goings-on" (by which she mainly meant adultery, homosexuality, and pornography; pedophilia would almost have been beyond her imagination) than New York. No longer. In this respect, my mother-in-law's part of the country is now incapable of protecting itself from the aggressions of my part of the country against the traditional moral standards which hers once upheld with all the force of law and social sanction and sometimes hypocrisy, acting as "the tribute vice pays to virtue."*

This is why we now have "culture wars." In contrast to most strictly political battles, these culture wars do arouse the passions of all those people who, in their wish to be left alone, are frustrated by forces and ideas that are repugnant to them and from which they cannot seal themselves off or—what is more infuriating—protect their children. I have done no formal survey research on the issue, but I would be willing to bet that even among people living the unexamined life, friendships have begun to be disrupted and even broken by disagreements over pornography and drugs as well.

In becoming thus aroused, these people are getting a small taste of what life is always like for an intellectual, by which I mean someone who, in the famous sociologist Nathan Glazer's memorable definition, lives for, by, and off ideas. Such a person takes ideas as seriously as an orthodox religious person takes, or anyway used to take, doctrine or dogma. Though we cluck our enlightened modern tongues at such fanaticism, there is a reason why people have been excommunicated, and sometimes even put to death, by their fellow congregants for heretically disagreeing with the official understanding of a particular text or

---

*I wrote about all this at some length in an essay entitled "My Mother-in-Law, *Lolita*, the Marquis de Sade, and Larry Flynt," which appeared in the April 1997 issue of *Commentary*.

even of a single word. After all, to the true believer everything important—life in this world as well as life in the next—depends on obedience to these doctrines and dogmas, which in turn depends on an accurate interpretation of their meaning and which therefore makes the spread of heresy a threat of limitless proportions.

We intellectuals are like that: not for nothing have we been called the "clerisy" of a secular age, and not for nothing are we unable to live amicably together when disagreements arise over the ideas that are so vitally important to us. This fear and hatred of the heretic, together with the correlative passion to shut him up one way or the other, is (to say the least, and in doing so I am bending over backward) as much a character trait of so-called liberal intellectuals as it is of conservatives. It was once thought that the concept of absolutistic relativism was an oxymoron or a contradiction in terms, but, thanks to the spread of "political correctness," the world has now, or should have, learned better. For we have seen that "liberal" intellectuals who tell us that tolerance and pluralism are the highest values, who profess to believe that no culture is superior to any other, and who are on that account great supporters of "multiculturalism" will treat these very notions as sacred orthodoxies, will enforce agreement with them in every venue in which they have the power to do so (the universities being the prime example of the moment), and will severely punish any deviation that dares to make itself known.

Furthermore, when intellectuals of the Left have been able to assume actual political power, as in most of the formerly Communist countries, where the leadership more often than not consisted of highly educated types, they have not hesitated to excommunicate and execute their own species of heretics. I would fear the same result in the thankfully unlikely event that my fellow intellectuals ever took over in this country. Which is why, like William F. Buckley, Jr., I would rather be ruled by the first two thousand names in the Boston phone book than by the combined faculties of Harvard and MIT. St. Augustine said that the virtue of children lies not in their wills but in the weakness of their limbs, and I would apply the same adage to intellectuals, the weakness of whose political power is more conducive to their democratic virtue than the content of their wills.

What happened in the 1960s was, to put it simply but not inaccurately, a mass conversion to leftist radicalism by the formerly liberal intellectual establishment and a commensurate seizure of enormous power by radical ideas and attitudes over the institutions controlled by intellectuals. These institutions, as everyone now knows, include the universities, the major media of information and entertainment (New York and Hollywood, the big newspapers and magazines, the movies and television), and increasingly even the mainstream churches. But if I am to explain how and why this development ultimately brought me such a wealth of ex-friends, I will have to stop for a minute or two and try to clear up the enormous amount of confusion about the word *liberal* that had its origins in this very same development.

Naturally, the radicals of the New Left hated the Right, but the Right was to them so self-evidently evil that there was no point wasting energy in fighting it. The real villain was "the liberal establishment," on whom the New Left heaped all the blame for everything that in its eyes was wrong with America: for starting and refusing to "end the cold war" and the "arms race" (and, a little later, the war in Vietnam); for perpetuating a social and economic system that fostered racism and poverty; for maintaining a middle-class culture based on repression (just as their socioeconomic system was founded on oppression); and for creating colleges and universities whose main purpose was to turn out slavish participants in that system and cannon fodder for its imperialistic aggressions in the Third World. To all these charges, the liberals, and especially those teaching in or administering the universities, in effect pleaded guilty with an explanation and threw themselves on the mercy of their young judges.

The terminological confusion arose when the victors in this aggression by the radicals against the liberals decided not only to occupy the territories once ruled over by the defeated enemy but to assume its previously despised name as well. The reason for this curious and entirely unexpected maneuver had everything to do with the exigencies of electoral politics. For in 1968 the radicals, in their own version of the Maoist "long march" through the institutions, tried to do to the Democratic party what they were already doing so successfully to the universities. In pursuit of this purpose they mobilized behind Senator Eugene McCarthy, who was challenging both Vice President Hubert Humphrey and Senator Robert F. Kennedy for the Democratic nomination for president. Not only did the radicals get "clean for Gene" (i.e., shave their beards and dress in more conventional clothes), but, realizing that radicalism had limited appeal among the voters, they also started (in a perhaps unconscious echo of the tag "liberals in a hurry" that had once been applied to the Communists) calling themselves liberals.

Four years later, with Senator George McGovern as their leader, these "liberals" actually did succeed in taking over the Democratic party. In the process, the term *liberal* itself underwent a—shall we say?—radical change of meaning and now signified on almost every issue a position almost the opposite of the one associated with liberalism a decade earlier. So deep and thoroughgoing was the transformation that by 1976, when Senator Edward M. Kennedy tried running for president, his policies both on the cold war and on the economy deviated by 180 degrees from those that had been pushed by his older brother John F. Kennedy fifteen years earlier. Indeed, JFK's own ideas were now much more closely approximated by those of a conservative like Ronald Reagan, who shared his Democratic predecessor's belief that a defense buildup was the best way to defend the liberties of the free world against the threat of Soviet totalitarianism and that a tax cut was the best way to ensure a prosperous economy at home.

As the stories that follow make clear, I, having been a liberal of the old style myself, participated in the conversion to radicalism, and it was when I lost faith in the teachings and practices of the radical (or, to use the confusing new designation, "liberal") "church" that I also lost all the friends I had made as a devoted communicant. They now looked upon me a dangerous heretic, which I certainly was from their point of view, and I considered them a threat to the well-being of everything I now held dear, which *they* certainly were—and still are.

No wonder, then, that there is hardly a one of my old friends left among the living with whom I am today so much as on speaking terms, except to exchange the most minor civilities if we happen unavoidably to meet (and often not even then).

Admittedly, not everyone would agree with this account of why and how intellectuals invariably become ex-friends when they fall out over ideas. For example, according to yet another famous sociologist, Daniel Bell, who is also another of my ex-friends (though we were never that close, and there were always difficulties between us even in the best of times), it is not "the ideas held by individuals but the way they are held," or the "temperament" of the holder, that matters most. Thus, he goes on, "I have retained my regard for Irving Kristol, for his wit and charm, though we have differed strongly in our political views."

Now, there can be no doubt that Irving Kristol (who, I am very happy to report, is *not* one of my ex-friends) possesses great wit and charm, as well as a temperament that is equable, cheerful, and almost relentlessly easygoing. Yet none of this prevented him from becoming a *bête noir* to the new liberals when he, a radical leftist of the Trotskyist persuasion during his student days in 1930s, emerged in the 1960s as the leader—or "the Godfather," as he was sometimes mockingly described—of the former leftists, myself in due course included, who became known collectively as the "neoconservatives." In fact, even as early as 1952, during the long phase of his political life in which Irving himself was a member in good standing of the old-style liberal community, most of his fellow liberals fell on him like ten tons of bricks when (in an article for *Commentary*, on whose editorial staff he then served)* he deviated from the orthodox liberal analysis of why Senator Joseph McCarthy's crusade against Communist subversion was proving so effective. As Irving saw it, the liberal community bore some of the responsibility for McCarthy's rise in that its failure to dis-

---

*Shortly thereafter, he went on to London to help found and co-edit (with the British poet and critic Stephen Spender) the monthly *Encounter*. Some years later, returning to New York, he became the editor of the biweekly *Reporter*, and still later, after its demise, he founded and co-edited (at first with Daniel Bell) a new quarterly, *The Public Interest*, devoted entirely to domestic affairs. Eventually he moved to Washington, taking *The Public Interest* with him. In Washington he also founded yet another quarterly, this one devoted entirely to foreign affairs and called *The National Interest*, of which he became the publisher (with Owen Harries as editor) while remaining (now with Nathan Glazer) co-editor of *The Public Interest*. All this activity could be ascribed to the statement he himself once made that whenever he thought something needed to be done, all he could think of doing was to start a magazine.

sociate itself unambiguously from the Communists, and to mount a much firmer opposition to them, was what had given the notorious senator from Wisconsin the running room he needed for his demagogic exploitation of the issue. For saying such a thing, Irving was never forgiven. At the time, he was vilified as a defender of McCarthy, and this slander is still being repeated to this very day. So much for the saving graces of wit, charm, and temperament.

Which brings me to the second question I am frequently asked and on which I hope to shed some light. If what in *Making It* I called the Family* did not fall apart when the neoconservatives broke ranks with it, what caused it to disappear and has anything come along to take its place? I will deal with the latter part of this question in the afterword, but to the former my answer begins with a consideration of the difference between ordinary friendships and those based on ideas.

In the normal course of events, people form friendships either through physical contiguity (growing up in the same surroundings or becoming neighbors as adults) or through shared enterprises (working together at a job or on some project or in the same profession) or through common cultural or recreational interests. Conversely, such friendships, even when they have become very strong, can be and often are dissolved by nothing more profound than a change in circumstances: childhood buddies drift further and further apart as they wind up pursuing different paths in life; a neighbor who has become an intimate moves to another city vowing to keep in touch, but as time goes by, the contact becomes less and less frequent; a co-worker changes jobs and after a while is no longer heard from; great pals starting out in

---

*For the record, it was the columnist Murray Kempton who coined this term, but it was only when I used it (with due acknowledgment) in *Making It* that it came into currency. The same thing happened to "dirty little secret," which was also plucked from obscurity by *Making It*. I borrowed the phrase, also with due acknowledgment, from D. H. Lawrence (he had used it not in one of his novels but in an essay about sex in the Victorian age, and I then applied it to the ambition for worldly success in contemporary culture). It soon became, and remained, a tiresome cliché whose origins were undoubtedly unknown by those who kept applying it with less and less precision or relevance to more and more inapposite things.

the same profession become rivals, and envy and bitterness gradually replace affection and loyalty; the election campaign ends, and the warm camaraderie it fostered among the participants fades away for lack of continued nourishment from the source that originally fed it.

The ties between people that are forged of ideas may be reinforced by any or all these factors, but they differ in one crucial respect: they do not necessarily rest on personal affection. On the contrary, they can endure and even remain strong in the teeth of mutual dislike and even detestation. It was by virtue of sharing a common culture, and not because they were fond of one another, that the writers and intellectuals whose work once appeared mainly in *Partisan Review* and *Commentary* became a Family. They had all read and tended to value books which had relatively few other readers in the culture at large, and they not only were conversant with the great works of literature, music, painting, and philosophy of the past but also were at home with and sympathetic to the avant-garde currents in the arts and in the intellectual sphere that the general public found too difficult or esoteric or irrelevant or even repulsive.

In politics, too, the "New York intellectuals" stood at a peculiar angle.* In contrast to most other Americans, they were neither De-

---

New York intellectuals was the term that one of us, the critic Irving Howe, preferred to *Family,* though we were not all from New York and not all of us even lived there. Even so, Howe insisted on "The New York Intellectuals" as the title of the article I persuaded him to write for *Commentary* in the early 1970s. This was during the few years when he and I (previously somewhat strained in our relations) became allies and friends through our common opposition to the New Left and the counterculture. But since his opposition amounted to a factional dispute with what he considered a deviation from the true leftist course, the minute he sensed that my own disaffection, which had originally resembled his, was beginning to spread to the Left in general, he too became an ex-friend. Even worse were his relations with Irving Kristol, who had been one of his Trotskyist comrades when they were both students at the City College of New York (CCNY) in the late 1930s. Long after Howe himself had ceased being a Trotskyist and become a social democrat or a democratic socialist (a creed that in his case had grown all but indistinguishable from McGovernite liberalism), he continued to think of Kristol (who had wound up opposing not just Communism but socialism and even liberalism!) as an apostate. And in *Arguing the World*—the documentary film that was made about the two of them and two of their CCNY contemporaries, Daniel Bell and Nathan Glazer, and that came out after Howe's death—Howe could not resist taking a swipe at Kristol's 1952 article in *Commentary* as "a back-handed apology for McCarthy."

mocrats nor Republicans nor even independents. But this is putting it much too blandly. The attitude of most of his fellow members of the Family was summed up by Dwight Macdonald's derisive dismissal of the two major political parties, in a piece he wrote at my urging for *Commentary* in the early 1960s, as "Tweedledumb and Tweedledumber."

Interestingly, Macdonald was throwing bricks from inside a glass house. In the 1930s, when he too was a Trotskyist (though from Yale rather than CCNY), his own leader, the great Leon Trotsky himself, had once issued the following pronouncement from the exile into which he had been driven after being beaten out by Joseph Stalin in the fight for succession following Lenin's death: "Everyone has a right to be stupid but Comrade Macdonald abuses the privilege." It was typical of Macdonald's good humor and sometimes clownish antics that he reveled in this insult. So much so, indeed, that he printed it on the front page of every issue of *Politics*, the magazine he founded and edited after quitting the editorial board of *Partisan Review* in the late 1930s when his colleagues Philip Rahv and William Phillips came out in support of American intervention in World War II. Still hewing at this point to the Trotskyist line, Macdonald regarded that war as a clash between two equally retrograde imperialistic systems that would end in mutual destruction. This would then set the stage for a true Communist revolution, led by Trotsky, that would redeem what Stalin, his old rival (and future murderer), had betrayed.

In 1945, before he had become world famous as the author of *Nineteen Eighty-Four*, George Orwell, himself the veteran of a mild flirtation with Trotskyism, would say of several similarly egregious misjudgments concerning the progress of World War II: "One has to belong to the intelligentsia to believe things like that; no ordinary man could be such a fool." But by the time Macdonald founded *Politics*, he had deserted Trotskyism and had moved on cheerfully and with characteristic insouciance to pacificism and anarchism. Still later, in the 1950s, he would become a fierce anti-Communist cold warrior and, later still, an even fiercer opponent of the Vietnam War and a great enthusiast of the student radicals of the 1960s.

As is obvious from all this history, everyone within the Family of

New York intellectuals was on the Left, the spectrum ranging from revolutionary Marxism of one stripe or another, through democratic socialism and communitarian anarchism, and all the way to a rather heterodox brand of liberalism. But what is often overlooked is that many of the poets and novelists who were literary heroes and mentors to these leftists were either men of the Right, like T. S. Eliot, Ezra Pound, and D. H. Lawrence, or at least anti-Left (W. B. Yeats and William Faulkner, for example).

It was this admiration for what would decades later be called "politically incorrect" writers that led *Partisan Review*, which had been founded in the early 1930s as the organ of a Communist "front" (the John Reed Clubs), to break with the party. The two main editors, Phillips and Rahv, rebelled against the efforts of the party's cultural commissars to prevent the magazine from publishing or praising writers whose political views were "reactionary" or whose formalistic experiments and often obscure work violated the officially approved canons of "socialist realism."*

After breaking with the Communist party, *Partisan Review* went on to form a loose association with Trotsky, which lasted until the outbreak of World War II. Though anti-Stalinist, in other words, the magazine remained within the revolutionary Communist fold while at the same time identifying itself with the modernist movement in the arts. Here the connection with Trotsky helped. For of all the major Communist leaders, Trotsky was the most congenial to young radical intellectuals with a passion for the arts. Himself a highly distinguished intellectual and a very good writer, he had once said that in his eyes "authors, journalists, and artists always stood for a world that was more attractive than any other, a world open only to the elect." Even more to the point, in his

---

*Once in the 1930s, the literary theorist Kenneth Burke, whose writings were very arcane and obscure, was marching through Union Square in downtown New York in a May Day parade sponsored by the Communist party. A fierce little man, Burke was calling attention to himself by energetically waving a placard, both sides of which bore the inscription WE WRITE FOR THE WORKERS. Another critic, Harold Rosenberg, towering in his great height over the dense crowd lining the parade route, spotted Burke and his placard. "Kenneth," the anti-Stalinist Rosenberg yelled with all the sarcasm he could get into his voice, "*you* write for the *workers?*" To which Burke yelled back, "It's an ambiguity on the preposition *for!*"

youth this extraordinary future leader of a Marxist revolution had once called down "a curse on all Marxists, and upon those who want to bring dryness and hardness into all the relations of life."

Lenin too—whose true heir Trotsky never ceased claiming to be, from the time he went into exile until the time Stalin finally sent an agent to Mexico to dispose of him once and for all by burying an ice pick in his head—understood that there was a conflict between the love of art and the "hardness" required of a Communist revolutionary. As he confessed to the writer Maxim Gorky after the two of them had sat enraptured through a performance of a Beethoven sonata, he could not "listen to music too often. It affects your nerves, makes you want to . . . stroke the heads of people. . . . And now you mustn't stroke any-one's head. . . . You have to hit them on the head, without any mercy."

In any event, among the closest literary friends and allies of the Family were Southern critics and poets like Allen Tate and John Crowe Ransom, who were politically very conservative indeed. What brought these apparently opposing groups together was the same thing that kept the Family of New York intellectuals together despite its own internal or sectarian differences: a similar set of standards in the arts. But they also shared a common disdain—stemming in the Family from Marxism and in the Southerners from an idealized and romanticized conception of the agrarian society of the pre–Civil War South that differed from the picture of that world in *Gone with the Wind* only in being more abstract and intellectually sophisticated—for the middle-class or "bourgeois" civilization in which they all lived. It was a civilization they saw as entirely philistine, materialistic, and puritani-cal. Dominated by businessmen and their values, it had no use, they felt, for people like themselves, people who cared about ideas and art more than they cared about anything else and who had "never met a payroll." Necessarily estranged or "alienated" from such a civilization, they huddled and remained together even in the teeth of personal ani-mosities and serious political disagreements.

To be sure, there were limits: Communism (or Stalinism, as it was usually known in that world) on the Left and Fascism on the Right. Throughout this book, I explore the nature and the contours of the limits on the Left. Since, however, I will have much less to say about the limits on the Right, I think it may be worth pausing here to cite an interesting and somewhat bizarre incident as a case in point.

This occurred when the 1948 Bollingen Prize for Poetry was awarded to *The Pisan Cantos* by Ezra Pound, who was then living in St. Elizabeth's, a mental hospital in Washington to which he had been sentenced for making radio broadcasts on behalf of Mussolini during World War II.* Without questioning Pound's eminence as a poet, the philosopher William Barrett, one of the editors of *Partisan Review*, wrote a piece in protest against honoring the man—a man who had sided with Mussolini and Hitler in a war against his own country and whose work, including *The Pisan Cantos* itself, was shot through with fascist ideas and anti-Semitic sentiments of an especially crude variety. (Barrett quoted a few choice examples from *The Pisan Cantos*, such as this little gem, in which the Holocaust becomes a crime perpetrated for profit by the Jews on the gentiles: "the yidd is a stimulant, and the goyim are cattle/ . . . and go to saleable slaughter/with the maximum docility.")

Allen Tate, a member of the committee that had chosen Pound for the award, took offense at what he considered a slur by Barrett on his honor and announced in the pages of *Partisan Review* itself that he would henceforth settle such insults in traditional Southern fashion—by actually challenging the perpetrator to a duel. Evidently, he also wanted to issue the same challenge to the poet Karl Shapiro, who had served with him on the Bollingen committee but had voted against giving the prize to Pound. He even went so far as to ask the

---

*"One does not arrest Voltaire," quipped General Charles de Gaulle when, as president of France, he was asked why he did not take action against Jean-Paul Sartre for having broken the law in some leftist demonstration or other. Well, I know Voltaire, and though Sartre was then certainly France's most famous and influential intellectual, time will tell—is already telling—that he was no Voltaire. Neither was Ezra Pound comparable in stature to, say, Walt Whitman, despite the excellence and originality of some of his own verse. Yet it was out of the same principle enunciated by de Gaulle that Pound, though indicted for treason, was never prosecuted (he was spared on the ground that he was not mentally fit to stand trial). It was suspected then, and has been confirmed by research since, that the psychiatrists who saved Pound from such a fate by certifying him as "of unsound mind" did not believe him to be insane. Unlike de Gaulle, however, they lacked the power to act by fiat merely on the basis of a witty cultural reference and therefore had to rely on a dishonest clinical diagnosis.

critic George Steiner, then one of his students, to find out for him "whether or not a Jew was, in the context of his faith and morals, at liberty to accept a challenge to a duel." Presumably, no such question arose in connection with Barrett, who was raised by his immigrant Irish family as a Catholic.

Having just reread Barrett's editorial in the April 1949 issue of *Partisan Review*, together with the debate it triggered the following month, I cannot resist transposing Robert Warshow's phrase to this context and saying that "one could almost weep" at the contrast between the culture it embodied and that of the 1990s. The Pound affair showed the New York intellectuals and their relatives in other places at both ends of the Atlantic at their intellectual and literary best. Except for Tate's almost comically intemperate outburst, every one of the pieces on both sides of the issue was written out of loyalty to the autonomy of art while its author wrestled honestly with the almost insuperable moral and intellectual difficulties this ideal presented. The case of Pound exposed these difficulties with unusual salience, and the participants in the debate (including immediate Family members like Barrett himself, Irving Howe, and the art critic Clement Greenberg, along with "kissing cousins" from England like W. H. Auden and George Orwell) rose to the occasion with arguments of a complexity and prose of a delicacy that puts the literary world of the 1990s—the deconstructionists, the feminists, the Africanists, and the assorted multiculturalists—to even greater shame than its work does all on its own.

Incidentally, I had a curious experience with Pound myself when in 1969, shortly before becoming *persona non grata*, I was awarded an honorary degree by Hamilton College in upstate New York. Pound had spent a few years there as a student, and, having long since been released from St. Elizabeth's, he turned up as one of my fellow honorees. Possibly as a penance for his sins during the war, he had taken a vow of silence (that is, he would write but not speak), which at least spared me the social embarrassment of refusing to talk to this notorious fascist and anti-Semite. But I still had to decide what to do when, during the academic procession, I preceded him to the stage, where everyone else stood up and applauded as he came darting down the aisle. My decision was to stay put in my seat and refrain from joining in the applause.

No more than Will Barrett did I question the aesthetic distinction of Pound's poetry (or, to be more precise, his early poetry). Still less did I doubt that he had performed a very great service as a guide and mentor to other poets, who then turned out to be much greater than he ever was. Like everyone else familiar with twentieth-century literature, I knew that he had, for instance, edited T. S. Eliot's "The Waste Land," which Eliot then dedicated to him with a phrase from Dante: *il miglior fabbro* ("the better craftsman"). An even greater debt, in my opinion, was owed him for the role he played in relentlessly encouraging W. B. Yeats to move beyond his early pre-Raphaelite and "Celtic twilight" beginnings and to start using a tougher, more colloquial, and (as one critic has called it) more "athletic" idiom. By taking this advice, Yeats, who had up till then been not much more than a good lyric poet, went on to produce some of the greatest poems ever written. Nor, finally, could I help feeling a secret thrill at the sight of this almost mythical figure from what seemed the distant past: it was as though history itself were suddenly being made flesh. Yet, like Barrett, I could not bring myself to honor the man. Pound, with only three years left to live but still possessed of sharp and burning eyes even in his dotage, turned them fiercely on me as a sign that he had noticed my thin little gesture of protest, but I had the impression (probably mistaken) that his inquisitorial stare was not altogether disapproving.

Still, it was rare for things to go so far as they did between Barrett and Tate in the Pound affair, and even when splits occurred—even when the parties involved ceased to be on speaking terms—they remained stuck with one another. For who else cared so much, or even at all, about the issues they were debating? Who else could properly understand the things they were writing and saying and the ways in which they were writing and saying them? By the same token, it was precisely when others began appearing on the scene who both understood and appreciated them that the Family's world started falling apart. In fact, this new cultural development was steadily eroding the foundations of the Family's communal interdependence by the time the political wars of the 1960s erupted. Those wars accelerated the process of cultural disintegration already going on within the Family and finally led to its complete dissolution.

Probably the main factor here was the enormous expansion of the colleges and universities in the aftermath of World War II. Thanks to the GI Bill, millions upon millions of Americans who would never have gone to college before were now exposed to a higher education, which in those far-off days still actually meant higher. This in turn led to an expansion of the audience for serious books and magazines and high culture in general. It was still a small audience as compared with the one that consumed the products of mass and middlebrow culture, but it was a lot larger than it had been before. It was now large enough, for instance, to make inexpensive paperback reprints of classic works a commercially viable proposition and to put a difficult and previously obscure highbrow novelist like Saul Bellow on the best-seller list (I vividly remember the shock of amazement, not untouched by envy, that ripped through the Family when his *The Adventures of Augie March* appeared on that list in 1953).

The upshot was that there were now other people to talk to and write for and other places to go. One of these was *The New Yorker*, where, beginning in the 1950s, veterans of *Partisan Review* and *Commentary* like Dwight Macdonald, Mary McCarthy, Harold Rosenberg, and even Hannah Arendt, the most abstruse of them all, began appearing fairly often. What made this migration all the more remarkable was that the Family had always regarded *The New Yorker* as the quintessential middlebrow publication, even though highbrow critics like Edmund Wilson, Alfred Kazin, and (once in a great while) Lionel Trilling had reviewed for it. (Fiction was another matter: no comparably highbrow story writers appeared in *The New Yorker* until later.)

That the old hostile attitude toward *The New Yorker* persisted among intransigent highbrow purists became clear to me from the disapproval of most of my literary friends when I myself began reviewing for *The New Yorker* in the mid-1950s. Nor were they altogether mistaken about the lingering middlebrowism of the magazine, at least among the old guard. My own editor there, a man with the central-casting name of Rogers Whittaker, once asked me whether there was a special typewriter in the offices of *Partisan Review* with a key containing the word *alienation*. On that occasion I retaliated by asking him whether it was true that John O'Hara had thrown a knife at him because he had tried to rewrite a sentence in one of O'Hara's stories. "Yes," Whittaker replied in his inimitably dry tone—the driest it has ever fallen to me to hear—"but it was only a butter knife."

Of course, the question of whether the likes of Harold Rosenberg were as fully understood by their new audience as by their old remained open. Harold himself told me that shortly after becoming *The New Yorker*'s regular art critic, he was summoned into the office of its then editor, William Shawn, for a frank discussion. Shawn confessed that half the time he simply did not know what Rosenberg was talking about. "What difference does that make?" replied Rosenberg pleasantly. "The only thing that matters is whether *I* know what I'm talking about—and I do."

The only other writer I have ever run into who could have matched, or perhaps even topped, this display of placid arrogance was Paul Goodman. At lunch one day a young admirer of his, to whom I was introducing him, timidly ventured a gentle demurrer about something Paul had written. I forget whether it was a novel or a poem or an essay, since he worked regularly in all these forms (though it was as a social critic, and especially as the author of *Growing Up Absurd*, published in the early 1960s with more than a little help from me, that he would make his deepest mark). Without missing a beat and smiling benignly, Paul puffed on his pipe and said, "Well, some day you'll learn to read better."

———————

For all the faults of the kind of intellectual community whose adventures are recounted in the pages ahead, its disappearance and the absence of anything resembling it today is a great loss to our culture. It is also, as I will later explain, a loss to me personally.

But for now what I want to stress is that I have found great consolation in a few old friends in whose company I broke ranks with the radical Left in the late 1960s (others of this group, alas, went on to break ranks with *me* because, like Nathan Glazer, they decided that I was moving too far to the Right).* There has also been the joy of reconnecting with other old friends from whom I had for a few years become estranged in moving to the Left—notably Irving Kristol and his wife, the historian Gertrude Himmelfarb; the writer-turned-diplomat-turned-writer H. J. Kaplan; the indefatigably anti-Communist journalist Arnold Beichman; and the at least equally relentless philosopher Sidney Hook. And I have not yet mentioned the many new friends, inveterate denizens of the conservative world, who have been added to the rediscovered old. Here, in what is for me a rare submission to the principles of affirmative action, which dictate that I should strive to achieve greater name-dropping "diversity," I will single out Henry Kissinger and William F. Buckley, Jr.

In spite of our failure to form ourselves into a cohesive family, we have managed to join forces as a dissenting minority of "heretical" intellectuals who are trying to break the virtual monopoly that the worst ideas of my ex-friends hold (even from beyond the grave) over the cultural institutions of this country. We have not succeeded, not by a long shot, but we have made much progress.

In the meantime, I never stop counting the blessings with which I have been showered—as a husband, a father, a grandfather, an editor, a writer, and indeed as a friend—since I shouldered the burden of challenging the regnant leftist culture that pollutes the spiritual and cultural air we all breathe, and to do so with all my heart and all my soul and all my might.

---

*It should be noted that those of us in America who broke ranks with the Left in the late 1960s had our counterparts in Europe. The two most famous were probably those two incredibly prolific polymaths, Paul Johnson in England and Jean-François Revel in France. Both also became and—since they never concluded that I was going too far in my recoil from the Left, perhaps because they themselves were in some respects going even farther—remained good friends of mine. Johnson and Revel were responding to the same general situation that we in America were, but the driving forces in both their cases also had local variations and names. Johnson, the former editor of the left-socialist weekly the *New Statesman*, was given a great push by his alarm over the metastasizing power of the trade unions. Where Revel, also a former socialist, was concerned, the decisive factor seems to have been a growing disgust with the readiness of his fellow intellectuals on the French Left—most prominently Jean-Paul Sartre and his disciples—to apologize for the Soviet Union's crimes and to portray the United States as the greater threat. Not only did Revel and Johnson not see the United States as a threat, but they both became great admirers of it.

CHAPTER ONE

AT WAR WITH
ALLEN GINSBERG

"ALLEN GINSBERG, MASTER POET OF BEAT GENERATION, Dies at 70," proclaimed the headline on the front page of *The New York Times* for April 6, 1997. Reading it, I was moved more deeply than I would have expected—not to grief (though an unmistakable touch of sadness did briefly make a surprise appearance) but, rather, to an overwhelming feeling of wistfulness. It came over me that I had known this man for a full fifty years—fifty years!—and that for at least forty of them I had been at war with him and he with me. It came over me too that even now, with Ginsberg himself carried off the field, his work and its influence would still be there and the war would still go on.

Perhaps the best place to begin in telling the story of that war is a Saturday night in the fall of 1958, when I was twenty-eight and had just left my job as an associate editor of *Commentary* to work on a book while also trying my luck as a freelance writer and editor. At about 7:30 P.M., after hanging around the house all day in the sloppy old clothes I usually wore on weekends, I shaved, put on a clean white shirt with a button-down collar, a rep tie, and a three-piece charcoal-grey flannel suit from Brooks Brothers, and headed down by subway from the Upper West Side of Manhattan to an apartment in Greenwich Village, where Ginsberg and his friend and literary sidekick Jack Kerouac were waiting for me to arrive.

———————

I had never met Kerouac before, but Ginsberg I had first encountered when we were both undergraduates at Columbia in 1946. As a freshman, age sixteen, I had submitted a long poem about the prophet Jeremiah to the college literary magazine of which he, nearly twenty and in his junior (or senior?) year, was the editor, and to my great delight he had accepted it for publication.

Many years later, I happened upon the issue in which that poem appeared, and its callowness set my teeth on edge. It also got me wondering how so crude an imitation of Walt Whitman could have met with the approval of Ginsberg, who in those days (like almost every other aspiring young poet in the English-speaking world) was still trying, and quite successfully, to sound like T. S. Eliot. But from a recent glance through the first section of his *Selected Poems: 1947–1995*, I have discovered that he was already making moves toward his famous rejection of Eliot in favor of my then-beloved Whitman. Might he have thought that in trying to sound like Whitman instead of Eliot, I was ahead of him and on to something new?

If so, he could not have been more mistaken. When he later abandoned Eliot for Whitman, he was defiantly repudiating what was then the academically correct model and aggressively embracing an unfashionable and largely frowned-upon tradition. (I say "largely" because even at the height of Eliot's influence, Whitman had his defenders, among them one of Ginsberg's Columbia mentors, Mark Van Doren, himself a famous poet. I vividly recall Van Doren raising his eyes to heaven and waxing rhapsodic over "Whitman's great poems about death.") I, on the other hand, was only just becoming acquainted with Eliot, and I did not yet know enough to know how retrograde my adolescent Whitmanesque frenzies actually were.

It was not long, however, before I found out, and as I did, I also began to suspect—with a little help from teachers and friends—that I was better at writing *about* poetry, and about literature in general, than

I was at writing poems. And so, having as a freshman launched my literary career at Columbia with the publication of a poem which in later years made me cringe, I ended it with the publication as a senior year of a precociously poised and accomplished critical essay which, when I came upon *it* in later years, made me smile.

From Columbia I went on to three years of graduate study at Cambridge University in England. While there, I began publishing reviews and essays in academic journals and intellectual magazines on both sides of the Atlantic: *Scrutiny* and *Essays in Criticism* in England, *Commentary* and *Partisan Review* in America. After leaving Cambridge for a two-year hitch in the army, I took a job as a junior editor at *Commentary*, and I resumed writing about contemporary literature for a number of more popular magazines as well, including *The New Yorker, The Reporter,* and *The New Republic.*

By this time Ginsberg and I had long parted company, and in more ways than one. At Columbia my friends tended to be straight, in both senses of that term, whereas Ginsberg, a middle-class Jewish boy from New Jersey in the process of discovering himself as a homosexual, fell in with an assortment of hustlers, junkies, and other shady or disreputable characters who were always getting themselves and him into trouble.

Prominent among the latter was Kerouac, a Columbia dropout who had already run afoul of the law through a friend of his named Lucien Carr, whom he had originally met through Ginsberg. Carr had stabbed a homosexual suitor to death in the course of repelling an advance, dumped the body into the Hudson River, and then sought out Kerouac to help him dispose of the evidence. Thanks to the botch they made of the job, Carr wound up in prison, though Kerouac, who had been arrested as a material witness, got off scot-free. Shortly thereafter, Ginsberg and Kerouac were caught in bed together in Ginsberg's room in one of the college dormitories. Ginsberg protested (truthfully, it seems) that they "hadn't done anything," but his pleas of innocence fell on deaf ears and he was hit with a year's suspension.

This was Ginsberg's version of the episode. The official reason for the suspension, however, was not a sexual dalliance with Kerouac but a prank Ginsberg had played on a cleaning woman who, he claimed, had refused to wash the windows of his dormitory room. To retaliate against her, writes one of his biographers, Michael Schumacher (confirming the story as I heard it around the Columbia campus), Ginsberg "had traced the words *Butler has no balls* into the grime, Butler being Nicholas Murray Butler, president of the university." Furthermore, suspecting her of anti-Semitism, he had, with characteristic perversity, "also printed the legend 'Fuck the Jews' into the dirt, and capped off the display with drawings of a skull and crossbones and male genitalia." In those unenlightened distant days, this was, as the dean of the college put it in a letter to Ginsberg's father, an "enormity" and by itself alone grounds enough for disciplinary action.

His exile over, Ginsberg was readmitted to Columbia, but before long he had progressed from getting himself suspended for undergraduate prankishness to getting himself arrested for possession of stolen goods. According to his obituary in *The New York Times*, they were found in his apartment, where they had been stored by one Herbert Huncke, a con man who was Ginsberg's Virgil in exploring the lower depths of Times Square and with whom he was then living; according to contemporaneous Columbia rumor (again confirmed by Schumacher), the stolen goods were in a car in which Ginsberg was a passenger and which attracted the attention of the police when the driver (a friend of Huncke's) brilliantly turned the wrong way down a one-way street.

This time Ginsberg was in serious danger of going to jail, but thanks to the intervention of several Columbia professors, including Lionel Trilling and Mark Van Doren, he was sent to a psychiatric institution instead. The eight months he spent there were subsequently put to good literary use in "Howl," the poem that would make him famous upon its publication in 1956 in a little paper-covered booklet entitled *Howl and Other Poems*.

Not having seen Ginsberg since Columbia, and not having heard much about him in the intervening years, I was at first a little surprised to receive an advance copy of *Howl*, together with a note from him suggesting that I review it. Evidently, though, he had kept close enough track of me to know that I was now an established literary critic and therefore in a position to do him a certain amount of good.

I never did review *Howl* itself, but within the next year or so I wrote no fewer than three highly critical pieces—one for *The New Republic*, another for *Partisan Review*, and a third for *Esquire*—about the group which had originally been hailed as the "San Francisco Renaissance" but which soon came to be much better known as the Beat Generation. Ginsberg was one of its two main leaders and spokesmen. The other was Kerouac, whose novel *On the Road* was now being acclaimed as the counterpart in prose to the literary and cultural revolution heralded in verse by the title poem of *Howl*.

Of the three pieces I wrote about the Beats, the one that appeared in 1958 in *Partisan Review* under the title "The Know-Nothing Bohemians" made the most noise. There my main literary target was not Ginsberg but Kerouac. Through a detailed analysis of his prose (the "spontaneous bop prosody" Ginsberg had sung his praises for creating) and the uses to which it was put in *On the Road* and *The Subterraneans* (which had quickly followed its best-selling predecessor into print), I tried to demonstrate that Kerouac's "prosody" was a cover for his "simple inability to express anything in words":

> The only method he has of describing an object is to summon up the same half-dozen adjectives over and over again: "greatest," "tremendous," "crazy," "mad," " wild," and perhaps one or two others. When it's more than just mad or crazy or wild, it becomes "really mad" or "really crazy" or "really wild."

And the "same poverty of resources," I went on to show, was apparent in his treatment of character and plot.

Neither in "The Know-Nothing Bohemians" nor anywhere else did I make any comparable literary charges against Ginsberg. The reason was that in my judgment Ginsberg, unlike Kerouac, was a genuinely gifted writer. Even as an undergraduate at Columbia, he had won my admiration with the amazing virtuosity that enabled him to turn out polished verses in virtually any style: love lyrics with an Elizabethan flavor, heroic couplets in the manner of Dryden and Pope, sonnets or rhymed stanzas reminiscent of Keats and Shelley. Now, through a fusion of Walt Whitman, Christopher Smart, William Blake, and William Carlos Williams, he had evidently found his own true voice. Hysterical and unmodulated, it was not a voice I liked; nor did I believe that the poems constituted the great literary break-through Ginsberg vociferously kept insisting he had achieved. Never-theless, I could not help being impressed by the sureness of his rhythms and his phrasing in "Howl" and by the wit, the humor, and the unexpected imaginative leaps that enlivened some of the other poems in this little collection, especially "America" and "A Supermar-ket in California."

Consequently, in *The New Republic,* where the first of my pieces about the Beats was published, I singled out Ginsberg as one of the three good poets of the San Francisco Renaissance (the other two were Robert Duncan and William Everson, a.k.a. Brother Antoninus, both destined to become even more obscure in the future than they were then). In that piece I characterized "Howl" as a "remarkable poem" whose "asssault on America is a personal cry that rings true" and whose "hysteria is tempered with humor," and a year later I also exempted Ginsberg from the severe literary strictures I directed at Ker-ouac in "The Know-Nothing Bohemians."

By then, however, I had changed my mind about Ginsberg's impli-cation in what I called the "ethos" of the Beat Generation. In *The New Republic,* I had said that Ginsberg shared with all the other writers of the San Francisco group "the conviction that any form of rebellion against American culture . . . is admirable" and that he too regarded "homo-sexuality, jazz, dope-addiction, and vagrancy as outstanding examples of such rebellion." But unlike the rest, Ginsberg did not, I thought, "glamorize" the "dope-addicts, perverts, and maniacs" he wrote about, and this struck me as an important and redeeming difference.

On further reflection, and after closer study of *Howl and Other Poems,* I realized that I had been misreading Ginsberg here. By the time I wrote "The Know-Nothing Bohemians," it had become clear to me that he was just as undiscriminating as Kerouac in his wholesale em-brace of the Beat ethos and that the two of them together were placing themselves at the head of a "revolt of the spiritually underprivileged and the crippled of soul" against "normal feeling and the attempt to cope with the world through intelligence." Indeed, Ginsberg was in certain respects a more sinister figure than Kerouac:

> At one end of the spectrum, [the Beat] ethos shades off into violence and criminality, main-line drug addiction and madness. Allen Ginsberg's poetry, with its lurid apocalyptic celebration of "angel-headed hipsters," speaks for the darker side of the new Bohemianism. Kerouac is milder [though he too] is attracted to criminality.

Having thus forged a link between the Beats and "the spread of juvenile crime in the 1950's," I concluded with a ringing declaration of war:

> Being against what the Beat Generation stands for has to do with denying that incoherence is superior to precision; that ignorance is superior to knowledge; that the exercise of mind and discrimination is a form of death. It has to do with fighting the notion that sordid acts of violence are justifiable so long as they are committed in the name of "instinct." It even has to do with fighting the poisonous glorification of the adolescent in American popular culture. It has to do, in other words, with one's attitude toward intelligence itself.

It was a scathing indictment, and it bothered Ginsberg so deeply that he would never get over it. And I mean never. Here, for example, is the first paragraph of an article about him that was published in *The New York Times* on the occasion of his seventieth birthday, only six months before he died:

> Sometimes the poet Allen Ginsberg still fantasizes about his old Columbia College friend Norman Podhoretz, who became the conservative editor of *Commentary* magazine. In Mr. Ginsberg's fantasies, Mr. Ginsberg is yelling at Mr. Podhoretz that the C.I.A. is selling drugs in Los Angeles and yelling that Mr. Ginsberg's epic poem "Howl" cannot be read on the radio during most daylight hours because of Federal limitations on obscenity. And he is warring with Mr. Podhoretz, who once called Beat poets like Mr. Ginsberg "know-nothing bohemians," about the very nature of poetry itself.

It was on that Saturday night in 1958 that all this yelling first began, and more than a quarter of a century later, in 1985, Ginsberg would tell an interviewer how and why it did:

> Podhoretz had written his attack on Kerouac and what he called "the know-nothing bohemians," this big chunk of leaden prose which people took very seriously as a statement of civilized values. It was in *Partisan Review*, but then the idea spread like trench mouth and finally wound up filtering down to *Life* magazine and the Luce empire. . . . Kerouac's response was "This is really too bad. That guy's article will probably wind up confusing a lot of people, and he himself is confused. Why don't we have him to tea?" So we called up Podhoretz and invited him over.

The call, which was placed not by Ginsberg himself but by Kerouac's girlfriend, I at first thought must be a practical joke ("I'm here with Allen and Jack who would like you to come see them tonight"). But then Ginsberg got on the line, and the minute I recognized his voice and realized that this was no joke, practical or otherwise, I caught myself desperately fishing for some graceful way to avoid what was sure to be a very unpleasant encounter. No such luck: the fear of seeming cowardly (in my own eyes as much as in his) was at least as strong as my apprehensions over the nasty scene he was undoubtedly preparing for me, and curiosity then also weighed in to tip the scales in favor of my accepting this unexpected and wholly unwelcome challenge.

But no sooner had I done so than it occurred to me that if I were to arrive at his apartment needing a shave and dressed in threadbare chino pants and a rumpled old shirt, it would be as if I were donning the enemy's uniform for a foray into his own territory. Worse yet, I might in some sense seem to be currying favor. And then there was another consideration. In "Howl" Ginsberg said that among the "best minds" of his generation who had been driven mad by "Moloch" (that is, life in America) were those "who were burned alive in their innocent flannel suits . . . & the mustard gas of sinister intelligent editors." I suspected that he might have been thinking of me in invoking those "sinister intelligent editors,"* and so changing into the uniform of "Moloch" before sallying forth from the Upper West Side to the Village seemed the only honorable and self-respecting thing to do.

Ginsberg's apartment turned out to be much as I would have imagined it: a walk-up in an aging building, sparsely furnished, and badly in need of a paint job. Though he had not yet become a Buddhist, he was already "into" Eastern mysticism, and he was sitting on the floor in what looked to my admittedly inexperienced eyes like some approximation of the lotus position. In addition to Kerouac, there were two other people present whom Ginsberg (in what I took to be a sophomorically deliberate affront to my bourgeois expectations) never bothered introducing. One of them was obviously the girl who had placed the call; the other was a young man who seemed to be paired up with Ginsberg. I no longer remember the girl's name, though I do remember that she said not a word the entire time I was there and lacked only the knitting to complete the impression she gave of a Madame DeFarge making sure that I would be sent to the guillotine when the revolution finally came. As for the young man, he was (as I discovered through the simple expedient of asking him) Peter Orlovsky, to whom Ginsberg would remain married for all practical purposes—other, of course, than sexual fidelity—for the rest of his life.

Kerouac was even handsomer in the flesh than in the pictures of him that had been appearing for months in such mass magazines as *Life* and *Time.* Unlike the others, all three of whom (especially Orlovsky) were predictably and ostentatiously scruffy, Kerovac had on clothes that, though casual, were neat and clean. Abnormally conscious as I was at that moment of the issue of personal appearance, and accustomed to the photographs in which he always had a two- or three-day growth of beard, I was also amazed to find him as clean-

---

*Actually, according to the elaborately annotated edition of "Howl" that was published in 1986, there *is* an allusion to me there, but this is not it. In referring in line 8 of the first draft to "Post-war cynical scholars" (altered in the final draft to "the scholars of war"), Ginsberg seems to have had me in mind—which was, I must admit, rather prescient of him, given that in 1956 I had not yet developed into the cold-war hawk I was subsequently to become.

shaven as I myself was. Had he perversely cleaned himself up for this meeting, just as I had done?

I had anticipated a tense and unpleasant evening, and Ginsberg did not disappoint me. The festivities began with his aggressive insistence that I smoke marijuana with them. I refused. Not, as Schumacher claims, because doing so would have been "tantamount to a passing of the peace pipe between factions of warring tribes" but for the same reason I had shaved and changed my clothes before setting out. Presumably relying on Ginsberg's recollection (which had me acting "a little stiff but polite"), Schumacher also claims that "the encounter was civil." But there again he gets it wrong.

In later life, Ginsberg would adopt a sweet and gentle persona, but there was nothing either sweet or gentle about the Allen Ginsberg I had last seen at Columbia ten years earlier, and there was even less evidence of those qualities in the Allen Ginsberg I met again that night. As an undergraduate he had been arrogant and brash and full of an in-your-face bravado; now, just into his thirties, he was still all those things and more, but there was also a fury in him that I had not detected in the past. "In those days," as he himself would later recall, "I'd go into towering rages over literary matters because I was in the middle of a big fight with the whole New York Establishment . . . and I was on my high horse." That night it was I in whom "the whole New York Establishment" was concentrated, and the rage was directed at me.

Some months earlier, the novelist Herbert Gold, who had also been at Columbia with us, had accused me of betraying what he considered one of my main responsibilities as a literary critic. I had written admiringly about the early critical essays of Edmund Wilson, Gold said, but instead of following the example the young Wilson had set in supporting and encouraging the novelists and poets of his generation, all I ever did was attack or belittle the work being produced by my own contemporaries.

Ginsberg (for all I know, having discussed the matter with Gold) now lashed out at me in similar terms. All night long he hectored and harangued me for my stupid failure to recognize both Kerouac's genius and his, and the more I fought back, the harder he tried to make me see how insensitive I was being. It was I, he kept railing, who was the know-nothing, not they.

Rather than rely on what is after nearly forty years a hazy memory, I want to quote from a letter Ginsberg wrote shortly before this encounter. It was to another mutual friend of ours from Columbia, the poet and critic John Hollander (through whom we had, in fact, met), and it gives a very good picture of what he said that night and the tone in which he said it:

> [Podhoretz lacks] even the basic ability to tell the difference between prosody and diction (as in his . . . diatribes on spontaneous bop prosody confusing it with the use of hiptalk not realizing it refers to rhythmical construction of phrases & sentences). I mean where am I going to begin a serious explanation if I have to deal with such unmitigated stupid ignorant ill willed inept vanity as that—someone like that wouldn't listen unless you hit him over the head with a totally new universe, but he's stuck in his own hideous world, I would try, but he scarcely has enough heart to hear—etc etc—so all these objections about juvenile delinquency, vulgarity, lack of basic education, bad taste, etc etc, no form, etc I mean it's impossible to discuss things like that—finally I get to see them as so basically *wrong* (unscientific) so dependent on ridiculous provincial schoolboy ambitions & presuppositions and so lacking contact with practical fact—that it seems a sort of plot almost, a kind of organized mob stupidity—the final camp of its announcing itself as a representative of value or civilization or taste—I mean I give up, that's just too much fucking nasty brass.*

But if the task was so hopeless, why did Ginsberg go ahead and try to explain himself to me anyway? According to Schumacher, he did it not because he aspired to win my "approval of [his] literature or lifestyle," but because I was an "influential member of the new critical establishment, and . . . it would have been, in terms of literary politics, a coup if [Ginsberg] had been able at least to gain a measure of respect from the camp" I represented.

---

*Sic to Ginsberg's eccentric punctuation here and elsewhere. The entire letter to Hollander can be found in the annotated edition of "Howl."

No doubt this consideration did play a part. (So relentless a self-promoter was Ginsberg that as he lay dying he asked his agent to do something about getting his latest collection reviewed in *The New York Times Book Review.*) And yet, as I could sense even then and as his weirdly unremitting fixation on me was to prove, he *did* crave my approval of his work, and even of his "lifestyle." For he did not limit himself that night to literary matters or to throwing the accusation of know-nothingism back in my face. He also harped on, and expressed incredulity over, my defense of the "square" way of life (or what today would be called middle-class values) against the Beat assault.

Here Schumacher for once gets it right when he says that I "was hearing nothing of . . . Ginsberg's harangues against middle-class living and values." Intransigent as I was in turning a deaf ear to his literary counterattack, I was even more determined to stand my ground on the moral and cultural issue between us. This was not because I was an uncritical admirer of "middle-class living and values." As it happens, I myself in that period was full of complaint about the "flabbiness of middle-class life" in Eisenhower's America (even using that very phrase in "The Know-Nothing Bohemians"). I also thought that my own generation was much too sober and mature for its own good, and (in a piece for *The New Leader* in 1957) I had predicted that we might soon "decide to take a swim in the Plaza fountain in the middle of the night."

Yet whatever I may have intended in invoking the example of F. Scott Fitzgerald and the youthful spirit of the 1920s symbolized by his drunken hijinks, it was certainly not the "know-nothing bohemianism" of Ginsberg and Kerouac. Indeed, to judge by the way I was living my own life, it was not any kind of bohemianism at all. At the age of twenty-six, the year *Howl and Other Poems* was published, I married a woman with two very small children, thereby assuming responsibility for an entire family at one stroke; and by the time "The Know-Nothing Bohemians" appeared in 1958, a third child had come along (with a fourth to follow in due course). To support this growing family, I was relying on three different sources of income: a full-time job as an editor, freelance writing at night and on weekends, and lecture engagements whenever I could get them.

Inevitably, then, and along with everything else, it was myself I was defending in fighting the Beats. Ginsberg sensed that there was an extraliterary, personal element in my opposition, but in his various attempts over the years to pin it down so that he could dispose of it once and for all, he kept looking in the wrong place. For instance, in a 1987 interview, he would attribute my hostility to disappointed ambition: "So then . . . Norman realized that . . . he wasn't [a poet]. So he had to go some different way for power, and he got very perverse thoughts and started taking revenge on poetry power." To still another interviewer in the 1980s, he would add an almost comically desperate variation on this theme: "Now, [Podhoretz] may have justifiably resented me because when I was twenty and editing *The Columbia Review* I'd published a poem of his by cutting it in half to the good part without asking him, which was a mistake, a very juvenile stupidity on my part."*

But the truth was that my gratitude to Ginsberg for publishing my poem far outweighed my shock at his cutting of it; and if I was ever "taking revenge" on anything connected with him, it was not his verse but what he himself called his "vision," which, as he would eventually come to recognize, was "provocative and interesting" to me.

How could it not have been? As against the law-abiding life I had chosen of a steady job and marriage and children, he conjured up a world of complete freedom from the limits imposed by such grim responsibilities. It was a world that promised endless erotic possibility together with the excitements of an expanded consciousness constantly open to new dimensions of being: more adventure, more sex, more intensity, more *life*.

God knows that as a young man full of energy and curiosity, and not altogether averse to taking risks, I was tempted by all this. God knows too that there were moments of resentment at the burdens I had seen fit to shoulder, moments when I felt cheated and when I dreamed of breaking out of the limits I had imposed upon myself. Yet

---

*The critic Paul Berman has gone so far as to dig up the two poems of mine that were published in *The Columbia Review* while Ginsberg was there. In a silly piece in the on-line magazine *Slate*, Berman quotes lines from both poems that he thinks Ginsberg might have inserted. But flattering though it is to my youthful efforts as a poet to have them attributed to Ginsberg, it was only "Jeremiah" that he edited, and all he did was cut.

at the same time, I was repelled by Ginsberg's world. In the abstract, he spoke for freedom from the oppressions of arbitrary social constraints, but his own work made no bones about the concrete consequences of this freedom: they were madness, drugs, and sexual perversity. In praising him at first for not "glamorizing" these consequences, I had failed to grasp just how radical he really was. But now I finally understood that to his antinomian mind, going mad in America was the only way to be sane, to get high on drugs was the only way to be sober, and to "scatter . . . semen freely to whomever come who may" was the only way to experience sex.

I was, to say the least, no antinomian. Although fantasies of promiscuity were only too appealing to me when I was still in my late twenties, I never imagined that there would be anything virtuous or praiseworthy about surrendering to them. And even if in some part of me I envied "N.C." (Neal Cassady), the "secret hero" of "Howl"—that "cocksman and Adonis" who had "sweetened the snatches of a million girls" and brought "joy to the memory of his innumerable lays"—and even if I also resisted the then-regnant Freudian interpretation of "compulsive Don Juanism" as a neurotic symptom, I did not consider such behavior healthy, let alone heroic. To portray it as such struck me as nothing more than a rationalization—and a morally tawdry and intellectually dishonest one at that.*

Where homosexuality was concerned, Ginsberg did not so much glorify as beatify those among the allegedly best minds of his generation "who let themselves be fucked in the ass by saintly motorcyclists, and screamed with joy/who blew and were blown by those human seraphim, the sailors, caresses of Atlantic and Caribbean love," and so on. In attributing saintliness and angelic status to his homosexual characters, as well as in other matters, Ginsberg was probably influenced by the use of similar imagery in the novels of the French writer Jean Genet—"another literary cocksucker," as Ginsberg affectionately

---

*In this connection, it is interesting to note that according to Barry Miles, another of Ginsberg's biographers, Cassady was once clinically diagnosed as sexually sadistic. Cassady, by the way, was not only the "secret hero" of "Howl" but, in the guise of Dean Moriarty, also the hero of On the Road.

called him. (Genet was himself canonized by no less prominent a cultural power than Jean-Paul Sartre, who wrote a nine-hundred-page book about him actually entitled *Saint Genet.*) Here again, as with heterosexual promiscuity, but with even greater antinomian conviction, Ginsberg was turning the tables and declaring that the perverse was infinitely superior to the normal.

So deeply did Ginsberg believe this that I even suspected him of having become a homosexual not out of erotic compulsion but by an act of will and as another way of expressing his contempt for normal life. This suspicion was less silly than it may sound. Ginsberg spoke freely about being homosexual to straight classmates like Herbert Gold and John Hollander, but unlike most of the other homosexuals at Columbia who (though necessarily closeted in those days) were easy to spot, he always struck me as straight. (And, indeed, as I learn from his biographers, he slept with a fair number of women while he was in his twenties.) Nor was I alone in taking Ginsberg for straight. Even someone as close to him as Neal Cassady thought (as Ginsberg himself put it in an early poem) he "was not a queer at first."

While I am at it, I might as well also admit to another outlandish suspicion about Ginsberg's homosexuality that I once entertained. This one, having more to do with literature than with ideology, was put into my mind by a crack that Philip Rahv, the co-editor of *Partisan Review,* once made about Robert Lowell. Always cynical about writers, and especially poets, Rahv professed to believe that the only reason Lowell had converted to Catholicism was out of the hope that it would help him write poetry as good as T. S. Eliot's became after *his* conversion to Anglicanism. Well then, might not Ginsberg, with his eye on the great romantic tradition of the *poète maudit* as exemplified by the likes of Arthur Rimbaud, have willed himself into homosexuality out of an analogous hope?

The answer was no. For whereas Lowell left the Church after a while (because, said Rahv with a triumphant smirk, it had failed to do the trick), Ginsberg remained an active and enthusiastic homosexual once he had given up his youthful struggles against it and stopped sleeping with girls.

Not that he ever accepted the current party line of the gay-rights movement that homosexuality is always inborn and never a matter of choice. Peter Orlovsky, whom he once went so far as to list as his "wife" in his entry in *Who's Who*, was, he said, "mostly straight" but decided to make a life with him. Kerouac too, though straight, "was willing to sleep with me occasionally." So was Neal Cassady. This was the same N.C. who "sweetened the snatches of a million girls," but he "made a big exception and we slept together quite a bit." And once Ginsberg became famous, he had no trouble luring "lots of straight young kids" into his bed.

Ginsberg also dissented from another of the current twists in the party line of the gay rights movement: the idea that homosexuals are exactly like heterosexuals in every respect other than erotic orientation and that they want all the same things, including monogamous relationships cemented by legally sanctioned marriages. In spite of his relationship with Orlovsky, the Ginsberg of "Howl" would have seen such an embrace of middle-class values as a suicidal surrender to Moloch. Nor did advancing age or the pressures of gay political correctness induce a conversion to monogamy. Even as late as the last week of his life, when his nurse told him he was HIV-negative, he replied, "That's surprising, given that I've had quite a lot lately," and his very last poem, written when he was on his death bed, dwelt almost entirely, and in his usual graphic fashion, on his "lovers over half century."

Of a piece with his beatification of homosexuality was Ginsberg's glorification of insanity. "I saw the best minds of my generation destroyed by madness," he announced in the opening words of "Howl"—but destroyed, as we immediately discover, only to be reborn into a state of grace, of sensitivity and wisdom, beyond the reach of anyone really crazy enough or sufficiently beaten down to be considered sane in the kingdom of Moloch. I thought this was heartless nonsense. Far from being in touch with a higher reality, the crazy people I had known—and I had known a few—were cut off in the most frightening ways from themselves and the world around them. There was something cruel about drafting such pitiable creatures into the service of an ideological aggression against the kind of normal life to which they would have given everything to return. And it was all the more heartless for parading itself as compassion.

Then, finally, there was the related issue of drugs. As a young man, I was a fairly heavy drinker, as were most of the literary people I knew. It was regarded as manly to drink a lot, and one took pride in being able to hold one's liquor. But we never for a moment doubted that drinking was bad for us—that indeed was the whole point. Nor did we ever mistake alcohol for an aid to literary composition ("I never try to write a line when I'm not strictly on the wagon," said Eugene O'Neill, one of the champion literary alcoholics of all time). By contrast, Ginsberg, who wrote "Howl" and a number of other poems under the influence of various drugs, never tired of declaring that they were the route to a higher and deeper consciousness.

From the few serious users I had by then come across, it was obvious to me that this was another egregious lie. Hard drugs like heroin (about which even Ginsberg himself, having "tried it a number of times," would subsequently develop second thoughts) and hallucinogenics like LSD (of which he would always be an enthusiastic propagandist) were dangerous to the mind and crippling to the spirit, quite apart from the degrading dependency they created.

As for marijuana, I knew from my own experience with it (which was limited but certainly did include inhaling), and from what I could see of its effect on the mental processes of others, that what it mainly did was generate an illusion of heightened awareness, which as often as not issued in the solemn utterance of hackneyed "insights" and pretentious banalities. I accepted that it was not necessarily addictive, but that did not mean it was not habit-forming. Moreover, persuaded by propagandists like Ginsberg that they could try marijuana with impunity, untold numbers of kids were getting hooked on it, and a certain percentage of these, having thus dipped a toe into the drug culture, would soon plunge into the deeper and more dangerous waters of LSD or heroin or cocaine.

For nearly four hours that Saturday night in 1958, Ginsberg and I had at each other on all these issues. As Ginsberg would later recall it, Kerouac tried talking to me but "couldn't make a dent"; eventually I "went home and that was the end of it." As I remember it, however,

Ginsberg himself did most of the talking and Kerouac, like his girl-friend, hardly said a word. Nor did I just go home. Sometime after midnight, Kerouac suggested that we all troop over to see "Lucien," who would just be getting off from work. Obviously, he was referring to Lucien Carr, who I had thought must still be in jail for the famous murder he had committed back in the 1940s. But it emerged that he had only served a brief term for manslaughter and had been set free many years before. Tired though I was and eager to make an end of what had been a tense and difficult night, I could not resist this chance to meet a legendary figure from my college days. Neither Ginsberg nor the others felt like going out, and so I wound up walk-ing alone with Kerouac to a nearby building in the West Village.

Once, when Hilton Kramer was chief art critic of *The New York Times*, he found himself seated at a dinner next to Woody Allen, who asked him whether he felt embarrassed when he ran into people whose work he had attacked. "No," replied Kramer, "I expect *them* to be embarrassed for doing bad work." Lacking Hilton's magnificent self-possession, I have indeed always felt embarrassed in such cases, and there have even been times when I have had to stifle an impulse to apologize. This was one of them. Ginsberg's defense of Kerouac as a writer had, just as he later said, failed to "make a dent" on me; if anything, the aesthetic argu-ments in support of "spontaneous bop prosody" seemed even more nonsensical coming from Ginsberg's mouth than they had coming from his pen. But, disconcertingly, Kerouac was as likable in the flesh as he was repellent in print. In contrast to the seething Ginsberg, who went at me with everything he had, Kerouac (in spite of being the aggrieved party) was so easygoing and charming that I could not help regretting the nasti-ness with which I had treated him and wishing I could say that I had been won over and now saw his novels in a new light.

But of course I could not and did not say this. Instead, what I did as soon as we were alone together was ask him about growing up in New England in a French Canadian family. Having been stationed for a while in that part of the country when I was in the army and having had a girlfriend in his own hometown of Lowell, Massachusetts, I was genuinely curious about this subject, and since he was happy to talk about it, the ploy worked. By the time we reached our destination, my discomfort had all but disappeared—only to be replaced by disappointment over Lucien Carr. In my teenage imaginings, he had been a larger-than-life character, but the man I now met seemed colorless; he surprised me even more by having a wife and a child (or possibly two).* If not for the air of squalor pervading the place, it might have been taken for a conventional bourgeois establishment, and the lingering traces of romance that had been attached to Carr faded away forever in the hour or so I spent there in his company.

It was about 3 A.M. when Kerouac and I left together. He walked me to the subway station in Sheridan Square, and we parted with pleasant words, which stood in the sharpest possible contrast to the ominous parting words Ginsberg had flung at me a few hours earlier just as I was leaving his apartment: "We'll get you through your children!"

I never saw Kerouac again, but there was more yelling by Ginsberg about a year later at a very big party thrown by Norman Mailer (the same party which became notorious when it ended with Mailer stabbing and nearly killing his then wife, Adele). In one of those interviews of the 1980s from which I have already quoted, Ginsberg would allege that early that evening I came over to him and said that if he would only get rid of friends like Kerouac, I could help him become "part of the larger scene" and advance his career in New York. Hostility transmuting his normally golden poet's ear into tin, he paraphrased me as follows: "Why aren't you working with us instead of these people that are so nowhere?"

It is inconceivable that I could actually have said this to Ginsberg, let alone in the words he put into my mouth. After all, though still controversial in some literary circles, he was already a very well known and widely acclaimed poet, and even if I had been as great a fool as this story makes me appear, I would also have had to be completely crazy to imagine that I was in a position to further his career. What I actually *may* have been foolish enough to do was repeat what I had already said several times in print—that I thought he was one of the few Beat writers who had genuine literary talent and that his relentless

---

*I recently discovered that one of these babies grew up to be the well-regarded novelist Caleb Carr.

evangelizing on behalf of the others was obscuring the difference between his work and theirs.

Not that I failed to understand why Ginsberg was doing all this
evangelizing. Much influenced by Ezra Pound in his poetry, as well as
in his prose (and especially in his letters, down to the eccentric punctuation and the use of idiosyncratic mock-comic locutions), Ginsberg
also, I recognized, saw himself as playing for his own literary movement the same role Pound had played almost a half-century earlier in
tirelessly promoting the avante-garde (or "modernist") writers of his
own generation, to whom he was at once a leader, an exemplar, and a
mentor. The difference was that Pound had had W. B. Yeats, T. S.
Eliot, and James Joyce to push and promote (not to mention a host of
lesser but still very important figures) whereas all poor Ginsberg had to
work with were the likes of Jack Kerouac, Gary Snyder, and Lawrence
Ferlinghetti. And while many of the writers Pound sponsored were
greater than he was (vicious though he was in his politics, where literature was concerned he could often be supremely selfless), Ginsberg was
the best of his gang—such as he was and such as they were.

In any case, if there may have been a tiny germ of truth up to that
point in the story he was telling about our encounter at Mailer's party,
most of the rest of what he said was pure hallucination:

> I suddenly saw myself in a B movie out of Balzac, with me as the dis-
> tinguished provincial being tempted by the idiot worldly banker—
> "We'll give you a career if you renounce your mother and father and
> your background." It was so corny, like being propositioned by the
> devil or something, . . . so I started screaming at him, "You big dumb
> fuckhead! You idiot! You don't know anything about anything!" Now,
> true to his particular nature, Podhoretz thought I was going to get vi-
> olent, because that's all he thinks about. . . . Podhoretz yelled, "He's
> going to get violent," and Mailer came over and took my arm, so I had
> to reassure him I wasn't going to hit anybody.

That he screamed abuse that night at me was true, but the idea that
I would be afraid of trading punches with Allen Ginsberg reminds me
of what James Cagney (a former street kid like me) once said about a
similar possibility involving Humphrey Bogart (who, like Ginsberg,

was raised in the middle class, albeit on a higher economic rung): "When it comes to fighting, he's about as tough as Shirley Temple." Nevertheless, I tell the story here because, like Ginsberg's letter to John Hollander, it conveys a vivid sense of the sinister role I played in his paranoid fantasies. Indeed, to Ginsberg himself, this was "an epiphanous moment in my relation with Podhoretz and what he was part of—a large right-wing protopolice surveillance movement."

Here, too, however, as in his allusion to me in "Howl," Ginsberg was being anachronistic. In 1985, when he recalled this "epiphanous moment," I had long since settled into the conservative position to which I am still firmly committed, but in 1960, when we met at Mailer's party, I was in no sense part of anything that could remotely be described as right-wing. On the contrary, I was then in the final stages of a process that had been carrying me from the liberalism with which I had grown up to the radicalism with which I would be identified for most of the decade ahead.

At the time, Ginsberg was well aware of this development. He knew that while opposing the Beats, I had been championing the novels of Mailer and other cultural radicals, such as the revisionist Freudian philosopher Norman O. Brown and the communitarian-anarchist social critic (and openly homosexual) Paul Goodman, all of whom differed from Ginsberg's crowd in their intellectual rigor and complexity. It would seem, though, that my break with the Left in the late 1960s (which included the belated realization that intellectual rigor and complexity did not make bad ideas any less pernicious) gave Ginsberg a chance to read a right-wing motivation back into my criticisms of Beat writing. This political explanation then joined the other two theories he had come up with (my lingering resentment over his editing of "Jeremiah" and my disappointed ambition as a poet) in trying to to get over his endlessly nagging worry over my refusal to acknowledge the greatness of the literary school of which he was the founder and the head.

To this day, I have trouble figuring out why my opposition should have bothered Ginsberg so much. It is perhaps understandable that he would crave my approval when he was just starting out and I was "an influential member of the new critical establishment." But why should he still have needed it when I was no longer even in the game (having pretty much shifted my attention from literary matters to politics and foreign affairs) and the rest of the world was falling at his feet with praises ("Ginsberg is responsible for loosening the breath of American poetry at midcentury," ran a typical comment by the eminent critic Helen Vendler, who assigned him "a memorable place in modern poetry"); heaping laurels on his head (including, among many others, the National Arts Club Gold Medal for lifetime achievement, a National Book Award, and election to the august American Academy of Arts and Letters); and even showering him with riches (a publisher's advance of $160,000—for poetry!—and $1.2 *million* for his papers from Stanford University)?

Was he so disturbed by me because in his heart of hearts he knew that, no matter what he kept saying aloud, my rejection of his extravagant claims to greatness as a poet and my arguments against his antinomian ideas could not be dismissed out of hand as the ravings of an ignorant philistine who was part of a "right-wing proto-police surveillance movement"? Did those arguments go on sticking so painfully in his craw because he could never come up with answers that truly satisfied him? Might he at moments even have feared that I might be right?

Unlikely as this seems, it is entirely possible. Once, for example, under the influence of yage, a psychedelic drug he took repeatedly while in Peru in the early 1960s, he had a vision in which it came to him that his "queer isolation" was the price he was paying for his flight from women, which was itself tied to "my lack of . . . contact with birth—my fear to be and to die—to bear life." I myself could not have done better than this in describing what I believed then—and still believe today—to be the spiritual etiology of homosexuality or in stating the deepest of all arguments against Ginsberg's usual antinomian view of it as superior to heterosexuality and everything entailed by a life of involvement with women.

This change in attitude was only fleeting, but while it lasted it found expression of a kind in a poem called "This Form of Life Needs Sex," and it thoroughly alarmed William Seward Burroughs, who, long before achieving great fame as the author of *Naked Lunch*, was a role model and mentor to Ginsberg, especially in the matter of drugs. Schumacher writes:

Knowing . . . that Allen, as a result of his yage experiments, had decided he should be kinder to women, Bill would go off on long, wicked antiwoman routines, repeating his theory that women were extraterrestrial agents sent by enemies to weaken the male species. They had "poison juices dripping all over 'em," Burroughs said, and if Allen . . . knew what was good for [him, he] would stay away from women.

Burroughs, incidentally, thought that if Ginsberg were cut open, Lionel Trilling, the Columbia professor to whom he had been closest as a student, would be one of the shaping forces found within him. This may provide another possible clue to Ginsberg's compulsive contention with me, since after he left Columbia I became Trilling's favorite student and (in my early days as a critic) his most loyal disciple. In being so exercised over my opinion of his poems and his ideas, then, Ginsberg may have been using me as a stand-in for Trilling, whose judgment of *Howl and Other Poems* had actually been much harsher than mine. Whereas I had at least pronounced "Howl" remarkable and thought that Ginsberg had found his true voice in it, Trilling told him in a letter that the poems in the collection were "dull." Furthermore:

> They are not like Whitman—they are all prose, all rhetoric, without any music. What I used to like in your poems, whether I thought they were good or bad, was the *voice* I heard in them, true and natural and interesting. There is no real voice here. As for the doctrinal element of the poems, apart from the fact that I of course reject it, it seems to me that I heard it very long ago and that you give it to me in all its orthodoxy, with nothing new added.*

Be all that as it may, there came a day when, all of a sudden, in the blink of an eye and out of the blue, a wholly new idea about me entered Ginsberg's mind. Here is how he would describe it in 1987:

> I had a very funny experience a couple of years ago when I dropped some Ecstasy . . . and I suddenly remembered Norman Podhoretz. And I said, Gee, good old Norman, we went to college together. . . . If

---

*Like the Hollander letter quoted above, this one can be found in the annotated edition of "Howl."

he weren't there like a wall I can butt my head against, I wouldn't have anybody to hate. And why hate him? He's part of my world, and he's sort of like the character Mr. Meany or the Bluenose or the Blue Meanie. At the same time, he has some sense in him. . . . But did I ever really hate him or was I just sort of fascinated by him?

I also saw him as a sort of sacred personage in my life, in a way: someone whose vision is so opposite from mine that it's provocative and interesting—just as my vision is interesting and provocative enough for him to write columns against it in the newspaper. In fact, maybe he's more honest than I am because he attacks me openly. So I should really respect him as one of the sacred personae in the drama of my own transitory existence.

This amazing interview, originally published in an obscure literary quarterly in Kansas City, Missouri, came to my attention only when it was reprinted about a year later in *Harper's* under the title "I Sing of Norman P." By that time, Ginsberg and I had not laid eyes on each other for something like twenty years, and I was naturally bowled over by this transformation in his attitude toward me. But it now also occurred to me that I might have had an inkling or two of it long before.

As far back as the mid-1960s, for example, when I would run into him now and then at a party or a meeting, Ginsberg would sometimes startle me (and perhaps himself as well) with a relatively cordial greeting. In that same period, we also had a curious encounter in Paris, where I was spending a few days on my way to a conference in Yugoslavia. Walking on the Boulevard St.-Germain, I spotted him coming toward me from the other direction, and having no wish to be yelled at yet again, I decided I would pretend not to have noticed him and pass on by. But before I could execute this evasive maneuver, he waved, ran up to me, and warmly insisted that I have a drink with him at the nearby Café de Flore. This was, of course, the hangout of Sartre and his circle, but so far as I could tell from looking around once we were seated, Ginsberg himself was the only famous writer in evidence. And famous by now not only in America but throughout the world. In recent months alone, as he told me with an excitement seeming to suggest that he thought I would share in his pleasure, he had been lionized in Havana and Prague before being expelled in turn by the Communist governments of those two countries for various forms of homosexual exhibitionism.*

From the drink I had with Ginsberg in the Café de Flore, I got the feeling that he no longer regarded me as the enemy. But this time it was I who was being anachronistic. I infer from Schumacher that the real reason he was so eager to sit down with me that day was that "After weeks of nonstop activity and celebrity limelight, he was on his own again, feeling lonely, his ego a bit bruised because he was not as recognized on the avenues of Paris as he had [just] been in England."† I also gather from Ginsberg's own statements that his hatred of me was still fresh and remained strong for at least another twenty years, probably even intensifying when I really did begin moving to the Right in the late 1960s.

The feeling was mutual. After "Howl," I pretty much lost interest in Ginsberg as a poet, the novelty having, so to speak, worn off. "Kaddish," his elegy on the death of his mother (regarded by many as his best poem), had affecting moments, but everything else, including much of "Kaddish" itself, seemed to be one kind of propaganda or another for the new radical movement of the 1960s passing itself off as

---

*It has always struck me as odd that so many of the dissidents in Czechoslovakia, all of whom were passionate anti-Communists, should have made heroes out of Ginsberg and other icons of the counterculture, all of whom were equally passionate anti-anti-Communists. Thus, when on a visit of my own to Prague in 1988 I was taken to meet Vaclav Havel, then the most prominent of the dissidents (and later, of course, to become president of a free Czech Republic), the first thing that hit my eye upon entering his apartment was a huge poster of John Lennon hanging on the wall. Disconcerted, I tried to persuade Havel that the counterculture in the West was no friend of anti-Communists like himself, but I made even less of a "dent" on him than Ginsberg had made on me thirty years earlier.

Conversely, I always thought the Communist governments were stupid in failing to understand that cultural radicals like Ginsberg, who did everything in their power to undermine American resistance to Communism, were their *de facto* allies in the cold war. I mean, when Ginsberg ridiculed the cold war in a poem like "America" ("The Russia wants to eat us alive. The Russia's power mad. She wants to take our cars from out of our garages" and so on), whose political purposes did Havel on the one side and Castro on the other think were being served?

†In 1993 the French made up for this by awarding him the medal of Chevalier de l'Ordre des Arts et des Lettres.

poetry. In fact, Ginsberg became one of the leading spirits of that movement, and the mounting disenchantment that ultimately led me to break ranks with it was in no small part caused by the triumph of everything he represented over the kind of radical spirit which ten years earlier I had hoped might emerge and which I wanted to help develop.

Now, in the mid-1960s, as before, the major difference between us had to do with our wildly contrasting ideas about America. Ginsberg's anti-Americanism of the 1950s had been bad enough, but the form it took in the 1960s as it exfoliated (or perhaps metastasized would be a better word) was even worse. His disciples and friends now extended way beyond the relatively narrow circle of the Beats to encompass the entire world of the counterculture—from rock musicians like Bob Dylan to hippies and yippies like Abbie Hoffman and Jerry Rubin to a variety of "gurus" peddling one form or another of Oriental mysticism. What they all had in common was a fierce hatred of America, which they saw as "Amerika," a country morally and spiritually equivalent to Nazi Germany. Amerika's political system was based on oppression, to which the only answer was resistance and revolution; and its culture was based on repression, to which the only answer was to opt out of middle-class life and liberate the squelched and smothered self through drugs and sexual promiscuity.

I simply could not stomach any of this, least of all the disgusting comparisons to Nazi Germany. Even when I was at my most radical, I still loved America, and my own utopian aspirations were directed at perfecting, not destroying, it. It went without saying that there were problems and flaws, above all the plight of the blacks and the poor, but I was confident that they could be effectively addressed through programs of radical reform within the going political system.

As for Vietnam, like Ginsberg and his friends I was opposed to the war, but unlike them, I thought it was a mistake, not a crime. I hoped for a negotiated settlement that would allow us to salvage our honor by withdrawing without abandoning the South Vietnamese to the Communists of the North, whereas in their hatred of America they yearned for us to be defeated and humiliated and the Communists to win.

In general, and over and above the specifics, I believed that the revolutionism of the New Left was both futile and dangerous, and as the

1960s wore on, I came increasingly to regard the counterculture as a species of nihilism that was wrecking the lives of more and more of the young people who were following through on the injunction of Ginsberg's great friend and fellow pusher of LSD, Timothy Leary, to "turn on, tune in, and drop out."

I was right about the counterculture, but I was wrong in thinking that my own utopian fantasies of perfection through radical reform had any better chance of success than any other brand of utopianism or that they could compete, especially among the young, with the seductively tantalizing promise of freedom from the responsibilities and constraints of a normal adult life. Back in 1958, as I was leaving his apartment, Ginsberg had shouted, "We'll get you through your children," and so it was turning out. Not, thank God, where my own children were concerned. Two of them would still be too young to feel the impact of the 1960s, while the older two, both girls, would escape with minimal damage. But some of their friends—bright, beautiful almost-women whose families were prosperous enough to send them to a fashionable private school in New York—would not be so lucky. One would suffer a drug-induced breakdown and go on to spend years of her life in and out of a series of mental hospitals; another would become a hopeless junkie; and a third would be raped and murdered while recklessly hitchhiking on a lonely road in the dead of night. And then there were the young men who would run off to Canada to avoid the Vietnam draft or leave college to join a commune or hang out in cesspools like Haight-Ashbury, where the drugs were plentiful and the sex was easy, and who would never manage to climb out of the hole of failure they had been encouraged by Ginsberg and his disciples in the counterculture to dig for themselves.

As the 1960s wore on, I came more and more to see all this as a new kind of plague, and when in the late 1970s I wrote a book about my break with radicalism, I ended with a lament for the victims it had claimed among the "especially vulnerable" young. They had, I said, been inoculated against almost every one of the physical diseases which in times past had literally made it impossible for so many to reach adulthood. But against a spiritual plague like this one they were entirely helpless.

Nor could they count on any help from their parents, who had themselves been so blinded by the plague that they mistook their children's "contemptuous repudiation of everything American and middle-class . . . for a form of idealism" and "went on insisting, even when the evidence of sickness and incapacity stared them full in the face, that the children were models of superior health." Shades of the antinomian propaganda Ginsberg had done as much as anyone else in America to spread.

So too with the teachers of the period, who surveyed a mass of desperately disordered and disoriented young people refusing to take their appointed places in the world and then proceeded to pronounce them, in the unforgettable words of Professor Archibald Cox of the Harvard Law School, "the best informed, the most intelligent, and the most idealistic" generation ever born in America. Again, what was this but a toned-down version of the opening words of "Howl" translated into the language of the liberal establishment?

An even more telling sign of the degree to which the hated establishment wound up capitulating to the Beats came in 1987, when the city council of Lowell, Massachusetts, decided to build a new park dedicated to the memory of Jack Kerouac, its famous native son. I happened just then to be in the middle of a four-year stint as a syndicated weekly columnist with my home base in the *New York Post*, and I devoted a piece to expressing my amazement at the fact that the people of Lowell should wish to memorialize the author of a series of books heaping abuse on the way of life lived in, precisely, places like Lowell. It was true that for a few years before he died in 1969 at the age of forty-seven, a very ill Kerouac had settled down in a suburb with his wife and mother, returned to the Catholic Church, and also moved to the Right in his political views. But it was not this Kerouac the world remembered and to whom the city of Lowell was preparing to build a monument; it was the younger Kerouac who, along with Ginsberg, had spawned the counterculture of the 1960s with its "hatred and contempt for everything generally deemed healthy, decent, or normal."

Around this same time, another and very similar event occurred about which I also wrote a column. On the twenty-fifth anniversary in

1986 of the publication of Joseph Heller's novel *Catch-22*, the Air Force Academy in Colorado staged a conference in its honor—in honor, that is, of a book viciously defaming the branch of the very service in which the academy was preparing its students to serve. The Air Force as Heller portrays it is an organization run by idiots and lunatics who send countless young boys to their death for no reason other than the furthering of their own personal ambitions and the lining of their own pockets. In honoring *Catch-22*, the Air Force Academy, an institution whose entire reason for existence was to teach the arts of war, was also implicitly endorsing Heller's justification of draft evasion and even desertion as morally superior to military service.

In the interest of full disclosure, I should add that I had written enthusiastically about *Catch-22* in *Show*—a glossy mass monthly for which I, already the editor of *Commentary*, was then moonlighting as a regular book critic—when it first came out. This piece expressed only one critical reservation, which was that Heller's comic nihilism did not go far *enough*. My review not only made Heller very happy in itself but also helped his book along, for, contrary to the notion that *Catch-22* was published to universal acclaim and took off like a rocket the minute it hit the shelves, it actually had a mixed reception and was a slow starter where sales were concerned. Robert Brustein, who was then still more a literary than a theater critic, and at the time a close friend of mine, probably pushed this first novel by an unknown writer harder than anyone else. But I did my share as well to establish its importance, and Heller quite naturally responded with warm feelings toward me. For a while, we were fairly friendly, but he (being far more politically Left than many of his readers ever realized) would become outraged by the increasingly insupportable heresies to which I began giving vent, and which (to give credit where credit is due) he was among the first to spot and denounce. After making his disgust with my political evolution clear in a letter to *The Nation*, he would cement our new ex-friendship with a savage caricature of me in one of his later novels. As for Brustein, he too eventually became an ex-friend, though the break between us had more to do with literary than with political matters.

My 1986 column on Heller aroused the ire of a number of readers, including a colonel teaching at the Air Force Academy who wrote a letter to *The Washington Post* lecturing me about the great importance of literature in general and satire in particular (though he never went quite so far as to claim that reading *Catch-22* was a good way to prepare for becoming a fighter pilot). The column I did on Kerouac about a year later also aroused ire, most notably that of the émigré Russian novelist Vassily Aksyonov, to whom I sounded like the cultural commissars he thought he had left behind in fleeing to the United States from the Soviet Union. But it had no such effect on Ginsberg. He referred to it in the interview in which he said that I was still speaking out in the newspapers against his own "vision" (and where he added that I was "still denouncing Kerouac as a moral degenerate"). Yet instead of being angered or offended, he spoke of me in respectful and even affectionate terms for the first time since we were both kids in college.

He then followed up—I forget exactly when—with a handwritten note very warmly inviting me to a seminar at the Naropa Institute in Colorado, a Buddhist college he had helped to found (and which became, much more suitably than the park in Lowell, a monument to Jack Kerouac under the name "The Jack Kerouac School of Disembodied Poetics"). *This* invitation, unlike the one some thirty years earlier to his apartment in the Village, I unhesitatingly declined, knowing that the new Ginsberg's lovingkindness would put me even more uncomfortably on the defensive than the young Ginsberg's rage had done.

I heard nothing further from Ginsberg until he once again described his new attitude toward me in that piece, cited earlier, which *The New York Times* did about him on the occasion of his seventieth birthday:

One day a few years back, a "light bulb went on in my head," Mr. Ginsberg said in the garden of his favorite Polish restaurant on the Lower East Side. "I thought of Norman. I thought how can I hate him? All those years he's had to suffer all my contumely in my head. It's served as an education, to make me think my thoughts. He's been a great help." Now, said Mr. Ginsberg, Mr. Podhoretz is "kind of a sacred object on my horizon."

Another invitation then arrived, not from Ginsberg himself but from a television producer who wanted to put us on the air together. But once more I passed up a chance to see him again. Six months later he was dead.

The rule is never to speak ill of the dead, but the obituarists and commemorators who wrote about Ginsberg upon his death could not have broken the rule even if they had wanted to, since they could see no ill in him to speak of at all. Except for George Will in his syndicated column and an anonymous editorialist in *The New Criterion*, everyone else reached lyrically for the stars. In *The New Yorker*, David Remnick, for whom "the distinguishing feature of Ginsberg's character was his generosity, his sweetness, his openness," accorded his work a place among the classics of the literary canon. In *The Washington Post*, Henry Allen also pronounced him "a great poet" who spoke "for the right and need of Americans to express personal and universal truth." In *Newsweek*, David Gates concluded that "Ginsberg's lifelong work was to say goodbye: in joy and sorrow, love and longing. And to remind us that ours is too." In *The Nation*, John Leonard said that "his ultimate role at every engagement in our second Civil War was as a nurse, like his buddy Walt Whitman."

And the encouragement Ginsberg gave to drugs and sexual licentiousness of every kind? To the extent that this was mentioned at all, it was breezily treated as a charming foible or as an expression of ideas that might have seemed a bit extreme in 1956, when (to paraphrase one elegist) "repression and conformity, and not the Russians and the Chinese, were the true enemies of America," but that were in the end revealed (in the words of another elegist) as "the beginning of a renewal of American values."

Ginsberg was also fulsomely praised as a pioneer of the gay rights movement, which indeed he was. Yet so far as I was able to determine, no one thought to draw a connection between the emergence of AIDS and the rampant homosexual promiscuity promoted by Ginsberg, with anal intercourse as an especially "joyful" feature that is described in loving (and sometimes not so loving) detail in poem after poem.

These poems are pornographic in the simple sense of providing descriptions of sexual activity in language that is highly explicit even by the lax and latitudinarian standards of our day. To such descriptions Ginsberg devotes a number of entire poems ("Many Loves," "Please Master," "Love Comes," "The Guest," and "Sphincter," among others). They are also to be found in passages scattered throughout Ginsberg's oeuvre, early and late—old age seeming not to have inhibited his compulsion to write in what I believe he himself would have acknowledged was the "dirtiest" possible way about his sexual encounters and fantasies.

In all fairness, I should take note of the fact that neither did old age have an inhibiting effect on the fantasies (heterosexual through and through in this case) of an infinitely greater poet than Ginsberg:

> What shall I do with this absurdity—/O heart, O troubled heart—this caricature,/Decrepit age that has been tied to me/As to a dog's tail?/ Never had I more/Excited, passionate, fantastical/Imagination . . .

But W. B. Yeats did not go on to describe the erotic details conjured up by his excited, passionate, and fantastical imagination.

Yeats also knew as well as Ginsberg that, as he put it in one of his greatest short poems, ". . . Love has pitched his mansion in/The place of excrement."* Yet somehow I doubt that, even leaving the issue of homosexuality aside, he would have approved of such direct elabora-

---

*I suppose it is necessary in this context to explain that Yeats meant, as is obvious from the poem as a whole, not to recommend anal intercourse but to desublimate the female tendency to romanticize sex and to strike a blow against "the heart's pride" (much as Freud said that Galileo, Darwin, and he himself had struck successive blows against human pride in removing the earth from the center of the universe, linking man to the animals, and demonstrating that he is always in the grip of irrational forces). The whole marvelous passage comes from a series spoken by a character Yeats calls Crazy Jane, who is in this poem speaking with a Bishop: "'A woman can be proud and stiff/ When on love intent;/But Love has pitched his mansion in/The place of excrement;/For nothing can be sole or whole/That has not been rent.'"

tions of this fact as the following passage (written by Ginsberg in his mid-fifties about an incident that had occurred when he was about twenty years old):

> . . . he fucked me in the ass
> till I smelled brown excrement
> staining his cock
> & tried to get up from bed to go to the toilet a minute
> but he held me down & kept pumping at me, serious & said
> "No, I don't want to stop I like it dirty like this."

Nor, I would presume to guess, would Yeats have approved of Ginsberg's countless references to "shit" and other variants in the vulgate for excrement. This one, for example, comes from "Violent Collaborations," a little number written to be sung in which Ginsberg clearly set out to go for the pornographic gold and (with the help of someone named Peter Hale) succeeded: "Fuck me & fist me/in your army enlist me/Poop on me when you're at ease."*

Finally, I could find only one mention (in *The Weekly Standard*) of Ginsberg's active sponsorship of the abominable North American Man Boy Love Alliance (NAMBLA), an organization devoted to the legalization of homosexual pedophilia. "I don't know exactly how to define what's underage," he once explained, quickly adding that he himself had "never made it with anyone under fifteen." Not that this prevented him from writing "Old Love Story," a poem taking issue with those who "think the love of boys is wicked" by invoking (in rhymed couplets, probably so as to suggest how traditional pedophilia was) the great men throughout history who lusted after the flesh of very young males.

There are writers of my generation with whom I dealt harshly

---

*I apologize for quoting such stuff, but I have felt it necessary to do so for two reasons. First, I want to demonstrate that I am neither exaggerating nor being unfair in using the word *pornographic* here. Secondly, because our debates over pornography—and still more about anal intercourse and other homosexual practices, like the fisting refered to in "Violent Collaborations," which the eruption of AIDS brought, as it were, out of the closet—have become so abstract and even, ironically, prudish, there is simply no other way of making clear what exactly we are talking about when we discuss these things.

when I was a young critic but whom, as we grew older together, I found myself reading with more sympathy and greater pleasure. As Ginsberg said of me, they were "part of my world." Because we cut our teeth on and were shaped by the same books and the same movies and the same radio programs and the same public events, we carried with us a shared frame of reference and we spoke the same language— even when we used it to disagree. As the years rolled by, and with the arrival of successive generations treading all of us down, this common background of experience bred in me a sense of kinship with these writers that I did not feel when we were young.

Of course, there was the additional fact that some of them, like Philip Roth and John Updike, developed into better writers than they were then. Roth, in particular, moved beyond the adolescent snobbery with which he used to regard everyone but himself and his friends and came to display a range of sympathetic understanding rarely even hinted at in his early work. Indeed, having once expressed a loathing no less ferocious in its own way than Ginsberg's for the life lived by most people in America, Roth (as I read his novel *American Pastoral*, published in 1997) finally landed firmly on the side of such people and against the intellectuals and academics who still maintained the sneering and patronizing attitudes that he himself had held in days gone by.

No such change ever came over Allen Ginsberg, for all the "generosity," the "sweetness," and the "openness" that David Remnick and others found in his character when he too was getting on in years. As a poet, he never grew or developed (even most of his admirers think that nothing he wrote after 1959 was as good as "Howl" and "Kaddish"), and he went to his death still preaching the same false and pernicious ideas about life in America with which he burst onto the scene in the 1950s and which spread (to borrow an image he once used about my ideas) "like trench mouth" through American culture in the 1960s.

Fortunately, these ideas were not by the time he died especially fashionable among the middle-class young. And yet there was enough resemblance between the situation at the turn of the century and the cultural climate of the 1950s to fear that his siren song might yet find its insidious way into the ears of yet another generation of restless kids, misleading and corrupting them as it did so many of their forebears in the all-too-recent past. And so at his death I was still inclined to say what I had said about ten years earlier in concluding my column about the park dedicated to Kerouac in Lowell:

> "I'm worried about a role model for kids," explained the lone member of the Lowell city council who voted against the Kerouac memorial. He is right to worry. After all, Kerouac and Ginsberg once played a part in ruining a great many young people who were influenced by their "distaste for normal life and common decency."

That last phrase, I hastened to point out, came not from the Lowell city councilman but from George Orwell, who was talking not about Ginsberg and Kerouac but about some of his own contemporaries in the England of the 1930s whose writings expressed many of the same attitudes. As against those contemporaries, Orwell insisted, "The fact to which we have got to cling, as to a lifebelt, is that it is possible to be a normal decent person and yet to be fully alive." Instead, we were memorializing Ginsberg and Kerouac, thereby further weakening our already tenuous grasp on Orwell's saving fact, and abandoning the field once again to these latter-day Pied Pipers, and their current successors, who never ceased telling our children that the life being lived around them was not worth living at all.

I was of course thinking there of the children through whom Ginsberg promised to "get" me and my kind as I was leaving his apartment that Saturday night back in 1958. In the end, having kept that promise, he decided to be magnanimous in victory and forgive me. But it was because of them, as well as all the others who I feared might be waiting in the wings, that I still could not bring myself to forgive *him*, not even now that he was dead.

CHAPTER TWO

GOING TOO FAR
FOR THE TRILLINGS

ASKED WHO WAS THE GREATEST OF ALL HIS COUNTRY'S poets, the French novelist André Gide replied, "Victor Hugo, alas." This grudging acknowledgment was not quite the spirit in which Lionel Trilling once said that I was the best student he ever had, but I have no doubt that there was at least a small trace of regret in his mind as he said it. Gide disliked and disapproved of Hugo and would have wished that someone more congenial might have won this particular palm, but what could he do against his own honest literary judgment, especially as honesty about his feelings was his main stock-in-trade? I am reasonably sure that Lionel Trilling never (well, almost never) actually disliked me, and there were certainly many times when, far from disapproving of me, he derived a veritably paternal pleasure and pride in what I was doing. Yet he was also disappointed in my failure to remain a true disciple of his as I grew older, and he was positively angry with me over certain disagreements that developed between us.

Devout Freudian that he was, he sometimes seemed to interpret these disagreements not on their own intellectual merits but as nothing more than rebellions against him as a surrogate father. So, and to a much greater and more consistent extent, did his wife Diana, who was also a literary and social critic. Having reportedly spent eighteen years in psychoanalysis, she was, if anything, an even more orthodox Freudian than Lionel, and my relations with her further complicated and sometimes disrupted my relations with him.

Oddly enough, considering the extent to which I came to be known as "Trilling's student," I only took one course with him when I was an undergraduate at Columbia, and that one not until my senior year. By the time I enrolled in this course in the fall of 1949, however, I already knew a lot about him, including the fact that he was the first Jew ever to be granted tenure in the Columbia English department. Professionally, he had not yet achieved the high standing or the fame within the academic and literary communities that was to come to him with the publication later in that very year of his collection of essays *The Liberal Imagination.* But my friends and I already looked upon him as the most important literary figure on the Columbia faculty, outdistancing even Mark Van Doren, who was then much more widely known than Trilling and was greatly admired both for his poetry and his criticism.

Unlike Van Doren, Trilling did not write poetry, but he had recently published a novel, *The Middle of the Journey,* and two of his short stories, "Of This Time, Of That Place" and "The Other Margaret," had come out in *Partisan Review,* where many of his essays had also originally appeared. Yet it was these essays, together with his books on Matthew Arnold and (to a lesser degree) E. M. Forster, that my friends and I most admired. We thought that (except perhaps for "Of This Time, Of That Place") he was far better as a literary critic than as a writer of fiction, and we made no hierarchical or invidious distinction between the two kinds of writing. The standard view in the literary culture was that criticism was subordinate to the "creative" works with which it dealt and off which it lived, but we respected the best literary critics more than we did most living novelists and poets.

Of course, this did not apply to a poet like T. S. Eliot or to such novelists as William Faulkner and Ernest Hemingway. Nevertheless, so far from idiosyncratic were we in exalting criticism to a higher position than it had ever enjoyed before that Randall Jarrell would soon disparagingly christen this period "the Age of Criticism." And yet Jarrell's own critical essays being more impressive than the many poems or the one novel he produced, he himself was a good case in point for our side of the debate. So was the fact that (the physical sciences apart) literary criticism may well have been the most vital intellectual activity in the years following the Second World War, and the most interesting branch of contemporary literature itself.

As I would later describe (in *Making It*) the way it was in those days, we awaited the arrival of the quarterlies in which criticism flourished—magazines like *Partisan Review* and *The Kenyon Review*—with the avidity of addicts. We seized upon the essays of such "New Critics" as Robert Penn Warren and Allen Tate with an excitement that far surpassed anything we felt about their own poems and novels and that often even equaled the passion aroused in us by the great works of the past that they were writing about. And if we could all quote at length from the poetry of T. S. Eliot, we also pored repeatedly over his critical essays, which in our eyes were hardly less significant (and, in truth, much more accessible) than the poems themselves.

The New Critics, whose most representative exemplar was probably Cleanth Brooks in his book *The Well Wrought Urn*, specialized in the explication and elucidation of difficult works (mainly poems), but they never departed from the texts themselves. To them the poem was a wholly autonomous organism, and in approaching it one was supposed to ignore all external factors, whether biographical, historical, moral, social, or political, and concentrate entirely on the way the strictly literary elements—structure, imagery, rhythm, sound—played on and off one another. One was also supposed to avoid committing the "heresy of paraphrase" by trying to say what a poem meant in words other than its own. There was no distinction between form and content: the form *was* the content. Or as Helen Vendler, one of the last surviving proponents of this dogma, would put it fifty years later, "I do not regard as literary criticism any set of remarks about a poem which would be equally true of its paraphrasable propositional content."

In studying the essays and books of the New Critics, we were thus taught how to appreciate literature in its own unique terms. We learned too how to unearth the hidden complexities and what the English critic William Empson famously called the "seven types of ambiguity" lurking beneath the surface of what often looked at first glance like easily intelligible texts. All this deepened our understanding of what literature was and how it differed from other modes of discourse; it also gave us the almost gnostic sense of power that came from seeing things that were invisible to the eyes of ordinary readers. (Unlike the "deconstructionist" literary critics of a later era, however, who would see things that, as they themselves would insouciantly acknowledge, were not actually there, we were very strict about submitting to the poet's imaginative intentions as realized in the text, even if the poet himself was not necessarily conscious of what his own imagination had put there. The rule we followed was once summarized in another connection by D. H. Lawrence: "Never trust the teller; trust the tale.")

After a while, however, we began growing restless with the uncompromisingly formalistic approach of the New Critics. We knew that they were mainly Southerners and that they were forthrightly conservative in their own social and political convictions. In *I'll Take My Stand*, an anthology of the 1930s, a group of Southern literary people had argued that the social and political order of the pre–Civil War South was superior to the society created by industrialism, capitalism, and democracy, and most of the New Critics still shared in that view. Thus, John Crowe Ransom, the editor of *The Kenyon Review*, where the New Critics held sway, once described himself as "an ex-agrarian ontological aesthete." Making even bolder and dispensing with the *ex*, Allen Tate—the same Allen Tate who wanted to challenge William Barrett to a duel over Ezra Pound—entitled one of his books *Reactionary Essays on Poetry and Ideas*. Yet since we could detect no connection between the literary formalism of the New Critics and what would several decades later be called their "paleoconservatism," it was not their politics that made us, as young men broadly of the Left, increasingly dissatisfied with their approach; it was, rather, the feeling that in the end there was something sterile in treating literature as totally self-contained. And here was where the kind of criticism written by Trilling and most of the other contributors to *Partisan Review*, as well as to the recently founded (1945) *Commentary*, came in.

Partisan Review had no quarrel with *The Kenyon Review* so far as the doctrine of the autonomy of art was concerned. On the contrary: although launched as a Communist magazine in the 1930s, *Partisan Review* had broken with the party over this very issue of artistic autonomy. Not only had it balked at accepting the party's dictation on literary matters, but it had also refused to judge writers merely on the basis of their political opinions. But leaving the Communist party and becoming "anti-Stalinist" was not the same thing as giving up on Marxism; and even in those cases where it was, the imprint of Marxist categories of thought remained in the mind. A person schooled in those categories of thought could easily reject the "vulgar-Marxist" idea of art as a "weapon" in the political wars, but he could not possibly rest content with a conception of literature as uninfluenced by any extraliterary factors and referring to nothing outside itself. Yes, a work of art was autonomous and had to be understood and judged on its own terms. But to the *Partisan Review* group it was not enough merely to "return to the text," as the New Critics had insisted upon doing in their rebellion against the old academic literary historians, who seemed to be interested in everything but the text. Such a return to the text had to be followed by a fresh departure from the text—into society, politics, history, and morality.

It was Trilling who took the lead in finding a way back to the interplay between literature and the various contexts from which it arose and to which it then returned, while at the same time (again unlike the deconstructionists and the various schools of "multiculturalist" criticism which would arise in the future) respecting its autonomy and aesthetic integrity. In doing so, Trilling was less influenced by Marxism, of which he had in any event never been a true devotee, than by Matthew Arnold, the great Victorian critic whose biography he had spent years in writing. Arnold's reverence for the aesthetic qualities that made for great literature was nothing short of religious, but this did not prevent him from defining poetry as a "criticism of life." Accordingly, he assumed the right—and, indeed, the duty—as a literary critic to examine his immediate cultural environment through the eyes of the masterpieces that served for him as "touchstones" of moral and intellectual greatness. By following Arnold in this, Trilling reintroduced all the breadth and vitality into the discussion of literature of which it had been robbed by the formalism of the New Critics.

Besides Trilling, there were two other members of the Columbia faculty who wrote mainly for *Partisan Review:* F. W. Dupee and Richard Chase. Having by now developed the ambition to become a critic of their ilk myself, I desperately wanted a stamp of approval from all of them, but especially from Trilling, to whom even Dupee and Chase deferred as the master. (Not, by the way, without a certain resentment: in later years, whenever Chase talked to me in private about Trilling, he would always refer to him in a sardonic tone as "Uncle Lionel," while Dupee would resort to his own subtler style of sarcasm when the mood was upon him.)

But if I knew all about Trilling when I enrolled in his course, he also knew all about me. I had no inkling of this until at the end of the year he let me in on the secret that my prowess as a student had been the subject of much discussion among his colleagues and that this alone was enough to put him on his guard. He was himself a notoriously tough grader, and he suspected that my success was due to some trick I had of pleasing my teachers by telling them what they wanted to hear. If I thought I could pull the same trick on him, I could think again.

The course was a seminar in nineteenth-century English poetry which met for an hour three times a week, and it featured lively and sometimes contentious discussions. There were no exams or formal papers. Instead, we were required as we went along to keep a journal of critical comment on each of the assigned readings and to hand the entire journal in at the end of the semester for grading.

Within the first week or two, I became convinced that Trilling had for some reason taken a dislike to me. My eager hand was often in the air, but he rarely called on me; when he did, he would respond frigidly to whatever point I might make. Things loosened up a bit as the weeks went on, and once in a while he would even seem to agree with something I said. But the coldness, which so far as I could tell I had done nothing to provoke, remained. Without exactly falling into despair, I was deeply worried about my failure to make a good impression on the one professor whose opinion was by now more important to me than any other's.

Meanwhile, I worked furiously at my journal, putting everything I had into it. By the end of the first semester, I had written more than two hundred pages of critical commentaries on selected works by the major Romantic poets. It came back from Trilling with exclamations of praise scrawled all over it.

So did the journal I kept on the Victorians in the second semester, during which Trilling's manner toward me in class not surprisingly became a lot warmer than it had been before. As the end of that academic year approached, *The Liberal Imagination* appeared, and just before graduating I did the long article about it for *The Columbia Review*, the college literary magazine (of which Allen Ginsberg had been the editor when I was a freshman). Trilling said that it was the most intelligent review the book had received, and when I asked him to autograph my copy, he inscribed it to me "in great admiration and high expectation." Together with the equally flattering commendations I had gotten from Chase the year before in his course on the American novel and the one I also got now from Dupee in his course on contemporary literature, Trilling's accolade made me positively giddy and confirmed me in my determination to follow in their footsteps as a critic and a teacher.

The *Columbia Review* essay was not the only article I was to write about Trilling. Upon graduating from Columbia, I was awarded two fellowships, which was what made it possible for me to spend the next three years at Cambridge University, where I went to sit at the feet of the dogmatic, pugnacious, and always embattled F. R. Leavis. Perhaps the greatest critic in England—greater, some said, than T. S. Eliot himself, an old ally turned adversary—Leavis was also the editor of the country's most formidable critical journal, the terrifying *Scrutiny*, graveyard (as I would characterize it years later in *Making It*) "of a thousand literary reputations, ancient as well as modern; incorruptible guardian of standards in a decadent culture; upholder of seriousness in a frivolous age."

As a critic Leavis had a good deal in common with Trilling, and studying with him served to intensify the sense I had already developed of how literature was related to the life around it and how, in being most fully itself and *only* in being most fully itself, it could act as an agent of moral, social, and political health. I confess never taking into account the problem presented to this puristic view by a novel like Harriet Beecher Stowe's *Uncle Tom's Cabin,* whose contribution to the abolition of slavery had little to do with its merits as a work of literature. Nor do I think that Leavis ever grappled with this problem, though Trilling may well have done so in the privacy of his own mind. One thing is for sure: when Abraham Lincoln said upon meeting Mrs. Stowe in 1861, "So this is the little woman who wrote the book that started this great war," he was not speaking as a Leavisian literary critic.

Be that as it may, so thoroughly did I absorb what Leavis had to teach that before the end of my first year at Cambridge, he bestowed the ultimate accolade of inviting me to write for *Scrutiny*—and the article he invited me to write was about Lionel Trilling.

Flattered down to my toes though I was by this invitation, it surprised me even more. I was well aware that, for all the similarities between their ideas about the relation of a work of literature to its historical, social, and cultural context and in spite of their common alertness to its moral implications, Leavis was suspicious of and even slightly hostile toward Trilling. (For his part, Trilling had no such feelings about Leavis and was puzzled to learn that Leavis thought less well of him than might have been expected.) I believed then, and I still believe today, that the problem was rooted in Leavis's not altogether inaccurate perception that Trilling set a lesser value on literature in general than he did. To Leavis, literature was what the Bible had been to his puritanical Huguenot ancestors, and criticism for him became both a method of establishing the true canon (much as the rabbis of old had done in deciding which ancient books had been written under divine inspiration and which were either apocryphal or heretical) and a substitute for devotional meditation and scriptural exegesis. It was for this reason that he was so dogmatic in his critical judgments and so intolerant of disagreement. Indeed, one could fall into permanent disfavor with him for liking the "wrong" poem or admiring a novel that he had not included in "the great tradition."

This kind of thing was totally foreign to Trilling's temperament. If in their respective attitudes toward literature, Leavis resembled an unwavering and fanatical devotee, Trilling was like a man of faith who was constantly assailed by uncertainty and doubt as to whether the works to which he was devoting his life were really all that important. In fact, he once said that there were times when he felt that he would rather do almost anything than read a book. It was inconceivable that such an impious statement could ever come out of Leavis's mouth, and his uneasiness about Trilling may well have grown out of an intuition that it *was* possible to imagine it coming out of *his*.

After all these years, I am still uncertain as to why Leavis, who must have been confident that I would produce a favorable account, chose me to write an article about Trilling when *The Liberal Imagination* was published in England. Probably he had concluded that, on balance, Trilling could be considered an ally, and he therefore wanted to make a conciliatory gesture toward him. In any case, the piece I wrote, aiming to "place" Trilling for a British audience whose familiarity with the American literary scene could not be taken for granted, was very different from the one I had done for *The Columbia Review*. It tried to explain why Trilling was the most "significant" of all American critics, and it concluded with the following words:

> T. S. Eliot has remarked that if [Matthew] Arnold were alive today, he would have to do his work all over again. Of *The Liberal Imagination* and of its author, it is possible to feel that they are doing for America, at least, the work Arnold himself might have done.

In comparing Trilling to Arnold, I was also hinting that he resembled Leavis, who saw *himself* as doing Arnold's "work all over again" for England. As he did not hesitate to inform me, Leavis thought this comparison excessively generous to Trilling, but he let it stand. He did, however, cut a paragraph praising an essay in *The Liberal Imagination* about Wordsworth's "Ode: Intimations of Immortality from Recollections of Early Childhood." Trilling, like practically everyone else in the world, considered the Immortality Ode (as it was usually called) a great masterpiece and a glory of English literature, but to Leavis it was one of the poems no truly good critic would admire. Nevertheless, having removed any evidence of this deplorable lapse both on my part and Trilling's, and having done a fair amount of grimacing and grumbling about the piece in general, he decided in the end that it was on the whole "intelligent" and that he would print it under the formidable title "The Arnoldian Function in American Criticism." It was, then, in connection with Trilling that, at the age of twenty-one, I made my first appearance in print as a professional literary critic.

I also kept in touch with Trilling while I was at Cambridge with long letters about my life there, to which he would unfailingly respond with long letters of his own. Then in 1952, after two years away, I returned home for the summer and was immediately invited to visit him in Westport, Connecticut, where he and Diana were vacationing. I have a dim recollection of being told later that I was the first student Diana had ever permitted into their home. But whether or not I was the first, my visit was certainly a rare occurrence, a result of the curiosity she had developed about this intellectually precocious young man who seemed to have a special affinity for her husband and who had made an unusually deep impression on him.

Diana Trilling was nothing if not presumptuous, and before I left Westport that day, she had already decided to take me in hand and tell me what to do. On this occasion she lectured me about the advantages of going to law school, but that turned out to be only the first in a long series of such confidently offered pieces of advice covering everything from my personal life to my career, with a good deal of political instruction thrown in along the way. I always listened politely and promised to give serious consideration to whatever it was she had more or less ordered me to do. But the truth was that I thought she had a skewed sense of reality, and half the time I found myself humoring her as though she were a little crazy. Even so, and mainly because she was determined to have it that way, a close relation developed between us that was independent of my friendship with Lionel (as I was by then given permission to call him).

With Lionel himself things were completely different. Unlike Diana, who so often seemed to be broadcasting on a different wavelength from the one to which I was tuned, he always understood exactly what I was trying to say, often before I had finished saying it, and his responses were always perfectly pitched and to the point. He was a better writer than a talker (or teacher), but against very stiff competition I am still inclined to rate him, whether by his words on paper or in conversation, as the most intelligent person I have ever known.

In the fall of 1952, I returned to Cambridge with the intention of getting a Ph.D. there, which, I had reason to hope, would land me a job in the Columbia English department; there was also a strong possibility that I might be asked to teach at Cambridge. But as the year ground on, the idea I had flirted with for a while of becoming an expatriate lost all its appeal, and the doubts I had already begun to feel about an academic career grew stronger and stronger. With my doctoral dissertation (on the political novels of Benjamin Disraeli) only barely begun and even knowing that if I quit graduate school and went home I would be subject to the draft and possibly sent to fight in Korea, I still decided that this would be the best thing for me to do.

It took about six months for the draft board to get around to me, and during my time as what Saul Bellow had called "a dangling man" in his novel about a similar experience during World War II, Lionel again played a large role in my life. He was always surprising me, and this time it was by sympathizing with my reluctance to follow in his footsteps by embarking on an academic career. It was partly for this reason that he had already called me to the attention of his old friend Elliot Cohen, the founding editor of *Commentary*, and so well suited did I turn out to be for this magazine that I was able to contribute a piece every month until I was finally inducted into the army. Furthermore, before I left, Cohen asked me if I would be interested in joining the editorial staff of the magazine upon my discharge two years later, and I accepted the offer with great eagerness.

I cannot recall whether it was Lionel who also introduced me to Philip Rahv and William Phillips, by then the two top editors of *Partisan Review*, or whether they became aware of me through my work in *Commentary*. But they too knew that I was Lionel's protégé, and they too invited me to write for them. And so by the time I was discharged from the army in December 1955 (having been sent not to Korea but to Germany), I had already been adopted by the "Family" of New York intellectuals. The youngest member of the group, I was flatteringly treated as an intellectual peer. As such, I was welcomed not only into the pages of the two magazines for which most of them wrote but also to the parties they threw; and when, after I got married and was able to throw parties of my own, I invited them, and they came. Many also became close friends, but the closest of all were the Trillings. I saw them all the time and I was often on the phone with one or the other. When I needed advice, I went to Lionel; and whether I needed it or not, I kept getting it from Diana.

Like all the other members of the Family in the unusual interlude between the onset of the cold war in 1947 and the emergence about twelve years later of the new radical "Movement"—consisting of a not always comfortable coalition between the politically oriented New Left, led at first by the Students for a Democratic Society (SDS), and the beatniks, hippies, and sexual liberationists of the counterculture, to whose emergence Allen Ginsberg, as we have seen, made so important a contribution—both Lionel and Diana were engaged in a struggle against the leftist ideas and attitudes by which they had been formed in the 1930s. Unlike some of the others, who had been "card-carrying" members of the Communist party, the Trillings had been "fellow-travelers"—that is, unaffiliated but generally uncritical supporters of and apologists for the party and its ever-shifting "line." But in growing disillusioned they had become as passionate in their opposition to Communism as the ex-Communists generally were. Also unlike many of the others, they did not regard themselves as socialists or anti-Stalinist Marxists. They were liberals whose job it was to rescue liberalism from the fellow-travelers who had usurped its good name by associating it not only with sympathy for the Soviet Union but also with—to use a term that Lionel would in later years make famous—an "adversarial" relation to their own country and its culture.

The fact that I shared fully in this perspective when I appeared on the scene was undoubtedly one of the elements that made my friendship with the Trillings possible in the first place. They saw me as a true disciple, forcefully and articulately carrying their intellectual and political point of view forward into a new generation. So indeed I was. My earliest published writings were pervaded by Lionel's influence, not in sounding like him (which, as a prose stylist, I never did) but in taking a stand, and precisely as his kind of "revisionist liberal," at the "bloody crossroads" where, he had once said, literature and politics met.*

As I would later explain in my third book, *Breaking Ranks: A Political Memoir* (1979), this did not of course mean attacking Communism and pledging allegiance to America at the conclusion of every piece I wrote. But it did involve showing how often the prevalence of leftist dogmas led to the misrepresentation and simplification of life in America by the books I was dealing with (mainly contemporary novels). A case in point was an article on the novelist Nelson Algren for *The New Yorker*. Freely acknowledging his literary powers, I also criticized him for writing about America as though it contained only two kinds of people— the exploiting (and listless) rich and the exploited (but always vital) poor—when even a glance at his own commercially successful career revealed a reality more complicated and far more interesting than that.

On other occasions I would attempt to show how the same leftist dogmas often led to critical misjudgments of the works in question. Thus, in a piece on Nathanael West, also for *The New Yorker*, I argued that the reason so obviously gifted a novelist had been neglected and underrated was that his sense of life clashed with one of the great articles of faith of the "radical press"—the idea that all the miseries of the human condition could be cured by the right social and economic arrangements.

In these ways I was following Lionel into the bloody crossroads. At the same time, I was trying to write criticism that was also loyal to

---

*"Revisionist liberal" was my term, not his. "Cold-war liberal" and "liberal anti-Communist" were other terms that came into being to describe the same position. As for "bloody crossroads," I would borrow it from Lionel's "the dark and bloody crossroads" to use as the title of a collection of my recent essays on politics and literature that was published in 1986.

T. S. Eliot's definition of it as "the common pursuit of true judgment and the correction of taste" (a definition strongly endorsed by my other great mentor, F. R. Leavis).

I also followed Lionel (and, for that matter, Eliot and Leavis) in venturing from time to time beyond the confines of literature and grappling head-on with the social and political issues that I could deal with only indirectly or by implication in writing about novels or poems. Here, still speaking as Lionel's kind of "revisionist liberal," I more often entered into contention with the Right than with the Left, and specifically with the idea that America was the spiritual "wasteland" that Eliot had used as the defining metaphor of the modern world as a whole. For all the talk going on at the time about the "religious revival" supposedly sweeping America, Eliot himself, and many of those politically conservative Southerners who were so prominent in the 1950s (and not only as critics but also as novelists and poets), saw this country as, for all practical purposes, a secular society. As such, they said, it suffered from a loss of the values upon which the entire civilization of the West rested and that derived ultimately from religious faith.

I too thought that the religious revival of the 1950s never went very deep, but in a long piece for *Commentary* and then again in an article for *Partisan Review* I laced into the idea that secularism for most Americans involved an absence of values. My argument was that the values of a people were to be found not in the speeches they made or in their rhetorical professions of belief but in the way they lived their lives from day to day; and if American values remained invisible to most social critics, it was because, like our novelists, they were so blinded by preconceived notions about the American middle class— notions deriving in about equal measure from the Left and the Right—that they had never taken the trouble to look at how the people of this country really lived.

I also argued, and even more fiercely, against the political corollary of the antisecularist position (held most prominently by Whittaker Chambers and William F. Buckley, Jr.), which was that the main difference between the Western and the Communist worlds turned on the issue of religious faith. I did not, that is, accept the idea that the cold war was a war between "godless Communism" and the Judeo-Christian tradition. Expressing a view whose most powerful proponent was the philosopher Sidney Hook, I insisted that what separated us from them was that we were free and they were not, that our political system was democratic and that theirs was totalitarian. And I consistently maintained that liberal democracy was itself a value—a value that Americans wanted to live by and that they were even willing to die for.

Diana was, if anything, even more pleased than Lionel by the positions I was taking in these articles. As a writer she was less literary and more explicitly political than Lionel and, as in life so on paper, she was less modulated, blunter, more aggressive. Also more of an activist than he was, it was she rather than he who became involved with the anti-Communist American Committee for Cultural Freedom (ACCF).

The ACCF had originally been formed in 1949 in response to a conference at the Waldorf Hotel in New York in which prominent American cultural figures sympathetic to the Soviet Union joined with a delegation of Soviet artists and intellectuals to appeal for "peace" and "friendship" between the two nation.* The hypocrisy of this appeal—which was part of a desperate campaign to quash the first stirrings of American resistance to Stalin's expansionist designs—so outraged a group of anti-Stalinist intellectuals, mostly members of the Family, that they organized a counterconference. Its dual purpose was to refute the lies the Waldorf group was spreading about the international situation and to protest against the support given by so many writers and intellectuals both here and in Europe to a regime in which cultural freedom of every kind was ruthlessly and murderously suppressed. It was out of this counterconference that the ACCF was born, and for a while it embraced a wide range of people who were simultaneously passionate opponents of Communism and strong supporters of the American effort to draw a line against any further expansion of Soviet power and influence.

But it was not long before quarrels developed, leading to splits and further splits. The main issue under contention was the congressional

---

*Many years later it was learned that some of the Soviet delegates, most notably the composer Dmitri Shostakovich, had been coerced into attending and then gagged on the lying words that had been put into their mouths by Stalin's commissars.

investigations of Communist influence in various areas of American life that came to be known collectively as McCarthyism. No one in the ACCF defended McCarthyite methods, but to the "hard" anti-Communist faction—which included Diana herself, Sidney Hook, and the eminent historian of the Russian revolution Bertram D. Wolfe*— the fact that abuses of civil liberties were taking place did not mean that the Communist threat was a paranoid delusion or that a "witch hunt" was going on (witches, as one of them put it, being imaginary creatures while Communists were all too real).

This stance of opposition both to McCarthyism and to Communism did not, however, satisfy another faction within the ACCF— composed, among others, of writers like Dwight Macdonald, Mary McCarthy, and Richard Rovere—who considered the McCarthyites almost as great a threat to the country as the Communists. Unwilling to cooperate any longer with people they not so secretly accused of being "soft" on McCarthy (and who not so secretly returned the compliment by regarding them as soft on Communism or, more awkwardly, as "anti-anti-Communists"), they all eventually resigned, leaving the ACCF entirely in the control of the hard-liners.

It was this ACCF of which Diana became president and whose board she arranged for me to join once I was out of the army and had settled into my new life in New York. But the timing was all wrong. For starters, I was already developing doubts about the single-minded preoccupation of my fellow board members with the Soviet threat. I was also bothered by what seemed to me their intransigent refusal to admit that anything had changed since the death of Stalin and the "thaw" in relations with the West that had been inaugurated by his eventual successor, Nikita Khrushchev.

Apart from all that, I was beginning to grow restless with the general outlook on life that I had absorbed from Lionel (though not from him alone). This new feeling found expression in the piece I was asked to write in 1957 by *The New Leader* about my own generation of

---

*Wolfe, the author of the classic *Three Who Made a Revolution,* was an ex-Communist who as a young man had had the great honor of being kicked out of the party for insubordination by Joseph Stalin himself.

intellectuals. Though I opened with a sympathetic exposition of our idea that the real adventure of existence lay not in radical politics or in Bohemia but in the "moral life" of the individual, I suddenly switched into a different key when describing how these ideas were working themselves out in practice among my contemporaries:

> A great many of them married early, most of them made firm and decisive commitments to careers of a fairly modest kind, such as teaching; they cultivated an interest in food, clothes, furniture, manners— these being elements of the "richness" of life that the generation of the 30's had deprived itself of. As befitted responsible adults, there was nothing playful or frisky about these young people; their very presence and bearing announced that they were serious men and women with no time for fooling around, burdened with a sense of mortality, reconciled to the sad fact of human limitation.

I was, of course, talking not only about my contemporaries but also about myself. And when I concluded the piece by saying that this "restless generation" was beginning to feel cheated of its youth and was getting ready to break out of the bonds of "maturity" into which it had prematurely squeezed itself, I had my own life in mind as well.

Shortly after this article was published, I went to a small dinner party at the home of Richard Chase. The Trillings were already there when I arrived, and the minute I walked in, Diana, who had up till then always approved of everything I wrote, immediately began berating me for having launched what she took to be an unwarranted attack on Lionel (though his name had never been mentioned in my piece). For his part, Lionel, who clearly agreed with her interpretation, said very little, allowing her (as he often did in unpleasant situations) to do most of the talking.

In view of the course on which I was subsequently to embark, I think in retrospect that they had a point. But I certainly did not think so at the time, and I was offended by what seemed to me a self-centered and patronizing response to my work. (Diana even referred to the piece, with a pretense of teasing, as a kind of *bar mitzvah* speech declaring, in the traditional formula, that today I had become a man in my own right.) Richard, who was in the process of developing a culturally radical point of view that quite consciously represented a repudiation of "Uncle Lionel," and who had recently published an article in *Partisan Review* that really was a covert attack on him, leaped to my defense. But this only served to confirm the Trillings in their suspicion that a rebellion from within was brewing against Lionel, and the evening ended on a testy note.

Not that this had any lasting effect on the close relations between us. I continued seeing and talking to the Trillings regularly, and around this time Diana even cited the very article about which we had quarreled in singling me out as the "spokesman" for my "literary age group." The citation appeared in a footnote about me that was appended to the introduction of a selection of D. H. Lawrence's letters, which she had edited. Such a footnote was made necessary by the fact that she had written the introduction as a letter addressed to "Dearest Norman," a letter that took the form of an extended response to something I had said to her about Lawrence. It was a loving gesture, but, ironically, it led to a much greater strain in our relations than my piece on the young generation had.

What caused the trouble was the merciless teasing to which I was subjected by other friends of mine, and even some of hers, who thought that Diana was announcing that I was her "baby." And what made things worse was that so public an identification with her, even on a literary issue that did not directly impinge on politics, created the impression that I was still clinging to the hard anti-Communist position of which in those days she was one of the most uninhibited spokesmen. In fact, however, I was already moving away from it and toward the anti-anti-Communist camp, whose members, while retaining their high regard for Lionel, considered Diana a fanatic and ragged me endlessly for allowing her to make free with my name. Deeply humiliated, I decided, young fool that I was, that I was honor bound to tell Diana that she had embarrassed me, and she of course felt hurt and betrayed. When the introduction was reprinted, it was retitled "Letter to a Young Critic," and all references to me were expunged.

This ugly episode left its mark in bad feeling and mistrust, but not even it, bad as it was, put an end to my friendship either with Diana or with Lionel. We still saw each other frequently, and though there was less agreement between us than before, enough common intellectual ground remained to fuel a thousand interesting conversations. Moreover, though both Lionel and Diana strongly disapproved of the radicalization I was undergoing in those years, they (especially Lionel) also took it seriously as a sign of a general change in the cultural climate and tried very hard to understand what it was all about.

When, for instance, I wrote a long essay on Norman Mailer, who as a best-selling novelist and a fellow-traveler had never been taken seriously by the Family, I showed the manuscript to Lionel; and though he expressed certain reservations, he was sufficiently impressed to go back and read Mailer for (if I remember rightly) the first time. So did Diana, who would subsequently write admiringly about him herself. At my urging, Lionel also agreed to read Norman O. Brown's *Life Against Death.* Indeed, he even found grounds for producing a favorable review of this central text of the nascent cultural radicalism toward which he was in general antagonistic and which—with Mailer, Brown, and me in mind—he would dryly characterize as "the Norman invasion."

By then, Elliot Cohen had died, and in January 1960, at the age of thirty, I became (against Diana's advice) the new editor of *Commentary.* In spite of their best efforts to keep an open mind about the leftward direction in which I was taking the magazine, the change was very painful to the Trillings—and all the more so because under Elliot the magazine (except in its concentration on Jewish issues!) had been close to a perfect reflection of their political and cultural outlook. It was an outlook that combined hard anti-Communism with an enthusiastically positive attitude toward America. To be sure, there was no necessary logical connection between the two positions. After all, socialists like Irving Howe, who had founded *Dissent* in 1954, were simultaneously hard anti-Communists and highly critical of the American system.

Yet Howe and his comrades were for the moment an exception. For given the long history of "alienation" from America among the intellectuals, it was virtually inevitable that most of them would develop a new disposition to find virtues in the country which had emerged as the great bulwark against totalitarianism, first in its incarnation in Nazi Germany and now in its embodiment in the Soviet Union. Thus, in 1947 Mary McCarthy (who only six years earlier had not even been able to bring herself to support the United States in its war against Nazi Germany, and who would during the Vietnam War twenty years later become even more anti-American than she had been in the 1930s) wrote an article for *Commentary* entitled, with no ironic intent, "America the Beautiful." Thus, too, *Partisan Review*, the great bastion of the alienated intellectual, ran a symposium in 1952 on "Our Country and Our Culture," the pronoun saying more about the change it signified than any of the pieces in the symposium itself.

One of those pieces, by the poet Delmore Schwartz, held out against this change, insisting on the continuing relevance of the idea of alienation and on the need to maintain the "critical nonconformism" which had traditionally characterized the intellectual's attitude toward American society. But by 1958, even Delmore had come around:

> Clearly when the future of civilization is no longer assured, a criticism of American life in terms of a contrast between avowed ideals and present actuality cannot be a primary preoccupation and source of inspiration. For America, not Europe, is now the sanctuary of culture; civilization's very existence depends upon America, upon the actuality of American life, and not the ideals of the American Dream. To criticize the actuality upon which all hope depends thus becomes a criticism of hope itself.

Though Delmore was on the staff of *Partisan Review*, it was not his own magazine but, rather, *Commentary* under Elliot Cohen whose editorial policies most faithfully reflected the sentiments he expressed here. The editors of *Partisan Review*, and especially Philip Rahv and William Phillips, were by the late 1950s already growing uneasy about going too far in their recoil from the Stalinists and their liberal fellow travelers. They still regarded themselves as men of the Left, and they were stung by Irving Howe's attack on them as participants in the "American celebration" that (so he said in an article they themselves felt obliged to publish) was turning this into an "Age of Conformity."

Elliot Cohen, by contrast, no longer identified himself with the Left, and he had no such worries. From his *Commentary* one got the impression that the "actuality" of America, for all its imperfections (the persistence of discrimination against Jews and Negroes being the main one), was the best society a human nature beset and limited by its own built-in imperfections was likely to be able to build. To criticize it was not merely, as Schwartz charged, to criticize hope itself. It was also to give aid and comfort to the totalitarian enemy whose main ideological purpose was to demonstrate that American capitalism was both unjust and unviable, that American democracy was a sham, and that the country was in the grip of an anti-Communist hysteria which threatened to bring outright fascists into power and ignite a nuclear war.

In this perspective, which was clearly a forerunner of what would later be designated as "neoconservatism," both Lionel and Diana fully shared. But it was characteristic of them that he would be more subtle and more nuanced in espousing it than she, and it was also characteristic that she would be more insistent on continuing to identify both of them as liberals. When Lionel was accused of being a "conservative" (and in those circles in those days this was indeed an accusation), he would sometimes acknowledge that in certain respects he was. She, on the other hand, always took offense, angrily contending that his criticisms of the "liberal imagination," as well as her own unremitting attacks on the liberal culture of the day, came from within and were— just as Lionel had said in his book—intended to restore liberalism to its former glory. This was why she devoted so much time and energy to distinguishing herself from anti-Communists of the Right like William F. Buckley, Jr., in whose young magazine, *National Review*, McCarthy was defended. There too a number of converts from the radical Left to conservatism—like James Burnham, a former Trotskyist who had once been an editor of *Partisan Review*, and Lionel's old Columbia classmate Whittaker Chambers, an ex-Communist who had once served as a Soviet agent—had found a new home.*

---

*In the case of Chambers there was a complication. The Trillings disapproved of his association with Buckley and Richard Nixon, and their own secularist interpretation of what the cold war was about differed sharply from his basically religious conception. But they believed that he was telling the truth about Alger Hiss's involvement in espionage on behalf of the Soviet Union, and they strongly supported him in the fierce controversy aroused by that charge. One of the main characters in Lionel's novel, *The Middle of the Journey*, was based on Chambers, and years later (much to the consternation of Hiss partisans like Lillian Hellman) he would refer to Chambers as an honorable man.

But if the Trillings worried about being identified with the Right because their hard anti-Communism was in truth not always easy to tell apart from the conservative position, and because, like Buckley and his friends, they mainly directed their polemical fire at the liberal establishment, they remained more concerned about the resurgence of the Left in the late 1950s, and especially the part I was playing in it as the new editor of *Commentary* in the early 1960s. It was one thing for me to promote the *cultural* radicalism of Norman Mailer and Norman O. Brown, and they were even barely willing (at least at first) to tolerate my resurrection of the utopian anarchist Paul Goodman. A prolific writer, Paul had been almost entirely forgotten until I serialized his book *Growing Up Absurd* in the first three issues of the "new *Commentary.*" Having already been rejected by nineteen publishers, *Growing Up Absurd* was to become one of the bibles of the radical movement of the 1960s. In bringing it to light (while also endorsing its main ideas in my own writing and printing many other pieces of a similar stripe by such writers as Hans J. Morgenthau and Edgar Z. Friedenberg), I contributed mightily to the spread of precisely what Delmore Schwartz had warned against: a radical critique of the "actuality of American life" in terms of "the ideals of the American Dream."

Yet to the Trillings—and to many other people with whom I had formerly been involved through the ACCF—this was as nothing compared with some of the articles I began publishing about the cold war. One of the worst from their point of view was a piece by the radical historian Staughton Lynd which, in arguing that the Soviet Union under Stalin was not entirely to blame for the outbreak of the cold war, challenged the most sacred element of the hard anti-Communist creed. Just as bad was an article by another historian, H. Stuart Hughes, who provided an elegant justification for a view that was then being propagated more crudely under the slogan "Better Red than Dead." And perhaps worst of all was "The American Crisis," an article in the June 1960 issue by the famous sociologist David Riesman (written in collaboration with his young disciple Michael Maccoby). What made this article particularly noxious to the Trillings was that it came from the principal author of *The Lonely Crowd* (the junior collaborators in this instance being Nathan Glazer and Reuel Denney), which Lionel had praised as "one of the most important books about America to have been published in recent times [and] one of the most interesting books I have ever read." Yet here was Riesman actually reducing the Soviet–American conflict to a case of sibling rivalry, with the Russians cast as the younger brother trying to imitate everything we did. According to this analysis, the only reason the Soviets were building nuclear weapons was out of a desperate desire to prove that they were as good as we were. Consequently, if we were to disarm they would follow suit, and there was a good chance that if we were then "to show that our system [could] be mobilized to produce a better life, drawing its meaning from activity rather than consumption *per se* or from national might, we would eventually shift the emphasis of Soviet emulation" to the same "utopian" and "idealistic" goals.

Feeling a bit queasy about this analysis myself, I invited a number of people to answer it in the next issue, and Diana was one of them. But she refused, explaining why in a long and very candid letter:

> It's an appalling piece, Norman. It rather shocks me that you printed it and I can't believe you would have, Riesman or no Riesman, if it weren't that this is the approach to politics that you consider modern, flexible, the necessary corrective to the sterile anti-Communism of your predecessor generation. OK then, so you print it and no doubt the Zeitgeist is with you, maybe it even applauds you. But why should I answer it? So that you can deceive yourself that you are open-minded, that you are promoting intellectual debate? If you *were* truly open-minded, you would surely have judged this Riesman piece for what it is—a hodge-podge of non-thinking, a soft sentimentality, an intellectual insult.

On rereading Riesman's article today, I agree with every word of Diana's attack on it, but her attack on me was a little unfair. After all, the very same issue in which the Riesman piece appeared also contained an article by the noted Sovietologist Richard Lowenthal arguing that the Soviet Union under Khrushchev remained a totalitarian state. And in the monthly column I was then writing as an introduction to each issue, I myself expressed serious doubts about the part of Riesman's article that dealt with ending the cold war ("It is, of course, true that many changes have taken place in the Soviet Union since the death of Stalin. . . . But there seems to be no very compelling reason to believe that a desire to end the cold war must be included among those changes").

Unfair or not, however, Diana was still determined to maintain friendly relations with me. Alluding in the same letter to an unpleasant quarrel we had had at a recent party at my house, she assured me that she was no longer angry and could not even remember what it had been about. But, she went on, "the strains, the watchfulness, the touchiness we must both of us be aware of are something else again and I wish *terribly* they didn't exist but I just don't know what to do about them except hope things will get back to where they were before."

Instead, however, they got worse. In a public debate at which Diana and I were among the speakers, I was so provoked by the resistance she expressed over any move away from the arms race and toward nuclear disarmament that, to her understandable horror, I found myself pushed into a defiant defense of the "Better Red than Dead" position. This, despite the fact that I was just then putting all my editorial energies into seeking out alternatives to these two unacceptable choices.*

Then, a few months later, a fight broke out between me and the Trillings during which even Lionel grew so incensed that, for the first time in all the years I had known him, this normally soft-spoken man raised his voice and began to shout. The occasion was a dinner party at the home of a mutual friend, the eminent labor journalist Arnold Beichman, who was one of the staunchest of the hard anti-Communists and had by then succeeded Diana as president of the American Committee for Cultural Freedom (from whose board I had already resigned). I forget what exactly triggered the argument, but it soon turned into a gang-up on me for sponsoring the resurgence of ideas and attitudes that Lionel had spent so much of his life battling against.

---

*The approach I then favored was the one developed by the social scientist Charles E. Osgood under the acronym GRID, which stood for "graduated reciprocal initiatives toward disarmament." It formed the program of a peace organization headed by Robert Pickus, who, among the other extraordinary things about him, was both a pacifist and an anti-Communist.

I was also accused of betraying the tradition that *Commentary* under Elliot Cohen had established and that I had been expected to maintain
and develop.

Though no one said so explicitly, I could not help being aware
that the anger behind this assault was rooted in the fact that Elliot
had been Lionel's mentor just as Lionel had been mine. As a precocious young editor working in the 1920s on *The Menorah Journal*, a
magazine devoted to exploring Jewish culture and promoting Jewish
self-acceptance, Elliot had not only been the first to print Lionel's
work but had also influenced his political development. In the early
1930s he had led the way first into Stalinism and then shortly thereafter into anti-Communism, and he had in addition done a great deal
in the ensuing period to push Lionel away from the standard intellectual stance of "alienation" and in the direction of a more positive
attitude toward American culture and American society. "Indeed,"
Lionel had said of him in a eulogy at his funeral in 1959 (which I had
then published in my first issue as the new editor of *Commentary*), Elliot "taught the younger men around him that nothing in human life
need be alien to their thought, and nothing in American life, whether
it be baseball, or vaudeville, or college tradition, or elementary education, or fashions in speech, or food, or dress, or manners." Now I,
Lionel's disciple succeeding Lionel's own mentor, was declaring that a
great many things in American life were and should be "alien" to our
thought. But what was even more treacherous (and what became the
focus of that particular evening), I was also raising dangerous doubts
about the continuing validity of liberal anti-Communism, doubts
reaching all the way back to its belief that the sole cause of the cold
war was Soviet expansionism and all the way forward to its conviction
that Soviet domination of the world was the greatest of all possible
evils.

I defended myself by counterattacking. So rigid were they, I yelled
back, that they could not even countenance the raising of questions
and the search I was conducting for a way out of the narrow alternatives offered by their view of the world. I denied that I had gone over to
the pro-Soviet enemy, pointing to such articles I had published as
Richard Lowenthal's piece and a more recent one by the historian (and

ex-Communist) Theodore Draper arguing that the Soviet Union still entertained "unlimited aims" (i.e., that it still dreamed of conquering the whole world). On the other hand, I charged them with refusing to see and to test the opportunities for ending the cold war that had been opened up by the risks of a nuclear holocaust. These risks had grown to the point where the need to reduce them was bound to moderate the Soviet Union's ideological ambitions and lead to a negotiated settlement, and it was up to us to explore this possibility.

None of this (to their credit, I would now say) cut any ice with the Trillings, and there was more ill will between us as we parted that night than there had ever been before. Later I learned that they thought I had been the aggressor spoiling for a fight, while I remembered it as a joint assault on me. Yet whoever may have started it, the ugly displays of temper it aroused on both sides certainly increased the "strains, the watchfulness, and the touchiness" of which Diana had spoken in her letter about Riesman.

And yet, in spite of everything that was driving us apart, the Trillings and I remained in fairly close touch, if not as close as before, and over the next few years I persisted with some success in hounding Lionel for contributions to *Commentary*. In 1962, I even nagged him into writing a piece for me about the controversy that had erupted in England over a ferocious attack by F. R. Leavis on C. P. Snow, who was then at the height of his fame both as a novelist and as a sage.

Having myself written in praise of Snow's novels for *The New Yorker*, and having then entered into very cordial relations with him, I saw no way of taking sides without being accused of betrayal by either my old teacher or my new friend. I therefore turned down Leavis's request that I publish his piece on Snow in *Commentary* with the excuse that it was too allusive to be entirely comprehensible to an American audience. I then managed after a herculean effort to talk a reluctant Lionel into producing an account of the controversy, and I considered that in finally snagging him I had pulled off a great professional and personal coup. There was in my opinion no one in the whole world better suited for this job than Lionel. As an additional bonus, since the article would be coming from America's leading critic, I would not be held responsible (as I would have been if I had commissioned a lesser writer) for anything he might say that would offend either of the two warring parties.

I turned out to be right about Lionel's article, which was indeed as balanced—and as brilliant—as I had hoped, but about everything else I was wrong. Both Leavis and Snow flew into rages with me (greater even than the one they directed at Lionel). Leavis, who had been growing more and more unhappy with me anyway and had interpreted my rejection of his piece as an intolerable affront, now cut me off entirely. Snow, while also feeling that I had badly let him down, eventually forgave me—until, that is, he decided (this time with greater warrant, given the high opinion of his work I had expressed earlier) that I had betrayed him once again by omitting his name from a list of the best contemporary novelists in my first collection of critical essays, *Doings and Undoings* (1964).

Thanks also to *Doings and Undoings*, I, having been convicted of using Lionel to betray both Leavis and Snow, was now indicted for betraying him as well. The offending passage occurred in the introduction:

> It has become fashionable in certain quarters to dismiss the revisionist liberalism of the 50's—which is associated with names like Lionel Trilling [and] which exerted a considerable influence on the earliest pieces in this collection—as a species of conformist thinking developed by intellectuals who, motivated in part by a genuine horror of Stalinism and in part by an abject failure of critical nerve, took to celebrating the virtues of American society and the values of the middle-class spirit.

I then went on to endorse this view, and though I tried to soften the point by respectfully acknowledging that "revisionist liberalism had something important to say in the 50's" that still needed saying, this concession (which, as I now see, Lionel would have been entirely justified in taking as insolent and patronizing) did nothing to mollify him. He repaid me by remaining silent about the book as a whole, and by taking a few swipes at it in print without condescending to mention its name or mine. (In one of these swipes, I became an anonymous "young critic" who was given to using "the sad word sophisticated." This was true, but what was sad about the word, I have never been able to figure out.)

Yet so strong was the bond between us that not even this episode led to a break. We still saw each other, and when a year or so later, he wrote a memoir called "Young in the Thirties," which was to serve as an introduction to a new edition of a novel by his late friend Tess Slesinger, he offered it to me for pre-publication in *Commentary* and I accepted with the greatest enthusiasm.

About three years further down the road, I showed him the manuscript of my next book, *Making It*, in which I acknowledged "my immense debt to Lionel Trilling, who has taught me more than he or I ever realized—though not, I fear, precisely what he would have wanted me to learn." In adding this qualification, I had our political differences in mind, but I was thrown into a state of shock when I discovered that it applied equally to elements of the book in which I had blithely expected him to perceive and be pleased by the measure of his great influence over me.

Making It unapologetically told the story of my own hunger for success, and it was he, after all, who had first taught me that ambition, far from being the shameful "bourgeois" passion that so many literary people professed to believe it was, actually testified to a commendable spiritedness of character. On my first visit to him in Westport (which I described in *Making It* itself), he had startled me by asking what kind of power I was after, and when I piously replied that I had no interest in power at all, he said, "Don't be silly, everyone wants power. The only question is what kind. What kind do you want?" *Making It* was an extended answer to that question which at the same time explored the reasons the whole issue had become the same kind of "dirty little secret" that sex had been to the Victorians.

Then, too, Lionel himself had written with warmth and affection about a type in the nineteenth-century novel (perhaps best exemplifed by Julien Sorel in Stendhal's *The Red and the Black*) he called "the Young Man from the Provinces" who comes to Paris or London in the hope of achieving success in one form or another. Furthermore, he had even lamented the fact that his students no longer identified with such characters:

> For some time I had been increasingly aware that my students had no very great admiration for Stendhal's *The Red and the Black*, gave it nothing like the response that it had had from my college generation. Then one day a whole class, almost all its members gifted men, agreed in saying that they were bored by Julien Sorel and didn't like him. Bored by Julien Sorel! But didn't he, I asked, represent their own desires for pre-eminence, their own natural young ambition?

In addition to teaching me that ambition was an admirable quality of character, Lionel had also taught me that honesty was the supreme literary virtue. Unlike his view of ambition, which was rare among writers and intellectuals, the high valuation he placed on honesty was universally shared by them. Indeed, in the estimation of the modernist creed, shattering taboos and confessing to one's true feelings, especially if they were considered disreputable, was one of the most courageous and valuable things a writer could do.

And yet, notwithstanding all this, Lionel complained that I had "bought the whole package" and advised me to add a concluding chapter to my manuscript which would so soften everything I had said before about success as in effect to take most of it back (though he phrased this advice in much more subtle terms). Otherwise I ought not to publish the book at all. If it appeared in its present form, he warned (not altogether inaccurately), it would be ten years before I lived it down. Diana then added insult to injury by informing me that the book—which I thought was shot through with humor and irony—was completely humorless and lacked any touch of saving irony.

Now it was my turn to feel betrayed (though I did not then, and I do not now, take this as an act of revenge on their part). By the time I had brought the manuscript to Lionel, *Making It* was already creating a scandal. My original publisher, who had given me a substantial advance, had decided upon reading it that he wanted nothing to do with such a book. Then, except for Norman Mailer (who, as we shall see, would change his mind after it was finally brought out by another publisher), the few friends to whom I had turned for reassurance and support had been as shocked by its "tastelessness" as the most puritanical of readers would have been by hard-core pornography. Evidently the "dirty little secret" I was opening up was even dirtier than I had imagined. But that was cold comfort and did little to mitigate my naive disgust at the hypocrisy of the world in which I lived. Surely I could depend on Lionel of all people to respond differently. When, however, he surprised me yet again by dashing this expectation, I was of course hurt, but I was even more bewildered to see *him* doing precisely what he was advising me to do—taking back everything he himself had seemed to believe, and had encouraged me to believe as well.

Still, no more than my past betrayal of Lionel did his present betrayal of me cause a complete rupture in our relations. Around this time—in the late 1960s—I invited both him and Diana to participate in a symposium in *Commentary* in which I raised the question of whether there was any justice in the charge that the Vietnam War (which, like me and everyone else in the Family, they opposed) had stemmed from the liberal anti-Communism we had also all espoused. Both agreed to participate, and each of them wrote a testy response denying the charge and reaffirming the validity of the liberal anti-Communist position.

Around this time, too, Lionel and Diana and my wife and I went as part of a larger group on a trip to Germany sponsored by the Ford Foundation. The four of us formed a little clique of our own and we had a lot of fun together. Not long after our return to America, Columbia became the latest campus involved in a series of demonstrations featuring the takeover of buildings by student radicals and clashes between them and the police. With the "revolution" advancing so close to home, Diana's polemical blood began to boil, and she wrote a very long article denouncing the tactics of the students, exposing the fallacious moral and political assumptions on which they had operated (while conceding a point to them here and there), and sharply criticizing their supporters within the universities and the intellectual community in general. She sent this article to me, and I accepted it for publication without asking for cuts, even though, at twenty-eight thousand words, it would occupy many more pages of the magazine than was usual for a single piece.

I did not agree with every word of this article, but I did share its overall point of view. Indeed, even when I was still a strong enough supporter of the radical movement to be tacitly accused by the Trillings of having gone over to the enemy, I had published a critical piece by Nathan Glazer about the first of the great campus outbreaks, the one at Berkeley in 1964. Glazer was generally sympathetic to the radicals and he granted the legitimacy of many of their grievances, but he also raised troubled questions about their ideas, their tactics, and what he called in a subsequent defense of his piece "the moral quality" of their actions.

As was usual between Nat Glazer and me, and as would continue to be the case on one issue after another in the years ahead, I went further than he did in my opposition to the Berkeley rebellion, which created deeper misgivings in me about the new radicalism than I was ready to admit, even to myself, at so early a stage in my association with it. There was very little actual physical violence at Berkeley, but I was intellectually and morally offended by the violence against language and ideas in the speeches and manifestoes of the participants and their supporters. A decade later, in *Breaking Ranks*, I would spell this out in detail. Violence, I would say, was committed against the distinction between the black poor of the ghettos and the privileged and prosperous young on the campuses (as in a notorious document of the uprising, *The Student as Nigger*). Violence was committed against the distinction between democratic America and a tyrannical state and was then compounded by comparing the disciplines of an academic community—like required courses and grades—to prisons and chains. And violence was committed against the distinction between one political position and another, as when apologists maintained that the Berkeley radicals were merely trying to fulfill the traditional values of American liberalism which they themselves were openly bent on demystifying and destroying.

But Berkeley was not the only development that stirred doubts in me about the radical movement in which I had placed my hopes and invested so much of my literary and editorial labor. I had been among the earliest opponents of American intervention into the Vietnam War, but I felt no solidarity with those of my political allies who, as the socialist leader Norman Thomas once put it, loved the Vietcong more than they loved peace and who were increasingly setting the tone of the antiwar protests.

I had also been an early participant in the civil rights struggles, but I felt no solidarity with the "black-power" separatists and revolutionists like the Black Panthers and the misleadingly named Student Non-Violent Coordinating Committee (SNCC), who were becoming more and more dominant within the civil-rights movement (and who were also serving as a cover for the reintroduction of anti-Semitism into American public discourse). Nor could I countenance the degeneration of groups like Students for a Democratic Society (SDS), whose early utopianism was by the late 1960s finding its mutated expression in the bombs of the Weathermen.

This was not the kind of thing I had expected and worked for in associating myself with the radical movement, and it was what ultimately drew me into a public breaking of ranks. But this breaking of ranks did not take the form of a sudden conversion on the road to a political Damascus. It was a gradual process that began as early as Berkeley and did not reach its consummation for at least another five or six years (and even then there would be more to come). Along the way it involved much painful thought, much reconsideration of long-held assumptions, and much angry argument with close personal friends and political allies on the Left.

Conversely, it inaugurated a new stage in my relations with the Trillings—as well as a few other fallen-away friends from my days as a hard anti-Communist, like Sidney Hook, Arnold Beichman, and Irving Kristol and his wife, Gertrude Himmelfarb. It would be going too far to describe this new stage as a reconciliation with the Trillings, since, as I have repeatedly stressed above, we never actually cut one another off, not even when things between us were at their worst. Nor could my publication of Diana's article about Columbia be interpreted either by the Trillings or by anyone else as an announcement of a new turn in my own political thinking, since I had from the very first refused to go along with the radical "party line" where the universities were concerned. But from that article in combination with certain others I was now running in *Commentary*, as well as from my own writing (including, ironically, *Making It*, which expressed more dissatisfaction with the Left than either I or the Trillings fully recognized), I was beginning to be seen by them as the prodigal son who was finally coming back home.

By 1970 my growing doubts about radicalism had coalesced and come to a head in a conviction so blazing that it ignited an offensive against the Movement in *Commentary* that was free of the hesitations and concessions which had diluted and weakened the criticisms I had been making up to that point. Lionel, just back from a stay in England (where, as also in France, Germany, Italy, and Japan, radicalism had once against become all the rage in the universities and among intellectuals in general, even without benefit of a government at war in Vietnam or a society torn by racial conflict), told me, for the first time in years, that he was happy with what I had started to do. "I see," he said, "that it isn't all over yet." No, I replied, it wasn't, but I needed his help to finish the job, and he promised me that I would have it.

It was a promise that he was never to keep. All he ever did was allow me to publish one of the lectures he delivered at Harvard that were subsequently brought together in his book *Sincerity and Authenticity*. I featured it as a lead article even though it disappointed me in being so muffled in its attack on the idea of insanity as a species of rebellion against the spiritual oppressions of middle-class society. This idea had been from the beginning—in Allen Ginsberg's declaration that "the best minds" of his generation had been driven mad and in Norman Mailer's celebration of the psychopath (about which more later)—a central element of the new radicalism. It also still figured in the work of serious thinkers like the psychologist R. D. Laing and in more popular form in a novel like Ken Kesey's *One Flew Over the Cuckoo's Nest*, which, as a measure of its by then mass appeal, was turned into a very successful movie. And it was, finally, an idea profoundly repugnant to

Lionel. Yet he could only bring himself to an expression of this repugnance by a route so convoluted and difficult to follow that many readers were at a loss to figure out what he was trying to say.

Except for his participation in a roundtable discussion of "Culture and the Present Moment" I sponsored in 1974, the transcript of which I then published in *Commentary*, this attenuated blast on an uncertain trumpet was all the good he ever made on his promise to join the *Commentary* campaign against the Movement. Evidently, his initial enthusiasm had been the impulse of a moment, and it soon gave way to an unmistakable coldness toward the enterprise as I was conducting it.

The first indication of that coldness came when Lionel told me one evening (using the Yiddish word for soiled or besmirched) that Sidney Hook had *"beschmutzed"* his own name by going too far to the Right in his recoil from Communism and that I was in danger of doing the same to myself in my war against the New Left. Not the least amazing feature of this extraordinary statement was his resort to a Yiddish term: I could not recall his ever doing so on any other occasion or in any other context, and I still have no explanation for it. But hardly less amazing was his assumption that I would be frightened off by being compared to Sidney Hook, a revered figure among anti-Communists who in any case had never moved so far to the Right as to stop calling himself a socialist (just as I at that period was inclined to describe myself as a social democrat).

Here, then, was a dramatic reversal of roles. Ten years earlier Lionel had cautioned me against going too far with the radical critique of American society and American foreign policy. A little later, I had in turn accused him of having been driven by a horror of Stalinism into extolling "the virtues of American society and the values of the middle-class spirit" and thereby abdicating the intellectual's proper role as a critic of society. Now it was he who was accusing me (not bluntly but in the language of friendly concern) of overreacting to the excesses of the new radicalism by becoming an uncritical participant in what had once been derided by his own leftist critics as "the American celebration."

To me it seemed clear that Lionel had lost his appetite for another fight against the Left, and indeed he would admit as much himself in the roundtable discussion on "Culture and the Present Moment." Disagreeing with my statement that the collapse of the academic and intellectual communities in the face of the radicalism of the 1960s had been a sign of cowardice, Lionel said:

> There is a reason to say cowardice in individual cases, but as a general explanation of the situation Norman Podhoretz refers to I think the word "cowardice" might lead us astray. One has to conceive of it rather in terms of fatigue. . . . Subjects and problems got presented in a way that made one's spirits fail. It wasn't that one was afraid to go into it, or afraid of being in opposition—I suppose I am speaking personally—but rather that in looking at the matter one's reaction was likely to be a despairing shrug.

I had not intended to include him in the charge of cowardice, but little did I know how deep his "fatigue" went. Within a year, at the age of seventy, he was to contract the pancreatic cancer that would carry him off with the speed for which that horrible disease is noted.

Thankfully, we had both been so determined to avoid yet another quarrel that the latest strain between us remained mostly below the surface, and I was therefore able to see him a number of times in the six months between the diagnosis and his death. Though my main interest had already shifted away from literature and into politics, we now talked more about the former than the latter, especially as the end grew nearer and nearer. When I visited him in the hospital for what turned out to be our very last meeting, I mentioned that I had been rereading Thomas Mann, that I had especially been bowled over by *Doctor Faustus*, and that I had come to the conclusion that Mann might well be the greatest novelist of the twentieth century—not a widely shared view within the Family or any other sector of the literary world. From his bed of excruciating pain, Lionel smiled a sweet smile and said (as best I can remember his words), "How very interesting. You know we always found it hard to forgive him for becoming something of a Stalinist in the forties, and probably we underrated him because of it. But what you say about him now is so intriguing that I would love to take another look at him myself."

With only about two weeks left to live, he never got the chance.

Meanwhile, as Lionel lay dying, Diana made an extraordinary request of me. Like Lionel, Diana was the child of Jewish immigrants from eastern Europe,* and they were both very conscious of themselves as Jews, but only in a social sense. Unlike Diana, though, who had never been sent to any kind of Jewish school as a child, Lionel had been tutored for his *bar mitzvah* by an eminent Talmudic scholar named Max Kadushin (with whom, by an unlikely coincidence, I myself would later study Talmud for a while). Then as a young man he had begun his professional literary career by writing regularly for and even briefly working on the staff of *The Menorah Journal.* By 1944, however, while retaining the anti-Zionist position espoused by *The Menorah Journal,* he had turned his back decisively on everything else it represented by way of a favorable attitude toward Jewish culture. In a symposium published that year in the *Contemporary Jewish Record* (a scholarly quarterly which was published for a few years by the American Jewish Committee and which in 1945 was theoretically incorporated but actually supplanted by *Commentary*), he wrote that

> as the Jewish community now exists, it can give no sustenance to the American artist or intellectual who is born a Jew. And so far as I am aware, it has not done so in the past. . . . I know of no writer in English who has added a micromillimetre to his stature by "realizing his Jewishness," although I know of some who have curtailed their promise by trying to heighten their Jewish consciousness.

As for Judaism as a religion:

> Modern Jewish religion at its best may indeed be intelligent and soaked in universal knowledge, but out of it there has not come a sin-

---

*In an unusual wrinkle, however, Lionel's mother's family came from Poland to America via England, where she grew up, read a lot of Victorian literature, and developed airs that had an enormous influence on her son's personality and manner while also setting her snobbishly apart from her own Jewish contemporaries. An amusing example was her relation with the mother of Irwin Edman, who, though Jewish, had been made a full professor in the Columbia philosophy department long before the English department could bring itself to do the same for her Lionel. Mrs. Trilling took her revenge by refusing to call Edman "Irwin," always asking Mrs. Edman when they met how her "Irving" was doing.

gle voice with the note of authority—of philosophical, or poetic, or even of rhetorical, let alone of religious, authority.

And as for himself, he disclaimed any connection as a writer with his Jewish origins:

> I cannot discover anything in my professional intellectual life which I can specifically trace back to my Jewish birth and rearing. I do not think of myself as a "Jewish writer." I do not have it in mind to serve by my writing any Jewish purpose. I should resent it if a critic of my work were to discover in it either faults or virtues which he called Jewish.

In later life, these violently negative feelings would soften a bit, as evidenced by an essay Lionel wrote in 1950 on "Wordsworth and the Rabbis," in which, by discovering affinities between his favorite English poet and an ancient rabbinic text ("The Ethics of the Fathers"), he was finally able to say something good about something Jewish. He was also fascinated by the fact that I had taken the trouble to get a serious Jewish education by pursuing an academic degree at the College of Jewish Studies at the Jewish Theological Seminary at night while attending Columbia by day, and he spent a good deal of time asking me about it, always in the tones of a man wondering whether his own settled opinion might need to be reconsidered. (Once he challenged me to name anything good that had come out of the culture of the eastern European Jewish world. "You," I shot back, at which he had the good grace to laugh, if not to be convinced.)

Where his early anti-Zionism was concerned, however, a reconsideration did indeed take place, as I was gratified to discover when he telephoned to congratulate me one Sunday morning on a passionately pro-Israel article of mine in that day's *New York Times Magazine*. So unexpected was this compliment that I could not help asking what he liked about the piece: "Good doctrine and good prose," he answered, surprising me (yet again) with the former accolade and delighting me with the latter.

Still, this change in Lionel never went far enough to induce him to arrange any form of Jewish education for his son, James, the Trillings' only child, who at the time of Lionel's final sickness was in his twenties.

Nor, so far as I could tell, had Diana ever undergone even as mild a transformation as Lionel's in her own attitudes toward Jewishness. Which is what made it so extraordinary that she should ask me as Lionel's certain death approached whether I would be willing to teach Jim how to recite the Kaddish, the prayer that a Jewish son is obligated to read at his father's funeral service. The enthusiasm with which I agreed to this request amazed me almost as much as the request itself. I simply had not realized that I cared so deeply about this, and I suppose now that the reason was that, when all was said and done, Lionel—just as Diana had always maintained, much to my resentment at what I regarded as a piece of vulgar Freudian reductionism—had indeed been a surrogate father to me.

Jim could not read the Hebrew alphabet, and so I set about making an English transliteration and drilling him day after day in how to pronounce the words properly. Lionel died about a week after we had begun these tutorials, and by then Jim had mastered the whole text and could even translate it into English.

Yet for reasons I was never to unearth or to understand, Diana (possibly seconded by Jim) changed her mind about giving Lionel even a watered-down Jewish funeral. The service was held in St. Paul's Chapel on the Columbia campus and was followed by a cremation. And neither in this Christian building nor in the crematorium did Jim recite the Kaddish. Distressed as I was by this, I was positively offended by Diana's decision to omit even a eulogy from the funeral services. I knew as surely as I was sitting there that Diana had persuaded herself that this decision arose out of her infinite regard for Lionel: what could a eulogist, or ten eulogists, say in praise of him that would be adequate or commensurate with his greatness? But having so recently been soaked in the Kaddish, I remembered more vividly than I might otherwise have done the reference to God as *l'ailah min kol birkhata v'shirata, tushbekhata v'nekhemata* (beyond [or above] all blessings and hymns, praises and consolations). And because I understood this passage to mean that only God was above or beyond them, I thought it a mark of impious and even blasphemous presumption to treat a mortal man as though he were beyond or above them too.

Perhaps out of cowardice, or perhaps because I was *still* not prepared for the almost certain break it would entail, I never said any of this to Diana. But it continued rankling, and when about eighteen years later, in 1993, she published a book about the early days of their marriage (*The Beginning of the Journey*), which I, and not I alone, read as a covert attack on Lionel, I found myself borrowing from her own Freudian arsenal and reinterpreting the funeral she had arranged not as a mark of hubris in relation to Lionel but as an unconscious slap at him.

The word *unconscious* has to be stressed here because, except for her equally unconscious book, in the twenty-one years left to her after Lionel's death Diana became so ferocious a custodian of his reputation that I could easily see her as the central character in a story by Henry James that he might have called "The Widow." Thus, she edited and arranged for the publication of a uniform set of his complete works, including previously unpublished material; she tried, and sometimes even with success, to vet everything written about him, and when she failed she would invariably retaliate with public denunciations. When, for example, Joseph Epstein, the then editor of *The American Scholar*, on whose advisory board she sat, ran an article about Lionel, she resigned on the ground that it had not been shown to her in advance, even though board members had no such prerogative and even though the article in question was wholly respectful and uncritical to a fault. On another occasion, she wrote a letter to *Encounter* in effect calling Sidney Hook a liar for his account of a conversation he had had with Lionel decades earlier at which she had not even been present. And she did exactly the same thing to me when *Breaking Ranks* came out in 1979.

In the four years between the death of Lionel and the publication of *Breaking Ranks*, my relations with Diana were good, and she was happy to let *Commentary* have one of the previously unpublished manuscripts that she had found among Lionel's papers. This was a rather academic essay about the changing myth of the Jew in English fiction that he had written at the age of twenty-four—a period in his life when, as part of the *Menorah Journal* circle, he was still actively struggling with the issue of Jewishness. It was not up to the literary and intellectual levels he would soon reach (he himself had judged it "inferior and dullish"). Yet it possessed historical as well as indirect biographical interest, and my own piety toward him was such that I was just as pleased to publish it as Diana was to have me do so.

Then, only a few months before the appearance of *Breaking Ranks* would forever after make such a thing impossible, she herself sent me a memoir she had written entitled "Lionel Trilling, a Jew at Columbia." It was about his travails as a young member of the faculty when anti-Semitism was still widespread enough to delay his appointment to a tenured position in the English department on the grounds that (as I myself had once put it) while a Jew could teach Greek or even philosophy, no one with such shallow roots in Anglo-Saxon culture could be entrusted with introducing the young to its literary heritage.

But if my relations with Diana were once again good, they were by no means as good as they had been in the first phase of our friendship. As far back as I could remember, I had always felt the need, and been willing, to "humor" her when she would start on some line of talk that was out of touch with any reality I could recognize. But either she was getting worse or I was becoming less adept at pretending to take her seriously. This naturally made me uncomfortable in her presence, and it sometimes spilled embarrassingly over into our professional dealings. Her writing often suffered from the same fault as her conversation, and the problem was exacerbated by the tendency of her prose to grow clotted and twisted in making its points. Even so, it was certainly good enough to be published in *Commentary*—except when her wacky sense of reality got the better of her and I had to find a tactful way of telling her so.

The first time this happened was when she sent me a long manuscript speculating freely on the reasons why so many intellectuals had been protesting against the execution of a death-row inmate named Caryl Chessman. Surely, she argued, if anyone deserved the death penalty, it was a lifelong criminal who had kidnapped, raped, and murdered a young woman. The trouble was that Chessman had not murdered the young woman in question, and the "kidnapping" had consisted in dragging her from one car to another in a parking lot. Another time she submitted a manuscript about the Profumo scandal in England in which her entire analysis was based on the assumption that the socialists, being of the Left, were in favor of easy sexual morals. The trouble there was that the Fabians to whom she kept referring had all been as puritanical about sex as their Victorian forebears.

But since Diana had no legitimate gripe against the rejection of these two pieces, and since I was still humoring her by concealing my genuine shock at her gaffes, the final rupture between us was delayed until she read *Breaking Ranks.* This was the book in which I used my own experience—much as I had done with the theme of success in *Making It*—as a focus for examining the evolution of American political culture from the mid-1940s to the mid-1970s. There was a lot about Lionel in it (including the story of his conversation with me about *Making It*) and a fair amount, though much less, about Diana as well.

Amazingly, she never wrote or spoke to me directly about *Breaking Ranks,* but she told everyone that I had lied in saying that Lionel had advised me not to publish *Making It.* Yet (just as in the case of the same charge she had made about Sidney Hook) she had not been present at the conversation during which Lionel had given me precisely that advice. Perhaps he had not told her about it, and it may be that she had taken this as evidence against my report. Perhaps too the charge was a cover for her outrage at my general account of Lionel, and most especially his "fatigue" in response to the radicalism of the 1960's. In my own judgment (now in tranquil recollection no less than then, in the heat of the moment), this general account, though critical, was truthful and respectfully written. Moreover, every word about him throughout the book reflected the immense regard in which I had always held his work, and the personal and intellectual debt I had always felt to him.

But as one would have expected of the title character in "The Widow," my imaginary Jamesian story, Diana was so outraged by *Breaking Ranks* that she demanded of all our mutual friends that they repudiate the book, preferably in public but at least by assuring her privately that they shared her feeling and would have nothing further to do with me. Those who refused (like William Barrett, to whom she wrote a letter declaring that if he were an honorable man he would withdraw the blurb he had given to this mendacious piece of work and who thought as a result that she had gone completely crazy) were themselves banished from her presence and excommunicated. The pianist Samuel Lipman (to whom she had originally introduced me and whose career as a music critic I had then launched) was actually thrown out of her house when he tried ever so gently to persuade her that she might perhaps be over-reacting to *Breaking Ranks.*

After weeks of this kind of thing, my wife (who, after all, had a husband too whose good name she thought needed defending) could no longer restrain herself. Without informing me that she was doing so, she wrote Diana an angry letter that would have resulted in the burning of any bridges that had not already gone up in flames. Yet even if any had remained standing, there would have been little likelihood of ever crossing them again.* For if Lionel thought I had already been going too far to the Right in the early 1970s, when I still regarded my-self as a centrist liberal or a social democrat, Diana (as I kept hearing) felt confirmed in her extreme hostility toward me when, in the years following *Breaking Ranks,* I finally surrendered myself to the "neoconservative" label and even became a great supporter of Ronald Reagan.

It was not that she ever gave up calling herself an anti-Communist or insisting on the moral and political superiority of that position. On the contrary, she had gotten into a big fight (before our own break), with her publisher, who was also the publisher of Lillian Hellman's *Scoundrel Time* (about which more later), when she refused to remove from a collection of her essays certain criticisms of that book bearing on this issue. Yet to the end of her life, Diana kept insisting with equal vehemence that she was still, and always had been, a liberal, even after that term had long since been hijacked by and become identified with the beliefs of the leftists and the anti-anti-Communists against

---

*One reason my wife was so angry was that she recalled a conversation during our trip together to Germany—a conversation at which Diana had been present and in the course of which Lionel repeated what he had previously told me *tête-à-tête* about pub-lishing *Making It.* If my wife's memory was accurate, then Diana was simply lying, and not fantasizing when she accused *me* of lying about Lionel's advice. But I continued to give Diana the benefit of the doubt on this matter, because although I did remember a difficult conversation the four of us had in Germany about *Making It,* I did not recall Lionel's repeating his advice not to publish it. Which does not prove, I hasten to add, that my wife's memory was faulty.

whom she had been contending for the past five decades and more. It made no difference to her that Reagan in the political sphere and his neoconservative supporters in the intellectual world were carrying on the same good fight. All she seemed to care about was refuting the people who had accused anti-Communists like her of lending aid and comfort to McCarthyism in the 1950s, and her way of doing this was to accuse anti-Communists like me of the same crime in relation to those forces that she regarded as McCarthyism's present-day legatees.

I realize how bizarrely sectarian all this must sound to ears not attuned to the ideological wars of the intellectuals. But an important issue was and is at stake here that reaches to the very heart of the relation between ideas and practical politics. In the world of ideas it is possible to keep one's political skirts clean. One can favor this and oppose that even when in the real world the "that" follows inexorably from the "this"; or one can support an end while refusing to back the only available means for getting to it. This is why intellectuals are so often drawn to "the third way" or "the third force"—that is, some currently nonexistent or utopian future alternative to the choices that are actually on offer in the here and now.

A vivid illustration came during the Vietnam War (about which I was to write a book in 1982), when certain people took the position that they were against both Saigon and Hanoi. What then were they for? The answer given in a piece written jointly by Irving Howe and the political theorist Michael Walzer, the editors of *Dissent*, after the war was over was that they had "hoped for the emergence of a Vietnamese 'third force' capable of rallying the people in a progressive direction by enacting land reforms and defending civil liberties." But since, as they themselves admitted, there was very little chance that this would happen, to have thrown their energies into opposing the American effort was tantamount to working for the Communist victory they said (in all sincerity) they did not want. Nothing daunted by this contradiction, they still awarded themselves moral congratulations on having been against the evils on both sides of the war:

> Those of us who opposed American intervention yet did not want a
> Communist victory were in the difficult position of having no happy

ending to offer. . . . And we were in the difficult position of urging a relatively complex argument at a moment when most Americans, pro- and anti-war, wanted blinding simplicities.

Yet considering the actual alternatives that existed, what did the urging of "a relatively complex argument" avail other than to make those who urged it feel pleased with themselves? If, as I added in my book, it served any purpose at all for the people of South Vietnam, it was to help deliver them over to the "blinding simplicities" of the totalitarianism whose hideous workings Howe and Walzer were now happy to denounce and protest against, even though there was no one in Hanoi or Saigon (now renamed Ho Chi Minh City) to listen or to hear.

I myself was no different from Howe and Walzer in my stance on the Vietnam War while it was going on, but I drew an entirely different lesson from the horrors that ensued when it was over. This lesson was that refusing to choose between the only alternatives before one because neither was perfect or pretty, or because one could envisage some future possibility that might or might not ever be realized but that was nevertheless uniquely worthy of one's support in the present, was not to act morally but to evade one's moral responsibility. And there was for me a corollary to this lesson, which was that one ought to join the side one was now on instead of engaging in a futile struggle to change the side one used to be on.

Thus it was that in the post-Vietnam period I discovered more and more common ground with the conservatives I had once opposed and less and less with the liberals and other leftists with whom I had once identified. True, there was still a brave band of Democrats loyal to the fervent cold warrior Senator Henry Jackson and to the then still relatively hawkish Senator Hubert H. Humphrey and opposed to the isolationism that had infected their party after its takeover by the leftist forces behind the presidential candidacy of George McGovern in 1972. I myself had joined with them in founding the Coalition for a Democratic Majority (CDM) in an effort to take the party back from the McGovernites. But we were vastly outnumbered not only by the McGovernites in our own party but by the proponents of détente among the Republicans. The upshot was that only among conservatives could I find genuine allies in the intellectual campaign I was now undertaking to help revive the American will to resist Soviet expansionism, a campaign against those in both major parties who were, as I put it in the title of an article I wrote in 1975, "Making the World Safe for Communism."

I had hoped that my old and close friend Daniel P. Moynihan, whose election to the U.S. Senate from New York in 1976 I had done my share behind the scenes to make possible, would assume the leadership of the Jackson Democrats and run for president in 1980. But when it became dishearteningly clear that he had no such intention and that he was in fact moving for political reasons of his own in the other direction, down the drain went the last traces of my resistance to the lessons I had drawn from Vietnam. I finally made a choice between the real alternatives on offer, while simultaneously joining the side I was on, by voting without any reservations whatsoever for Ronald Reagan in 1980 against Jimmy Carter.

How Lionel would have felt about all this if he had lived, I cannot be sure. Even though he had foreseen and worried about my move to the Right, the new circumstances that developed in the years after his death would probably have elicited an even more complicated response from him than Irving Howe and Michael Walzer had formed to the Vietnam War. After all, everything in the world, with the possible exception of Stalinism, was complicated to Lionel (I can hear him even now pronouncing the word, perhaps his favorite in the whole English lexicon, with his rather thin voice lovingly lingering over the first syllable). He always regarded himself as a liberal, but more often than not he would use the term in a pejorative sense; he believed in and celebrated society and its restraints, but he also wrote with great sympathy about the yearning for an "unconditioned" life; he loved literature above all things, but he was capable of complaining about how much he hated to read. Considering this doubleness in his nature, I can easily imagine him defending Reagan against liberal attack while at the same time shaking his head over the simplifications in which Reagan specialized, asking me to explain why I thought they were commendable, and listening skeptically but patiently as I did.

But I can imagine no such scenario featuring Diana. By the time she died in 1996 at the age of ninety-one, all the contempt and the ridicule to which she had once been subjected by the likes of Hannah Arendt and Mary McCarthy* (about both of whom I will also have much more to say later on), not to mention enemies further to the Left, had been forgotten, and she even came to be hailed by feminists as something of a pioneering heroine. *The New Yorker* ran a reverential profile of and several pieces by her; the book she wrote about her marriage to Lionel was on the whole extremely well received, as was the one she did earlier about the Jean Harris murder trial; and court was paid to her by a new generation of academics and intellectuals who knew not Joseph. It is inconceivable to me that she would have jeopardized all that by seeming in any way to sympathize with the Reagan conservatives or the Right in general, notwithstanding their (our) success in achieving what would surely still have been her most cherished political wish: the breakup of the Soviet empire and the defeat of Communism.

When she died I thought of attending her funeral, but I decided that it would be hypocritical of me to do so when I had not seen her in so many years (except across crowded chapels at several other funerals). Although I still consult Lionel's writings often and although I think about him a lot, always with admiration, gratitude, and indeed love, the best I can do with Diana is occasionally to remember her fondly. But not, in all truth, all that often or all that much.

---

*In the late 1960s, Mary wrote to Hannah that she had felt obligated to answer a letter from Diana about a piece of hers in *The New York Review:* "That woman is such a fool; if she didn't occupy her absurd place in the New York establishment, they would have thrown her letter in the wastebasket. . . . [My husband Jim] says she's an example of brain drain without geographical displacement." Of course, this remark came from "our leading bitch intellectual," as Mary has with justice been called, who moreover had a long history of opposition to Diana, going back to the split in the ACCF. Yet the fact remains that her malicious attitude toward Diana was widely shared within the Family, some of whose members, with no justice, even attributed Diana's "absurd place in the New York establishment" entirely to her connection with Lionel.

ANOTHER PART OF THE FOREST:
LILLIAN HELLMAN

WHEN I GOT TO KNOW THEM SOCIALLY, THE TRILLINGS lived—as they would continue indefinitely to do—in an apartment near the Columbia campus, where Lionel was by now indisputably the most eminent member of the liberal arts faculty. Like almost everyone else in the Family in the 1950s, they entertained a lot, sometimes with small dinners, but more often making use of their spacious living room for much larger pre- or postprandial gatherings at which the main refreshment offered was alcohol. It was at one of these after-9 P.M. parties, in 1957, that I began forming what would later strike many people as among the most unlikely and puzzling friendships of which they had ever heard.

Arriving a little late, I could see at a quick glance that all the many guests already there, milling around with drinks in their hands and chatting characteristically with animation and zest, were the usual mix of Family members and Lionel's academic colleagues. All, that is, except one. The stranger was a woman who, on the basis of photographs I remembered from book jackets and newspaper stories, seemed a dead ringer for Lillian Hellman. But since it was hard to imagine the Trillings associating with her, I was sure that it must be someone else, and my astonishment knew no bounds when, a minute or two later, I discovered that it was indeed none other than Lillian Hellman herself standing there.

I had good cause to be astonished. For one thing, Lillian (as, at her insistence, I soon began calling her) was the author of hit Broadway plays and Hollywood films and, as such, the kind of writer for whom literary intellectuals like the Trillings generally felt disdain and even contempt. In retrospect, I can see that her presence at the Trillings was a harbinger of a new cultural climate in which commercially successful "middlebrow" writers like her would no longer be automatically dismissed as vulgar popularizers contributing to the debasement of aesthetic standards and the corruption of literary taste. At the time, however, this attitude was still sufficiently prevalent among "highbrows" like the Trillings (though the fastidious Lionel would never have allowed such a word into his vocabulary) to arouse my wonder at the sight of her among them that night.

But this cultural divide, wide as it may have been, was as nothing compared with the fact that Lillian was (or at least had been the last time anyone looked) a "Stalinist." I have already used this epithet more than once in the preceding pages, but let me linger for a moment on it here in trying to explain why in those days and for years to come it was charged with a degree of meaning and portent that can scarcely be appreciated any longer by anyone under a certain age.

The term was originally applied to Stalin's supporters within the Communist movement by rival groups, also within the Communist movement, who thought that he had betrayed the Russian revolution of 1917 led by Lenin, and who now invested their hopes for redemption in the exiled Trotsky or some other less prominent claimant to the true Communist faith. But this very term had gradually begun to be adopted as a derogatory epithet by certain anti-Communists as well. These were socialists and liberals who found it useful as a way of characterizing others on the Left who, whether or not they were "card-carrying" members of the Communist party, definitely sympathized with the policies of the Soviet Union under Stalin and apologized even for the crimes he committed against his own people (about which more in a moment). In the pre-Stalin era, Lenin (who died in 1924) had ungratefully derided such fellow-travelers of his own movement as "useful idiots"; and later Whittaker Chambers, after his own break with Communism, would say of Stalin's fellow-travelers in the United States and the West generally that if they were not actually Communist party members, they were cheating it of dues.

Many of the anti-Stalinist socialists and liberals had once been Communists or fellow-travelers themselves whose belief in the Soviet Union as a utopia-in-the-making had been shattered by one "Kronstadt" or another.* The original Kronstadt was the armed suppression under Lenin by the Red Army of a sailors' revolt in the early 1920s, a suppression from which the long series of disillusioning episodes that followed took their name: the murder by Stalin of millions of peasants who resisted the collectivization of agriculture in the early 1930s; the show trials of the mid-1930s through which he executed his potential successors (all of them loyal lifelong Bolshevik comrades of his who had been tortured into false confessions of treason); and the pact that he, who had been touted by Communists everywhere as the only reliable bulwark against the Nazis and the fascists then being appeased by the Western democracies, signed with Hitler in the late 1930s.

After each of these "Kronstadts," a certain number of Communists in the West broke with the party and went into opposition against it, as did a contingent of fellow-travelers who no longer found it possible to swallow the rationalizations and the outright lies offered up to explain the horrors away. Nor did such breaks merely involve a change of mind about large political issues. More often than not, they

---

*This designation comes from Louis Fischer, one of the contributors to the highly influential compilation *The God That Failed* (1949), in which six writers (of whom Fischer himself was the least well-known, the others being Arthur Koestler, Ignazio Silone, Richard Wright, André Gide, and Stephen Spender) explained why they had broken with the Communist party. But the summary I provided of these "Kronstadts" in my own book *The Bloody Crossroads*, and which I am more or less reproducing here, was my own.

resulted in bitter personal quarrels leading to the destruction of friendships, love affairs, and even marriages with people who against all evidence remained stubbornly faithful to the Communist cause. The Stalinists regarded their fallen-away comrades as traitors and cowards who were acting from the basest of motives: they had "sold out" to the capitalist enemy and nothing was too scurrilous to say about them. For their part, the ex-Communists denounced the Stalinists as slavish devotees of a totalitarian regime to whose crimes they were willfully blinding themselves and in whose defense they would accept and spread any lie, no matter how blatant or egregious.

I have already said that neither Lionel nor Diana Trilling had ever been a member of the Communist party but that after a brief spell of intense fellow-traveling in the early 1930s they had become very fierce in their anti-Communism. Indeed, they (and especially Diana) were at least as fierce as any ex-Communist intellectual in sight.

As for Lillian Hellman, I strongly suspected (rightly, as will emerge in due course) that, in spite of her well-publicized denials, she had in fact been a member of the Communist party, but in any case there was no doubt as to where her political sympathies lay. A series of "Kronstadts" might have shattered the illusions of many others about the Soviet Union, but she had managed to weather each and every one. Kronstadt itself had come a bit too early for someone her age and background (I doubt that a girl of sixteen born and bred in the American South would even have heard of it). But she had certainly reached full political consciousness by the 1930s, and yet neither the millions of peasants slaughtered by Stalin in the early part of that decade nor the show trials of the later part had ever elicited a word of protest from her. The only words she uttered in public were in the statements she had signed affirming the justice of those trials and defaming the people who were trying to expose the ugly truth about them. And though she was Jewish, not even the Nazi–Soviet pact had shaken her faith in Stalin's regime.. True, she had put on her anti-Nazi play *Watch on the Rhine,* a big hit on Broadway that was also made into a successful movie, while the pact was still in force. She thereby defied the party line of the moment, which called for a muting of any criticism of Stalin's new ally. Even so, she defended the pact itself as a justifiable tactical move (and as will also emerge in due course, she may even have had the party's secret permission to stage *Watch on the Rhine* when she did).

All this might have been overlooked and finally forgotten when in 1941 Hitler violated his pact with Stalin by invading the Soviet Union, just as Stalin's own crimes were forgiven when he then forged an alliance with the Western democracies and his country went on to make an enormous contribution to the defeat of Hitler. But the glow of the wartime alliance faded when Stalin, breaking agreements into which he had only just entered with the West, established Communist puppet regimes in all the countries of Eastern Europe his troops had occupied in advancing toward Germany. And as if this were not ominous enough, he also began using the Communist parties in other countries as instruments of subversion and revolution.

Here, then, was a new type of Kronstadt, involving illusions not about the domestic character of the Soviet Union but about its role in international affairs. Thus, in seizing on the opportunity presented by his military successes in the Second World War to establish a new empire of his own, Stalin was giving the lie to the claim that the Soviet Union was the great opponent of imperialism in the world. And in maintaining his armies at wartime strength and seeking to extend his imperial sway beyond the domains of Eastern Europe (while the United States was demobilizing and "bringing the boys back home" as fast as it possibly could), Stalin was also demonstrating that far from being, as was also claimed, a peace-loving power, the Soviet Union was now the main threat to the peace of the world.

These international Kronstadts, which caused the onset of what soon came to be called the cold war, also opened the eyes of yet another batch of Stalinists and fellow-travelers to the Soviet reality. Not, however, Lillian Hellman's. Her response was to help organize the infamous Waldorf Conference of 1949—the very one whose purpose was to whitewash Stalin's actions and blame the United States for the tensions they had caused, and also the same one that provoked the formation of the anti-Stalinist American Committee for Cultural Freedom, of which Diana Trilling herself would later became president.

Around the same time, Lillian played an active part in supporting Henry Wallace, who had left the Democratic party to run for president on a platform wholeheartedly endorsing the Soviet line on the onset of the cold war and whose campaign, as she herself would admit many years later, was taken over and run by the Communist party. (A small but interesting measure of how Lionel Trilling felt about that campaign: when a rally for Wallace on the Columbia campus was scheduled for the same hour as one of his seminars, the rumor went forth that he would make sure to take attendance that day—something he almost never did—in order to show that, unlike a number of his colleagues on the faculty, he did not regard attendance at the rally as a good reason for cutting class.)

I did not know all these details of Lillian's past* when I first spotted her at the Trillings, but I knew enough to know that she was a perfect example of the type of person with whom it would only a few short years earlier have been unthinkable for them to associate. But as Diana explained in a postmortem phone call the next day, Lillian had made the overture, telling the Trillings that she would very much like to resume a youthful acquaintance, going back to the 1920s, that had been prevented by politics from developing into a real friendship.

---

*And there were many others as well. A more exhaustive list of events that Lillian either defended or was silent about would be compiled by Sidney Hook in reviewing her book *Scoundrel Time* for *Encounter* in 1976. Though it overlaps with the list of Kronstadts I compiled above, Hook's catalogue is worth quoting in full: "Moscow purge trials/Deportations and resulting famine in the Ukraine/The Nazi–Soviet Pact/The invasion of Poland and the destruction of the Baltic States/The invasion of Finland/The 1940 surrender to Hitler of German Jewish Communists who had fled Germany in 1933/The execution of two Jewish antifascist leaders as 'spies for Hitler'/The Katyn massacre of Polish officers/The mass execution of returning Russian prisoners of war/The overthrow of the Czech democratic government/The Zhdanov purges/The Berlin blockade/The crushing of the Hungarian revolution/The Berlin Wall/The incarceration of dissenters in insane asylums." Hook also charged Lillian with failing to speak out against Soviet anti-Semitism when "even the American Communist party, the most supine of the Kremlin's pensioners, had shown enough independence to make a feeble protest."

Nearly twenty years later, in *Scoundrel Time*, she would express amazement at the perversity of the Trillings' anti-Communist "political and social views," and she would accuse Lionel in particular of ignoring "facts" (!) in his championship of Whittaker Chambers as against Alger Hiss. She would also indict the entire circle of intellectuals to which the Trillings belonged—that is, the Family—for failing to defend her and her political friends when they were being hounded in the early 1950s, by Senator Joseph McCarthy in one branch of Congress and the House Un-American Activities Committee (HUAC)* in the other. But she said none of this to them now. What she said now was that she was not really a political person.

She said the same thing to me on more than one occasion after we had become close friends, and though I never took this claim at face value, I had reasons of my own for wanting to let political bygones be bygones.

The night I met Lillian, I was twenty-seven years old, and still a member of the board of the American Committee for Cultural Freedom along with the likes of Diana and Sidney. Though much too young to have participated in the political wars they had waged against the Stalinists and their fellow-travelers in the 1930s, I had in my own small and belated way followed a political trajectory similar to theirs. Thus, at the advanced age of thirteen, I had joined American Youth for Democracy (AYD), which was the new name the Young Communist League had adopted when the party began trying to broaden its appeal by concealing itself behind front organizations with blandly liberal titles. To be sure, it was not out of political conviction that I joined AYD. The main reason was that the editor of its magazine, to which one of my teachers in high school had suggested I submit a huge epic poem I had just written about the heroic Russian stand at

---

*I am adopting this way of referring to the committee because it was how Lillian herself, and practically everyone else on the Left, did. But if I may be forgiven a small pedantry, the proper name was the House Committee on Un-American Activities, or HCUA.

the battle of Stalingrad, had responded to my literary offering by sending for and then praising me to the skies.

So pervasive in the world around me was the "liberalism" of AYD that I never noticed anything special about it. Where I grew up, in the Brownsville section of Brooklyn and among struggling Jewish immigrants from eastern Europe whose struggles had been made even more desperate by the Great Depression of the 1930s, there were very few actual Communists. But everybody worshiped President Roosevelt and loved his great friend "Uncle Joe" Stalin, who were working together against the "reactionaries" to establish a new era of peace and friendship after the end of the war.

Things were not quite so monolithic in the high school I attended, where at least one of my teachers was actually a Republican, the first and only representative of that exotic species I had ever laid eyes on. But most of the others were like everyone else I knew, which was to say that they were liberals of the fellow-traveling variety (not that I was politically savvy enough to have put it that way). Nor was I sophisticated enough to recognize that a few members of the faculty were almost certainly Communists. One of them was the one who recommended that I submit my poem to the AYD magazine. Another was a particularly gifted teacher whose version of European history came, as I later realized with a combination of amusement and shock, straight out of Lenin's treatise on imperialism; this same teacher also used his classroom to defend the Soviet Union's position in the debates then being conducted on how to organize the newly established United Nations.

Upon graduation from high school in 1946, I won the scholarship that sent me to Columbia, where I not only met Allen Ginsberg for the first time but had many classmates who were World World II veterans attending on the GI Bill. Some of these were as much as ten years older than I was, and among them were a number of anti-Stalinist socialists and liberals who were then locked in a battle with the Stalinists for control of the newly founded American Veterans Committee. As I listened to the debates between the two groups, I became aware for the first time in my life that "liberal" and "reactionary" were not the only possible categories of political opinion. I was also surprised by how brilliant and knowledgeable some of these anti-Stalinists were, so ingrained in me was the idea that only know-nothings and bigots could be opposed to the self-evidently enlightened "liberal" or "progressive" position espoused by such fellow-traveling papers of that era as *PM* and the *New York Post*. And I was even more impressed when I learned that a few of the stars of the Columbia English department—including the three who would soon become my intellectual heroes, Lionel Trilling, F. W. Dupee, and Richard Chase—were all in the anti-Stalinist camp (though Mark Van Doren, the biggest star of them all until he was later eclipsed by Trilling, was a serious fellow-traveler, as I discovered when he turned up as chairman of the same Wallace rally that provoked Trilling into taking attendance that day in class).

Because I was still much more interested in literature than in politics, it took a while before any of this made a real impact on my thinking, such as it was, about the issues involved. Besides, I was too busy. Trying to keep pace with the very heavy readings assigned in my courses while struggling to catch up with my better-read classmates—some of whom seemed already to have digested the complete works of all the difficult modernist poets and novelists—I had neither the time nor the energy nor the interest to engage in a serious reconsideration of my comfortably settled political opinions.

So it was that I wound up at the beginning of my junior year at Columbia rooting for Henry Wallace against Harry Truman in the 1948 presidential campaign. Evidently, however, the anti-Stalinist perspective to which I had been exposed as a freshman had made its mark, since to my own surprise I was relieved and even pleased when Wallace did very badly (getting about a million votes instead of the ten million he had originally expected) and Truman won out over his heavily favored Republican opponent, Thomas E. Dewey.

Mutatis mutandis, the Wallace campaign turned out to be my own private little Kronstadt—though in this case the "God that failed" was not so much Communism as fellow-traveling liberalism. I now began reading *Partisan Review* and *Commentary,* which were the main centers of the intellectual war against the Soviet line and its purveyors both in and out of the Communist party, and I became a more and more enthusiastic partisan of the American side in the cold war.

Apart from the deepening of my literary education that came from the three years I spent at Cambridge University after graduating from Columbia, living in England in the early 1950s introduced me to the anti-Americanism that permeated the British political air and to one or another modality of which almost everyone I met or read seemed to subscribe. For some, mostly on the Tory Right but also including artists and intellectuals on the political Left, America was the source and fount of a barbaric culture that threatened to overwhelm and corrupt the precious civilization to which Europe was home and heir. (Never mind that America was in the opening stages of an especially rich period in the arts that would surpass anything being done in England or anywhere else in Europe.) For others, America was an imperial power whose pathological fear of Communism was in the process of turning it into a fascist country and whose paranoid obsession with the Soviet Union was dragging the world into a nuclear war.

Against this stood the conviction I had developed even before arriving in England that the United States was both morally and politically right in trying to resist any further expansion of Soviet power and Communist influence. Two books I read as I was settling into my new life in Cambridge greatly strengthened this conviction. One was Hannah Arendt's *The Origins of Totalitarianism* (entitled in its British edition *The Burden of Our Time*). From this great work I learned that the Soviet Union under Communism was fully comparable to Germany under the Nazi regime—in its internal organization, in the vast scale of its unspeakable crimes, and in its commitment to the eradication of liberty and democracy everywhere in the world.

The other of the two books was George F. Kennan's *American Diplomacy: 1900–1950*, which included and enlarged upon "The Sources of Soviet Conduct," an enormously influential article he had written for *Foreign Affairs* under the pseudonym "X." Kennan's view of the nature of the Soviet system and the intentions of its Communist rulers was fully compatible with Arendt's. But his focus, political rather than philosophical, was mainly on how the United States should respond, and the strategy of "containment" he outlined was the one that had been adopted and was now being implemented by Harry Truman's administration.

It was that strategy which had led Truman into the Korean War just as I was leaving home for Cambridge. As a graduate student I was exempt from the draft, much as would be the case with Bill Clinton at Oxford during the Vietnam War. Like him, I could have avoided military service altogether if I had stayed on in England for a while longer. Taking exactly the opposite course, however, toward the end of my third year in Cambridge I reached the decision to return home and make myself available to the draft.

Of course, unlike Clinton in relation to Vietnam, I supported the American intervention in Korea, but this was not the main motive behind my decision. Like most American kids who had been old enough at the time to be aware of World War II but too young to fight in it, I had a kind of yearning to see what the army would be like, to share in an experience so universal that one somehow felt incomplete without it; indeed, in those days men who had never been in uniform, let alone in combat, tended to be shamefaced about it, feeling that their masculinity had never really been put to a serious test. Accordingly, though I was of course relieved when the Korean War ended even before my induction into the army in 1953, I also enjoyed the luxury of a small disappointment when I wound up being shipped not to Korea but to Germany as part of the army of occupation.

While I was there, the Pentagon issued a directive ordering that all personnel be required to attend a series of lectures that would help them understand what the cold war was all about and would, hopefully, improve morale by making them proud to serve in such a conflict. The course was outlined in a group of pamphlets prepared by the Defense Department and was supposed to be conducted by an officer. But the poor second lieutenant to whom this job was handed in my outfit nearly had a nervous breakdown as he was delivering the first lecture and had to leave the podium before he even finished. After searching unsuccessfully for a replacement among his cadre of officers, our company commander found out that there was a lowly enlisted man on the base who had any number of college degrees. Desperate enough by now to go against the regulation calling for an officer, he offered to relieve me of my regular military duties if I would take the job. Which was how I came to spend nearly half of my two-year hitch in the army spelling out the differences between Communism and democracy in a series of lectures to audiences of soldiers numbering in the hundreds. In carrying out this assignment, I broke another regulation by discarding the intellectually primitive pamphlets the Pentagon had issued for guidance, relying instead on my own conception of how and why the cold war had broken out and why it was so important for us to fight it.

Not to be coy about it, these lectures made a great hit with the troops, very few of whom had ever been exposed to the material I covered or had glimpsed the power and importance of ideas in general. But the lectures also had an effect on me. After three years of contending with the scattershot arguments of the fellow-traveling Left, they helped me organize the information I had collected; and being forced to translate my ideas into terms that could be understood by people who knew little or nothing about the issues involved served to clarify those ideas for me as well.

I was discharged from the army on December 14, 1955, and the very next day, as previously arranged with Elliot Cohen, I went to work as an assistant editor at *Commentary*. In the sharpest possible contrast to what I had experienced at Cambridge, in the *Commentary* office I was surrounded by people who were, if anything, even more passionate cold warriors than I myself had become. But this intellectually comfortable situation was not destined to last. Only a few short months after my arrival at *Commentary* came the publication of Khrushchev's secret speech in which the new Soviet leader denounced Stalin for crimes both against his colleagues and against the Soviet people and announced that he intended to run the country in a more benign way.

This speech—confirming, and from the most authoritative source imaginable, the charges against Stalin that had been made all along by the anti-Communists and embarrassing and humiliating all the people who had for so many years been maintaining that such charges were malicious lies—finally seemed to be Lillian Hellman's Kronstadt. It was, however, a grudging Kronstadt at best: Carl Rollyson, one of her biographers, says that she at first "condemned Khrushchev for turning on the very leader [i.e., Stalin] who had been responsible for Khrushchev's successful career." (I am now also inclined to believe, for reasons I will eventually set forth, that it may not even have been a real Kronstadt at all.) Even so, the speech did for the first time permit her to admit, as she did to me in private and as she would later put it in *Scoundrel Time*, that she had "mistakenly denied" many of the plentiful "sins of Stalin Communism."

On me, the speech had a paradoxically converse effect. By suggesting that change in a more liberal direction was possible in the Soviet Union, Khrushchev had seriously undermined the theoretical foundation of the hard anti-Communist case in which I had come to put my intellectual and political trust. For according to that theory, only change in the opposite direction—toward tighter and tighter controls—was possible in a totalitarian society.

But if this was how I saw it, it was by no means how all my fellow hard anti-Communists did. My colleagues at *Commentary* and on the board of the American Committee for Cultural Freedom, for example, thought the whole thing was a trick, a tactical maneuver; and soon they could point to the tanks Khrushchev would send into Hungary, to suppress the revolt against Communist rule that erupted there in the wake of his own speech, as evidence that nothing essential had changed in the nature of the Soviet regime. In later years, I came to accept that they had been more right than wrong, and even at the time I still agreed with them in regarding Soviet Communism as the greatest threat on the face of the earth to political and cultural freedom. But I also now thought that we had entered a different world and that new possibilities were opening up for negotiating an end to the cold war. This meant that it was no longer necessary to keep fighting the old battles. In the past there had been many defenders of the Soviet Union to argue against, but against whom did the argument need to be conducted today? The American Communist party—discredited as a craven apologist for Stalinism by the supreme Soviet leader himself—was still there and still attempting to speak, but no one (or so it seemed) was listening anymore, not even fellow-travelers or Stalinists of old like Lillian Hellman. And just as the "thaw" in Soviet relations with the United States initiated by Khrushchev was opening up new possibilities for negotiation between our two countries, so on the level of personal relations there was now a chance to mingle with people with whom such encounters had been out of the question before.

All this explains my readiness to let political bygones be bygones when I met Lillian Hellman at the Trillings' party, and it is also why I felt a new expansiveness, a new sense of freedom, in chatting with her. Of course, she made it very easy for me from the minute we were introduced by responding with a look of recognition to the sound of my name and then—the surest way to any writer's heart—praising that piece I had recently published in *The New Yorker* about the novels of Nathanael West.* "Pep," as she called him, had been a good friend of hers (years later I would learn that he had also been one of her many lovers). In fact, while working as the night manager of a hotel owned by his father, Pep had given a free room to "Dash" (whom she did not identify any further, taking it for granted that I would not only get the reference to Dashiell Hammett but that I would know that the famously blocked author of *The Maltese Falcon* was for all practical purposes her husband). "Sid" (S. J. Perelman), Pep's brother-in-law, had also stayed there, and so had any number of other writers, including "Dottie" (Dorothy Parker) and "Bunny" (Edmund Wilson). In his lifetime, Lillian said, Pep had never achieved the recognition he deserved, and then after he got killed in that terrible automobile acci-

---

*Though West was a fellow-traveler of the Stalinists himself, and possibly even a party member, his work did not fare well with the critics who wrote for the Communist press in the 1930s. He was understandably bitter and puzzled about this, evidently not realizing how out of step with the party line was his view of life, especially as embodied in his best novel, *Miss Lonelyhearts.* But Stalinist though she herself was, Lillian would never have attacked a distinguished work of fiction on the ground that it ran afoul of the dogmas of economic determinism in its portrayal of character.

dent back in 1940 when he was only thirty-seven, it looked as though he might be entirely forgotten. *Now*—casting a significant glance at me as she pronounced the word—he stood a chance of being discovered by a whole new generation of readers.

It goes without saying that I was flattered. But more than that, I was dazzled by Lillian's easy references to legendary literary characters—so easy that they carried not the slightest trace of name-dropping—and the glimpse she afforded into a more glamorous world than any I had yet entered. When, as I hoped would happen, she called a day or two later inviting my wife and me to a party at her house, I could hardly wait for the designated evening to arrive.

Lillian would complain to me often and at length in the years ahead about how broke she was. First Hammett had been put on trial and convicted for contempt of court for refusing to answer questions about his membership on the board of a well-known Communist-front organization; then she herself had been hounded by HUAC, causing her to be blacklisted in Hollywood and costing her a fortune in legal expenses. From the books that have come out about her since her death in 1984, it is clear that she exaggerated both her financial difficulties and the extent to which they could be blamed on the blacklist or on HUAC. According to William Wright, another of her biographers, "films . . . had never been an essential source of her income, most of which came from the theater, where there was no effective blacklist." The main cause of the financial hardship of which she complained, says Wright, "was the poor showing her recent plays had made at the box office."

Yet even at the time, I found it hard to understand in what intelligible sense Lillian could be considered short of money. Certainly no writer I had ever met before—or, for that matter, would ever meet again—lived in as opulent a style as she did. Not even the few very rich people from whom, as a rising young critic and editor, I had just begun receiving dinner invitations had homes that could match the sumptuous elegance of the neo-Georgian house she owned on East Eighty-second Street and into which, about a week after our initial meeting at the Trillings, I set foot for the first of many times.

Everything about this house—its location, its proportions, its furnishings—reeked of money (and, as I would later discover, so, though more subtly, did her house overlooking the harbor on Martha's Vineyard). Lillian entertained often and her parties were lavish. Born and bred in New Orleans, where food was taken seriously, she always made sure that her guests were properly—and expensively—fed (and, again, as I was later to discover, on those special private occasions when she would prepare dinner herself, the meal would turn out to be as good as anything one had ever eaten anywhere). The company was usually as glittering as the surroundings. At that first party, and on subsequent evenings as well, there were famous theatrical personalities—producers, directors, actors, and actresses—with the women all richly begowned and bejewelled and the men radiating the special air of self-assurance that seems always to accompany the making of a lot of money. There were writers too (it was at Lillian's, for instance, that I first met Norman Mailer), but unlike the writers I knew, they were the kind who made a lot of money as well.

It was heady, it was exciting, and it was fun. But the most fun of all—playful, mischievous, bitchy, earthy, and always up for a laugh—was Lillian herself. Though she was fifty-two to my twenty-seven, so well did we hit it off that we became fast friends almost immediately, and over the next ten years or so we spent a great deal of time together. Hardly a party did she throw to which my wife and I were not invited; and unless she happened to be out of town, she also came to all of ours. Though Lillian barely managed to tolerate the wives of her men friends (whenever she referred to any of them, it was always dryly as "Madam"), she seemed to make an exception of mine. Sometimes when she was at loose ends she would call and invite us over then and there, or she would ask if she might drop by to our apartment for a drink and a chat, or we would go to a movie together.

Going to the movies with Lillian was an amazing experience, since this woman who was famous for the meticulous plotting of her plays could never understand what was happening on the screen. "Why did he say that?" or "Where did she come from?" she would whisper querulously, and between bouts of imperfectly suppressed laughter I would try to explain. On one memorable occasion, however, the positions were reversed. "Where did they find *him?*" I asked her *sotto voce* about a singularly untalented member of the cast in the film version of *West Side Story.* "In Jerry Robbins's bed, of course," she whispered back loudly enough to be heard from one end of the theater to another.

Being a great movie buff, I loved hearing about Lillian's own days in Hollywood. She was half amused by this and half disapproving, but with so appreciative an audience to hand, she could not resist telling stories about performers she had known, like the Marx Brothers, Fanny Brice (who used to do her hair), and Ann Sheridan (who, she assured me with a lascivious little grin, would be very flattered to learn of my interest in her). She was also full of stories about producers and directors like Sam Goldwyn, Sam Spiegel, and William Wyler (the last of whom she brought over to my apartment on the spur of the moment one Saturday night when I was sitting around after dinner chatting with an obscure young professor of political science from Syracuse, thereby giving the awestruck Daniel Patrick Moynihan—"Is *this* how you live in New York?"—a highly exaggerated sense of the routine glamor of my existence).

In addition to all this, Lillian and I, sometimes accompanied by my wife, sometimes not, took a number of trips together—to New England by car on a glorious fall weekend when some mutual friends with ancestral roots in Massachusetts decided that I needed to be introduced to the "real" America; to a conference in Puerto Rico, where she insisted on dragging me to a restaurant many miles away from our hotel because it had the best black bean soup in the world (and of course it did); and to another conference in Princeton, from which, her sense of direction being even worse than mine but her sense of humor being similar, it took us six hilarious hours instead of the normal two to drive back to New York.

Finally, there were the weekend visits in the summer to her house in Vineyard Haven on what I called, in tribute to the celebrity of her neighbors along the harbor, Murderer's Row. During these visits she would take us out in her boat to some remote cove for swimming and a picnic lunch, always beautifully packed, always delicious, and always accompanied by a thermos of the veritably ambrosial mint iced tea that she alone knew how to make. Then there would invariably be a star-studded dinner party at home on the first night and another on the next at, as it might be, the (Leonard) Bernsteins or the (William) Styrons or the (John) Marquands.

One winter Lillian offered me the use of that house when I needed a week alone to struggle with a recalcitrant book on which I was working. When I arrived, I found a memo entitled "Notes to a Jewish Traveler" waiting for me in the kitchen. The first item on this highly detailed list of instructions read: "To your left on the wall you will find a circular glass-covered object with numbers on it. This is known as a thermostat."

It was a measure of how close we had grown and how generous she could be when the spirit was upon her that Lillian would permit me, thus unsupervised, to invade her exquisitely appointed and most beloved sanctuary. ("God help you if you break anything up here," a mutual friend laughed in congratulating me on my courage as I was setting out. "I would never have the nerve to take such a chance.") But being that close to her was not always so easy or pleasant. Like a few other women I have known who were both famous and unattached, she could be extremely and unreasonably demanding. If she wanted to see me alone or if she asked me to chaperone her on some occasion or other, she did not lightly take no for an answer, and she managed somehow to let me know that she considered it tacky to plead the feelings or wishes of my wife (in spite of being relatively fond of her) or the needs of my children (whose existence she resolutely ignored) as an excuse for begging off.*

For some reason, however, I was spared another troublesome demand that I gather from her biographers Lillian made of all her other friends. This was never to associate with anyone who had "named names" or cooperated in any way with the congressional committees investigating Communist influence. Evidently, she broke with a number of people who refused to follow this injunction. Yet even though she chided me from time to time for having become friendly with the

---

*The only time I ever saw Lillian entirely lose her composure was when one of my daughters, then about nine years old, strode purposefully up to her as she sat on the couch in our living room and planted an unwelcome kiss on her nonplussed lips. As my daughter herself would have said if she had noticed, it "grossed" Lillian out.

director and screenwriter Robert Rossen (an ex-Communist who, after working abroad for some years, finally offered to testify because he saw no point in remaining on the blacklist when he had ceased believing in the cause that had put him there), she never did unto me what she did to a theatrical producer named Lester Osterman when he hired Rossen to direct a play in which she was not even involved. "When Lillian found out about it," Osterman recalled to William Wright, "she was beside herself. . . . How did I know that she considered him an archenemy because he was a friendly witness to HUAC? I knew nothing about it." Well, I did know about it, but Lillian neither screamed at me nor accused me of disloyalty nor insisted on pain of losing her friendship that I have nothing further to do with Rossen.

Apart from her sometimes troublesome demands, there was also the problem of her writing, which, try as I might, I simply could not bring myself to admire. I could see that her plays were very well crafted, but I could not see in what other respect they ever rose above the conventional theatrical fare produced and admired by the people she herself witheringly dismissed as "Broadway intellectuals." This was as true of plays like *The Children's Hour* and *The Little Foxes*, which had made her famous (and rich) in the 1930s, as it was of the two she wrote during the time of our friendship, *Toys in the Attic* and *My Mother, My Father, and Me*.

I was no more impressed by the memoirs she produced when, disgusted by the failure of *My Mother, My Father, and Me*, she finally decided to give up on the theater altogether. Much acclaimed for their honesty, to me these memoirs seemed self-servingly false. Her prose style (as I would say when I finally came clean about it years later in *Breaking Ranks*) was an imitation of Hammett's imitation of Hemingway; and the style was already so corrupted by attitudinizing and posturing in the original that only a miracle could have rendered it capable of anything genuine at this third remove. As for the stories she told in those books, they were often too good—too neat and self-congratulatory— to be true. No doubt Mary McCarthy went much too far when she later said (provoking Lillian to sue her for libel) that "every word [Hellman] writes is a lie, including 'and' and 'the.'" Yet the fact is that many details, some small and some large, would indeed (as I will relate in some detail below) subsequently be exposed as what could only be interpreted as deliberate lies.

It is a truth universally acknowledged in the literary world that the only way to remain on good terms with a writer whose work one does not admire is to pretend to admire it; and this is what I did with Lillian. It was—especially at that age—a very high price for me to pay, and I never could or would have paid it if I had been forced to review her work in the public prints. But so long as my praises were confined to private conversations between the two of us, I was able to pull off this unsavory trick without corrupting my own writing or betraying the standards that were everything to me as a literary critic. On the other hand, I was never able to pull it off without feeling ashamed and more than a little disgusted with myself.

There was, for example, the day I sat in her house on the Vineyard, having been summoned up there to read a draft of her first book of memoirs, the one that was later published under the title *An Unfinished Woman*. She was full of anxiety as she waited to hear my verdict, and my heart sank lower and lower as I read page after page of what sounded to me like one long outpouring of phony candor. Telling her the truth was out of the question, and so I lied and told her how good it was, making the lie more credible by throwing in a few honest editorial suggestions, for which she was as grateful as she was for my feigned enthusiasm.

I can even claim to have aided and abetted her in one of the most blatant and notorious of the falsehoods she wound up peddling about herself. At lunch one day in (inevitably) a very expensive and fashionable restaurant, she was in an unusually somber mood. When I asked her why she seemed so low, she replied that she had been struggling with herself over whether to write about a certain incident in her life that she felt a great inner pressure to deal with but that she had long ago promised never to make public. She then proceeded to spell the whole thing out, and by the time she had finished, I was left wondering what exactly the big secret was and why she should feel bound to keep it. "So you think it would be okay if I wrote about it?" she asked, and I said, "Absolutely. It's a great story and I can't see any reason not to use it."

Although I was giving her the answer I knew she wanted to hear, I was not in this instance being entirely insincere. It *was* a good (if not a great) story, and from what I had just heard, there was indeed no valid reason to continue hushing it up. But when, some weeks (or was it months?) later, she presented me with the manuscript to read, I had to revert once again to the by now old habit I had formed of faking my reaction to her work. The story as she had told it orally seemed genuine enough, but on paper it came out sounding as false as everything else she had written in the same Hemingway-via-Hammett prose style. Not, however, to the ears of her increasingly adoring public, which singled it out for special praise when it appeared under the title "Julia" in *Pentimento,* her second volume of memoirs.

But as was revealed long after we had ceased being friends, the prose style turned out to be the least of what was false about "Julia." Some years after its publication, and following the release of the movie that the Hollywood branch of the "Broadway intellectuals" made of it (with the politically, if not physically, appropriate Jane Fonda as Lillian), Lillian was charged with appropriating the story from another woman and then casting herself in a heroic role she had never actually played. Here then was the real reason for the hesitation to write about the incident that had seemed so puzzling when she first told me about it.

Yet another irritant in the relations between us was Lillian's attitude toward Jews in general and toward Israel in particular. She never denied being Jewish herself, and when she teased me, as she often did, about my own Jewishness (as in the instructions she left for me when I moved into her house in Vineyard Haven), it was usually in a good-natured spirit of fun. But she also had a streak of Jewish anti-Semitism which came out (especially while trading gossip with her great pal Dorothy Parker, who was only half-Jewish but twice as anti-Semitic) in cracks or sardonic comments about the vulgarity or the tastelessness of some "kike" or other. Though this kind of thing sometimes bothered me, it was so common among highly assimilated Jews of her generation— especially those who, like her, were of German origin and had always looked down upon Jews whose families stemmed from eastern Europe—that I never took it to heart or felt the need to protest.

Nor was I especially bothered by the role Lillian had played in the de-Judaization of the stage version of *The Diary of Anne Frank* written by Albert and Frances Hackett (whom she had recommended for the job after turning it down herself). According to the novelist Meyer Levin, his own adaptation had been rejected by the producer on Lillian's advice as "too Jewish." Levin connected this judgment with her ferocious opposition to any and all expressions of Jewish particularism, which he in turn connected with her Stalinist mentality. Later I became one of the numerous writers and critics he tried to enlist in his campaign to get his own version produced, and my normal inclination would have been to side with him on this issue. But I could not help feeling that he, a commercial writer himself, was trying to elevate a commercial decision (and one that was vindicated by the huge success of the Hacketts' play) into a question of high principle. The fact that he also seemed more than a little paranoid put me off as well.

In retrospect, I think Levin had a good case, and I must admit that even back then my own experience with Lillian lent plausibility to his charge against her. After all, it was this very issue of Jewish particularism that triggered the only two seriously unpleasant arguments I ever got into with her. One of them occurred at a big party to which Lillian and I had both been invited and where, to the acute embarrassment of everyone else in the room, I experienced one of my very rare losses of temper when (I forget in what context) she remarked irritably that Jews were not the only people persecuted by the Nazis; "radicals" (her favorite euphemism for Communists) had perished in the camps too. Another time we had a nasty exchange over Israel, toward which her extreme hostility (or perhaps *hatred* would be a better word) was fed by two sources of anti-Zionism, one flowing from her German Jewish background and the other from her "radicalism." Knowing that, for reasons she simply could not fathom, I was a passionate supporter of Israel, she usually tried to keep her own feelings under wraps if I happened to be around, and on this one occasion when her animus got the better of her self-control, my reaction was so violent that she never slipped again.

Troubled though I was by Lillian's attitude toward things Jewish, resentful though I sometimes was at the unreasonableness of her demands upon me, and uncomfortable though I always felt in the false position into which her writing put me, in the end it was none of these problems that led to my estrangement from her. Nor, so far as I knew then or know now, did our break have anything to do with the personal or literary problems she, on her side, had with me. She occasionally got petulant with me because I was not as attentive to her as she thought I should have been, and she may well have resented the fact that, unlike some of the other young men in her entourage, I never once made a pass at her, not even when she was at her most flirtatious. Moreover, my writing probably forced her into as much insincerity as hers did me. She always expressed admiration for my essays, and she stood loyally by me when *Making It* was being attacked from all sides (her only reservation being that I had written such a book too early in my career), but I doubt that she would have done so if I had been a stranger to her. On the other hand, I also doubt that these things were all that irksome to her.

Long after we had become estranged, I would often be asked how a hard anti-Communist like me and an unreconstructed Stalinist like Lillian could ever have become friends, and my answer would usually consist of some version of the story I have been telling here. But privately, between me and myself, I would have to admit that our friendship owed something to factors other than personal affection and affinity. For me, there was the attraction of the glamor and the glitter to which she offered easy access and in which, being full of ambition and youthful curiosity, I had a great yearning to swim. For her, with a literary career that was no longer going well—a decline she blamed entirely on the anti-Communist climate of the 1950s—there was an advantage in reputation to be gained through associating with a young literary intellectual like me who was in addition politically respectable by the standards of that period. (I was far from the only such young man she cultivated in those days.)

But these considerations played a significant part only in the beginning. As time went on, they gave way to the genuine fondness that developed between us and the delight we took in each other's company.

These feelings easily outweighed the problems which also developed between us, and chances are that this is how it would have continued to go if not for the outbreak in the late 1960s of the old political wars of the 1930s. It was these wars that eventually put an end to our friendship, exactly as they had done to so many other friendships (including Lillian's with the Trillings) the first time around.

Of course, in its second round the war took a new form and was fought on a different front. In the 1930s, the main issue between the Stalinists and their opponents on the Left had been the nature of the Soviet Union; this time the main issue was the nature of America. For in the 1960s the political and spiritual descendants of the Stalinists of the 1930s had little if any attachment to the Soviet Union. To the extent that they looked to the Communist world for inspiration, it was to China under Mao, or Cuba under Castro, or North Vietnam under Ho Chi Minh, and not to the Soviet Union under Khrushchev or Brezhnev. But what really drove them was not so much a love of Communism (a word they never used, preferring instead the blander term *socialism*) as a blind and blinding hatred of America such as I had not encountered since my days as a student at Cambridge. To them, no less than to Allen Ginsberg and his entourage, "Amerika" was evil in itself and a force for evil everywhere else in the world and only a revolution could save it.

In the early 1960s, as the newly appointed chief editor of *Commentary*, I had taken the magazine with me on the leftward course on which I had begun moving shortly after I first met Lillian (a change that, by the way, removed what would certainly have been another irritant in our relationship, even though we both generally shied away from talking about politics). In doing this, I also did more than my share to develop and spread the ideas that formed the intellectual basis of the New Left. But as I have stressed in various connections above, I could not abide the Movement's more and more vicious—and more and more mendacious—attacks on America. Still less could I stand the spillover of these attacks into the mainstream liberal culture, which once again served as a fertile breeding ground of fellow-traveling apologists for the more extreme positions to their Left. By the late 1960s, the complete consummation of this sorry process acted on me as yet another Kronstadt. Consciously following the example of the ex-Communists of the 1930s who felt obligated to tell the truth about the cause they had deluded themselves into serving, I now went public and launched my soon-to-become-notorious counterattack against the lies about America being spread by my former allies on the Left.

They did not, to put it in the softest possible terms, take kindly to this, and in due course most of them responded much as their political ancestors had done to the defectors from their ranks in the 1930s. Which is to say that they tried very hard to damage my professional reputation and blacken my name. In some cases, there were nasty quarrels either face-to-face or by letter; in others, where quarrels were avoided because of lingering personal affections or sheer distaste for confrontation, there was so much mutual discomfort that drifting apart became inevitable. Thanks to this discomfort, I now hardly ever received invitations to the big parties that were so common in those days, which was just as well since going to them would have meant avoiding or being avoided by most of the other guests in the room.

With Lillian the process of estrangement took a special form of its own. Like a number of other old-time Stalinists with whom I had become acquainted during my sojourn on the Left, she had never been wildly enthusiastic about the radical Movement of the 1960s. Naturally, she thought that it was a gigantic improvement over the McCarthyite "conformism" of the 1950s and was doing more good than harm, but, for all that, it was not her cup of tea. Though I cannot recall discussing the matter with her in any depth, I had the strong impression from hints and passing remarks that the New Left—as the political arm of the Movement had come to be designated precisely in order to distinguish it from the Communist-dominated radicalism on which she had cut her teeth—struck her as altogether too raucous and undisciplined. Even less to her taste was the scruffy drug-infested counterculture.

Feeling this way, Lillian was not all that exercised over the attacks on the New Left and the counterculture that began appearing in *Commentary* in the late 1960s. In fact, she even agreed with some of the minor criticisms that I and others were making. What bothered her—

and bothered her profoundly—was our use of the term *anti-American* to characterize the point of view not only of extremist groups like the Weathermen and the Black Panthers but even of a "liberal" publication like *The New York Review of Books*. This, at any rate, is what she told me over dinner one night in the grand Park Avenue apartment to which she had moved in 1970 from the house on East Eighty-second Street—a dinner featuring a goose which (nothing symbolic intended, I feel sure) she had taken great pains to cook herself, just for the two of us. Unfortunately, we were both so tense that neither of us could fully appreciate the fantastic job she had done in preparing this meal.

Having anticipated the worst when she had called to say that she needed to talk to me, I was much relieved to discover that her only complaint concerned the charge of anti-Americanism. I was also surprised to discover that she saw no difference between this term and the term *un-American*, which, she reminded me with a quavering voice, had done so much damage to so many people, herself included, in the past. To this I replied that to me the distinction was obvious: the charge of "un-American" had been used to rule out certain beliefs and activities as alien and therefore illegitimate whereas the position I called anti-American was one that denounced the entire American system itself as illegitimate and openly and frankly opposed everything the United States was doing everywhere in the world.

I got nowhere with her and she got nowhere with me, and though we both remained polite throughout the evening and parted with the usual hugs and kisses, I knew as I walked through the door that it was just about all over between us and that I might well never hear from her again.

About this I was both right and wrong. It *was* all over between us, but I did see her again a few years later coming toward me on the street. Before I could decide what to do, she settled the issue by saying, "Hello, Normie" (no one except the people I had grown up with in Brooklyn ever called me that, but Lillian always had), and then, with a slight shrug and a wistful half-smile, speeding up her pace when I started slowing down. After another ten years or so, shortly before she died, I saw her yet again, and for the very last time, being carried in the arms of a young man into her building on Park Avenue from a car. The pity of it hit me hard, and I had a powerful impulse to run over and plant a kiss on her forehead. By this point, however, we had become not just estranged friends who retained a lingering fondness for each other but passionate and bitter enemies, and I had long since forfeited the right to make any such tender or affectionate gesture. Besides, I was pretty sure that if I were foolish enough to try, she would have summoned enough strength, even in the moribund condition she was clearly in, to tell me to go fuck myself.

It was with the publication in 1976 of *Scoundrel Time*, the third of Lillian's four volumes of memoirs, that things had come to this pass between us. Even if we had still been friends when this little book appeared, it would certainly have precipitated a decisive break, since I could never have pretended to like it as I had done with its two predecessors. The falsity I found in those books was aesthetic, and it never popped into my head when I first read them that they were in many respects false in substance as well. But *Scoundrel Time*, while suffering from the same aesthetic flaw, dealt with issues of which I had first-hand knowledge. Hence, there was no need to wait upon scholarly researchers to expose the outrageous distortions and the far more serious lies contained in her account of her appearance in 1952 before the House Un-American Activities Committee.

Naturally, Lillian emerged from this account as a hero and a martyr: a hero for refusing to cooperate with the committee and a martyr for being blacklisted as a result. Moreover, to her the "scoundrels" of the title were not HUAC and the other McCarthyite committees themselves but the ex-Communists who, for no reason she could perceive other than to save their own skins, betrayed their former comrades by "naming names."

Needless to say, she never permitted it to enter her mind that some of these ex-Communists might have felt contrite over having aligned themselves with a murderous totalitarian regime and now wished to make up for it by broadcasting the truths they had since so painfully learned. The most prominent example was the director Elia Kazan, whose decision to become a "friendly witness" Lillian never hesitated to ascribe to the usual base motives. (Nor did the rest of the predominantly "liberal" Hollywood community ever credit him, or anyone else, with having acted out of principle, or hesitate to set up a—shall we call it?—blacklist of its own when it came to the giving of awards. Nearly a half-century after his testimony, an effort to present Kazan with what even his political enemies acknowledged was a well-deserved prize for lifetime achievement was voted down repeatedly by the Academy of Motion Picture Arts and Sciences. And so liberal were these great defenders of free speech that another "friendly witness"—not a "turncoat" like Kazan but someone who had been an anti-Communist all along—the actor Robert Taylor, was posthumously punished in the 1990s by the removal of his name from a building in Hollywood that had been dedicated to his memory.)

So far as I was concerned, however, the real scoundrels of Lillian's story were not the ex-Communists who had repented of their support for Stalin and his monstrous crimes but the Communists and the fellow-travelers who had persisted in defending Stalin and apologizing for those crimes. It was true that some of these people had suffered for this by going to jail or losing their jobs, but that did not justify their ideas or make their political activities any less reprehensible. It was also true that combatting those ideas and activities through demagogic congressional investigations, and by putting people in prison or throwing them out of work, was disgraceful and disgusting. And it was, finally, true (as I myself, in *Making It,* had long ago acknowledged, confessing, perhaps a little too exuberantly, to a "brutal insensitivity" on this issue) that the hard anti-Communists around *Partisan Review* and *Commentary* in the early 1950s had been more concerned with fighting against the ideas of the Communists and their liberal fellow-travelers than with defending them against their congressional inquisitors.

Even so, this did not mean, as Lillian made a special point of saying in *Scoundrel Time,* that "*Commentary* didn't do anything," that "no editor or contributor ever protested against McCarthy," and that "*Partisan Review,* although through the years it had published many, many pieces protesting the punishment of dissidents in Eastern Europe, made no protest when people in this country were jailed or ruined." For one thing, as William Phillips remarked in *Partisan Review,* "some *were* Communists and what one was being asked to do was to defend their right to lie about it." And for another, as I myself had also been careful to point out, "some of the most penetrating analyses of McCarthy and his methods to have been written at the time appeared in *Commentary*."

In any event, whatever *Commentary* and *Partisan Review* may or may not have done, it was nothing short of blasphemous to compare the fate of "dissidents in Eastern Europe" whose "punishment" consisted of execution, torture, or long years of imprisonment under conditions of hardship scarcely imaginable to Lillian Hellman with, say, the six months Dashiell Hammett spent in jail cleaning bathrooms, let alone with the luxury in which she herself lived even when she could no longer command huge fees for writing Hollywood films. If this was martyrdom, it was so mild a form that laying claim to it—as she subtly did in her ostentatiously understated manner—was ridiculous at best.

All this, and more, I would say three years later in *Breaking Ranks*, but at the time I was too agitated to set it down clearly and coherently on paper. Instead, I turned—as so often I had before and would again—to Nathan Glazer. Nat knew much more than I did about the congressional investigations of Communism in the 1950s, and so I asked him to review *Scoundrel Time* in *Commentary*, where he himself had some twenty-five years earlier published one of the best of those penetrating analyses of McCarthyism which I had mentioned in *Making It*. He was thus in a perfect position not only to make all the necessary points in answer to Lillian's version of the events in question but also to give the lie to her charge that the anti-Communist intellectuals around *Commentary* and *Partisan Review* had never "protested against McCarthy." This he did brilliantly, and he also provided a lucid account of Lillian's behavior before the Committee. I want to quote at some length from this account because the truth about it has been totally obscured by the false legend Lillian herself created in *Scoundrel Time*. But certain legal technicalities have to be rehearsed first.

Anyone called to testify before a congressional committee investigating anything (whether it be organized crime or the tobacco industry or Communist influence) cannot with legal impunity refuse to answer questions by invoking the protection of free speech under the

First Amendment. The group of screenwriters known as the Hollywood Ten, widely thought to be acting on orders from the Communist party, had adopted this strategy in 1947 and were cited for contempt of Congress, tried and convicted in federal court, and then sent to jail. The failure of this strategy led to a change in party policy, and thereafter party members who were summoned to testify before a congressional committee were instructed to remain silent by invoking the Fifth Amendment's protection against self-incrimination. They could in this way escape prosecution, and though they were hardly in a position to present themselves as martyrs to free speech (as the Hollywood Ten were entitled to do in standing on the First Amendment), they did so anyway—and quite successfully in the eyes of their sympathizers. Still, this was not a cost-free course, since, in Glazer's words, it "opened one to sanctions by private groups and individuals who could deprive one of a livelihood." As for Lillian, Glazer wrote:

> She offered in a letter* to tell the Committee anything it wanted to know about her, so long as it desisted from questioning her about others. If the Committee insisted on questioning her about others, she would take the Fifth Amendment. The Committee did, and she did.

This was exactly the path that was followed by numerous witnesses who had preceded her (many of whom, incidentally, had also requested the same deal and been turned down). Nevertheless, Glazer went on:

> She suggests that . . . she broke new ground in the strategies of witnesses before the Committee. Thus, she reports that a man in the audience during her appearance said loudly: "Thank God somebody had the guts to do it." One is puzzled. Do what? She has just explained that she had taken the Fifth Amendment in refusing to answer a question . . . as to whether she had been present at a certain meeting . . . , and as to whether she was a member of the Communist party (she

---

*This was the famous one in which she declared, "I cannot cut my conscience to fit this year's fashion."

tells us she was not). So one is left wondering what new ground was broken, and just what she had the "guts" to do.

Lillian responded to Glazer's article by telling Martin Peretz, the publisher of *The New Republic*, that I was part of an organized "anti-Communist conspiracy" against her book led by Daniel Patrick Moynihan (who had come a long way since she and the Wylers had first encountered him in my apartment). "From her experience in the Communist orbit," said Peretz, "she had a view . . . that everybody was under some kind of explicit or at best implicit or tacit discipline." Of course, the idea of a conspiracy, let alone one under discipline from on high, was as nonsensical as the charges about the past she had made in *Scoundrel Time* itself. Like them, however, it also contained a minuscule element of truth.

Roughly five years before the publication of *Scoundrel Time*, when Lillian and I had parted for good, my main concern had been to demonstrate that the much-abused American "system" was a precious thing which needed and deserved to be defended against the assaults of the anti-American Left. But more recently, I had also become alarmed by the mounting evidence that the Soviet Union was returning to a strategy of imperialist expansionism and that it was becoming militarily powerful enough to pose an even more serious threat to the democratic world than it had done in the first phase of the cold war. In the face of this evidence, my old anti-Communist passions came flooding back. Both as an editor and as a writer (through such articles as "Making the World Safe for Communism," which appeared in *Commentary* only two months before Glazer's review of *Scoundrel Time*), I now set out to help all I could in rebuilding the moral and political case for a renewal of American resistance to the spread of Soviet power and influence.

It was in this campaign that Lillian saw a conspiracy, and it was in the participation of Moynihan, who had been appointed as ambassador to the United Nations on the basis of an article he had written for *Commentary* and had then been elected to the U.S. Senate, that she detected the secret hand of government. There was no conspiracy and there were no orders from on high, but because *Scoundrel Time* was published when it was, the response to it among anti-Communists like me was inevitably colored not only by all the old debates of the past but also by the new debate going on in the present over Soviet Communism and the role America should play in relation to it.

―――――――

In 1984 a book came out by the psychoanalyst Muriel Gardiner in which she, the only person who could possibly have been the Julia of *Pentimento*, denied ever having been on the receiving end of the heroic mission to Nazi Germany that Lillian claimed to have taken on her behalf. Shortly thereafter I commissioned yet another article about Lillian, this one from Samuel McCracken of Boston University. McCracken drew partly on Gardiner's book and partly on an article Martha Gellhorn (an ex-wife of Ernest Hemingway who had been with him in Spain during the civil war there) had written in 1981. There Gellhorn had demonstrated that many of the details in *An Unfinished Woman* (including a few about experiences Lillian said she had had in Madrid and in the company of Hemingway) were what she sardonically called "apocryphisms." But mainly McCracken relied on his own extensive and meticulous researches (which included getting hold of and combing through such obscure and arcane documents as German railway timetables of the 1930s). The result, entitled "Julia and Other Fictions by Lillian Hellman," was an utterly devastating indictment that made mincemeat of the reputation Lillian had acquired as (in McCracken's words) "an ethical exemplar, and . . . a ruthlessly honest writer."

It was because the McCracken piece had just appeared when I happened upon the pitiable sight of an utterly helpless Lillian being carried into her building on Park Avenue that I stifled the impulse to approach and plant a kiss on her forehead. Yet if the the impulse itself signified that there was a spark of affection for Lillian left somewhere deep inside me, it was only a spark, with no combustible material around it to set on fire; and I would bet that not even that much was left in her for me.

For with the passions of the cold war raging once again, we had come full circle, back to where we had been before the "thaw" had made it possible for the political likes of her and the political likes of me to become friends. To her, I was a latter-day version of the "scoundrels" of *Scoundrel Time;* to me, she was a latter-day version of the Stalinist she had been in the past, if indeed she had ever really ceased being a Stalinist at any point along the way.

Earlier in this chapter, I said that when I first met Lillian in 1957, my guess was that, in spite of her many denials, she had been a member of the Communist party. Her reiteration of those denials in *Scoundrel Time* were not convincing, and we now know for certain that my original guess was right. In a confidential letter to Joseph L. Rauh, one of her lawyers, which came to light after her death, she admitted that she had joined the party in 1938 and had remained a member for about two years, until 1940. The letter contained no real explanation of why she had left, and in view of her continued loyalty to the cause, it is entirely possible that she quit, if she truly did, only because the party thought she could be more useful if she were not officially a member. If so, she would not have been the only Communist about whom this decision was made.

Nor would I be in the least surprised if other documents were to be unearthed showing that Lillian never actually quit at all but remained a secret member of the party not only after 1940 but even after acknowledging the "sins of Stalin Communism," as she quaintly described them in *Scoundrel Time,* and even beyond that. Her biographer William Wright agrees. "So great were the advantages of secrecy to both Hellman and the party," he writes, that "she may well have been encouraged in her few well-aired deviations from party policy—primarily her writing *Watch on the Rhine* when she did." Wright also proceeds to give a number of reasons for suspecting "not just a one-time but a lifelong membership" in the party. And he makes the interesting point that "her political postures—and that would include her silences almost more than her stated positions—take on a much needed logic" under the supposition that she was secretly "a lifelong Communist" who "enjoyed a customized membership that loosened the discipline."

But secret Communist or not, and notwithstanding her early reservations about the New Left, she cooperated in the last two decades of her life with these political and spiritual descendants of her old Stalinist comrades to stigmatize the United States as an evil force both at home and abroad and to head off its resurgent determination to resist the spread of Soviet power and Communist influence.

Her support for the Communist cause continued to find tangible expression even after she died. In her will she provided for the establishment of the Dashiell Hammett Fund to award grants to persons advocating "political, social and economic equality, civil rights and civil liberties . . . preferably here in the United States." So far so impeccably liberal, but she quickly went on to stipulate "that the fiduciaries in making such selections shall be guided by the political, social, and economic beliefs which, of course, were radical, of the late Dashiell Hammett who was a believer in the doctrines of Karl Marx." Not even from beyond the grave, then, could she summon the honesty to use the word *Communism* in describing the political faith to which Hammett was unquestionably committed to the end of his days and to which she also unquestionably subscribed from the early 1930s until the late 1940s and, I would now guess, to the end of her own days as well.

Lillian, I always suspected, was committed to Communism more out of loyalty to Hammett than out of loyalty to the Soviet Union. In many ways Hammett treated her very badly, even to the point of sometimes slapping her around and beating her up, and she was (in retaliation?) unfaithful to him many times over. But she never forgot the debt she owed him for encouraging her as a writer and acting as her literary mentor and editor. And even though they were never formally married, he was more her true husband than the one man to whom she was married for a few years (the humorist Arthur Kober). Furthermore, though no woman I have ever met was less romantic in the usual sense than Lillian, I think Hammett was and never ceased being her one true love (notwithstanding the fact that she would probably have been insulted by the application of so soupy a phrase to her).

In the 1930s, being a Communist did Lillian no harm. If anything, it worked to her advantage in the big-money Broadway–Hollywood world in which she was making her career as a writer and where her political views were almost universally shared. Later, with the onset of the cold war and the turning of the tide, her Stalinist political views did wind up costing her something—not nearly so much as she liked to claim, but enough to frighten her into pretending that she had given them up.

Then, when the tide turned leftward once again, she seized on the chance to represent herself as a hero and a martyr, and the big-money show business world (whose influence was now greater even than it had been the first time around) fell into paroxysms of veneration. I remember shaking my head in wonder when she made an appearance on the stage at an Academy Awards celebration in the mid-1970s and received a protracted standing ovation before a television audience of fifty million Americans, myself included.

The applause was swelled by a new crop of literary intellectuals who, like me, had been seduced by the pleasures of her company and the glamor and the glitz surrounding her but who, unlike me, never saw anything wrong with her political views, either in the past or the present. To them all her sins, even assuming that she had ever committed any worth mentioning, had been wiped clean for all time by her sufferings at the hands of the McCarthyite inquisitors.

As any reader of the obituary pages could testify, Lillian was not the only old Stalinist to whom this same absolution was extended. Almost anyone who had been targeted by the congressional investigations, even if he had apologized for or lied about Stalin's murderous crimes and still remained unrepentant, came to be regarded as a persecuted advocate of "political, social and economic equality, civil rights and civil liberties." Very few of these people were ever held morally to account, and Lillian perhaps least of them all.

Not that she lacked for critics, of whom at least some could not cavalierly be ignored as coming from the Right. In fact, it was precisely from the Left and as a socialist that Irving Howe rebutted her plaintive assertion that whatever "mistakes" she and her fellow "radicals" might have made, "I do not believe we did our country harm." Howe addressed her directly:

Dear Lillian Hellman, you could not be more mistaken! Those who supported Stalinism and its political enterprises, either here or abroad, helped befoul the cultural atmosphere, helped bring totalitarian methods into trade unions, helped perpetuate one of the great lies of our century, helped destroy whatever possibilites there might have been for a resurgence of serious radicalism in America. Isn't that harm enough?

Yet, as Wright sums it all up, the critics simply could not prevail "among her many distinguished friends [who] even after her death . . . were fiercely loyal." As for "Hellman enthusiasts in the public at large, the documented demonstrations of her dishonesty seemed to have no effect whatsoever."

There can be no question that this was indeed the case. In a literary-academic world even more permeated than it had been in the 1930s by leftist attitudes, a world whose reach was now extended even further by the feminist movement (for which, ironically, Lillian herself never had much use), her political record continued to be taken as a badge of courage; in a culture in which the old distinction between highbrow and middlebrow hardly retained even a vestigial existence and which was less and less capable of distinguishing between attitudinizing and genuine feeling, her counterfeit writings were accepted as real and valued far beyond their true literary worth; and in an age when the very concept of truth was being deconstructed by jesting critical Pilates and philosophical relativists alike, the self-aggrandizing lies she told about herself and her life were either dismissed as unimportant or justified on grounds of artistic license.

I for one will have none of this. Even though I can still be surprised by sudden rushes of warmth when I think of Lillian, and even though I am still capable of nostalgia for the good times I had with her when I was young and we were friends, nothing in that friendship repaid me so well as the cause for which I felt myself forced to give it up in spite of the fact that doing so could only be interpreted by her as an act of *personal* betrayal. The plain truth is that I remain proud of the part I went on to take in the fight against the political ideas and attitudes in whose service she corrupted her work and brought, as I now see it, lasting dishonor upon her name.

CHAPTER FOUR

HANNAH ARENDT'S JEWISH
PROBLEM—AND MINE

I ONCE QUIT A JOB BECAUSE OF HANNAH ARENDT, AND thereby hangs a tale. Because of Hannah, too, I changed my mind about the nature of intellectual activity, and thereby hangs another tale. Because of her, finally, I learned something about myself as a Jew, and thereby hangs the most important tale of all.

The job I quit was as an associate editor of *Commentary*, and the reason I did so was that a highly controversial article which Hannah had been commissioned to write proved, after a lengthy and complicated process of negotiation, impossible to get into the magazine in a manner that was acceptable to her. Technically, it was Hannah who withdrew the article, but in reality she had, for all practical purposes, been maneuvered by my colleagues into doing so. For my part, this episode, following upon a number of others that had already been making me more and more unhappy with the way things were going at the magazine, clinched my decision to resign.

The article in question grew out of a conversation one of my colleagues and I had with Hannah in the fall of 1957, just when violent local resistance was being mounted against an effort to integrate the schools of Little Rock, Arkansas, in accordance with the Supreme Court decision of 1954 in *Brown v. Board of Education.* I no longer recall where that conversation took place; probably it was over an editorial lunch. Nor do I recall precisely where and when Hannah and I first met. Chances are that it was at one of those big after-dinner parties that everyone in the Family of New York intellectuals was always throwing in those days. At twenty-seven, I was the newest and youngest member of the Family. Hannah, at fifty-one, was among the oldest and in some respects the least typical.

Like many of the others, she was Jewish,* but they had all either been born in America or come here at a very young age, whereas she, a refugee from Nazi Germany, had not arrived until 1941 at the age of thirty-five, and had never lost her heavy German accent. Of course, many German Jewish intellectuals had fled to the United States after Hitler came to power, and, by the 1950s they had become a highly visible presence in the universities. Of them all, however, Hannah (though she did wind up teaching at a number of colleges and universities) was the only one who, at least at first, found a more congenial home in the Family than in the academic world, and the only one the Family ever fully adopted as its own.

Nor was this the only way in which she differed from most of the other members of the Family. Although passionately concerned about politics, they were—with one or two exceptions, most prominently, her nemesis Sidney Hook—basically literary people who in the end cared more about the arts than about anything else, while her main interest was in philosophy and especially political theory. Until I read Elisabeth Young-Bruehl's biography of her (*Hannah Arendt: For Love of the World*), I never knew—though it did not surprise me to learn—that she had writ-

---

*I want to stress the word *many,* because there is a general impression that *all* members of the Family were Jewish. Not so. The following are only the most obvious exceptions: Dwight Macdonald, F. W. Dupee, Mary McCarthy, William Barrett, Richard Chase, and Elizabeth Hardwick; and to them can be added close relatives (or "kissing cousins," as I once liked to call them) like Robert Lowell, John Berryman, Robert Gorham Davis, Ralph Ellison, and James Baldwin.

ten a good deal of verse in German and that her grounding in German literature was very deep. While still in Germany she had co-authored an article about the poetry of Rainer Maria Rilke, and once settled in America she wrote pieces about the novels of Franz Kafka and Hermann Broch. She also worked hard to acquaint herself with poetry and fiction in English, helped along by the close relations she came to form with poets like Randall Jarrell and W. H. Auden and with the critic and novelist Mary McCarthy, who eventually became her most intimate American friend. Nevertheless, for the most part Hannah shied away from literature as a subject, concentrating her energies as a writer mainly on philosophy and politics.

Most of this writing was published not in academic philosophical journals but in *Partisan Review* and *Commentary,* and her social life too soon came to be centered in that milieu. As Young-Bruehl describes it:

> Arendt started going to parties and discussions with members of a loosely defined group—the New York literary and largely Jewish Left. She was excited, and a bit overwhelmed by her new milieu. . . . Political accord came quickly with her new friends and she praised them extravagantly to her European friends for their lack of fanaticism, their refusal to worship the God of Success and their commitment to a literary language accessible to readers of many persuasions and backgrounds.

My own guess is that "political accord" was the least of the factors that drew Hannah into the Family, since yet another respect in which she differed was that, unlike just about all the others, she was not then nor ever had been a Marxist or indeed any kind of serious leftist. Responding to a characterization of her as rooted in the German Left, she once wrote: "I am not one of the 'intellectuals who came from the German Left.' . . . If I can be said to 'have come from anywhere,' it is from the tradition of German philosophy."

To be sure, this was an exaggeration. For one thing, she had been raised by a mother who was a passionate socialist. Hannah herself once told me the story of how, as a little girl, she had stopped on her way home from school to watch a military parade and was then slapped in the face by her mother for having enjoyed so politically incorrect a spectacle. By contrast, as Young-Bruehl records, Hannah remembered how, at the age of thirteen, she was

> taken along by her mother, who was an ardent admirer of [the revolutionary Communist leader] Rosa Luxemburg, to the first excited discussions . . . of the news . . . that there had been an uprising. As they ran through the streets, Martha Arendt shouted to her daughter, "You must pay attention, this is a historical moment!"

From Young-Bruehl I also learn that as a young woman Hannah was closely associated with the German Left not only through a number of friends but also through both of the men she married. Her first husband, the writer and journalist Gunther Anders (né Stern), was a radical who had close ties with the circle of Communists around the playwright Bertolt Brecht, and her second, Heinrich Blücher (whom I came to know when they moved to New York), was still a Communist when she first met him in 1936. Before breaking with the party after the Moscow Trials and becoming a critic of Marxism in general, Heinrich encouraged Hannah to probe more deeply into the writings of Marx, Lenin, and Trotsky. Then, after arriving in America, she herself remained sufficiently interested in Marx to "set out to write a little study" about him (which, however, she never managed to finish).

Still, for all this, it was true that Marx had exerted a much smaller influence on her way of looking at the world than had been the case with virtually every other member of the Family. What Marx was to them, the two German philosophers with whom she had studied, Karl Jaspers (who later became a surrogate father to her) and Martin Heidegger (who at the time became her secret lover), were to her. On the other hand, if she at least respected Marx, she was altogether untypical in being positively disdainful of Freud, who supplanted Marx as the leading formative influence on Family thinking in the years following World War II. So far as I know, she never wrote about Freud, but I myself often heard her make fun of him and of psychoanalysis in general.

Of all my elders in the Family, there was none for whom I had a higher regard than Hannah. The intellectual quality I prized most at that stage of my life was brilliance, by which I meant the virtuosic ability to put ideas together in such new and surprising combinations that even if one disagreed with what was being said, one was excited and illuminated. Everyone in the Family had this ability—it was in effect the main requirement for admission—but I thought Hannah had it to a greater degree than anyone else. In my youthfully starry eyes, she even outshone the art historian Meyer Schapiro, whose lectures at Columbia were generally considered the *ne plus ultra* of brilliance.

In 1951, about five years before meeting Hannah in the flesh, I had been introduced to her intellectually through *The Origins of Totalitarianism*. It would be impossible to overstate the effect this book had on me. Reading it threw me into so fevered a condition of intellectual exhilaration that I had to keep putting it down every few pages in order to regain the composure to go on. It seemed to me—and I was far from alone in this—that Hannah Arendt had uncovered the interrelations among all the terrible things that had happened and were still happening in the twentieth century and that in tracing the development of these connections she had arrived at a new understanding of how they had culminated in the greatest evil of all. The name she gave to this evil was totalitarianism, and though she herself had not invented the term, she had made it her own through a more profound analysis of the phenomenon it signified than had ever been offered before.

When I first discovered the book at the age of twenty-one, the sheer intellectual excitement of following the play of the dazzlingly agile synthesizing mind at work in *The Origins of Totalitarianism* was similar to the aesthetic pleasure that I derived as a literary man from a great poem or a great novel. But here of course there was a political dimension as well, and it consisted of the demonstration that Nazism and Communism, usually regarded as standing at opposite poles of the political spectrum, one on the extreme Right and the other on the extreme Left, were in truth brothers under the skin. The two apparently opposed ideologies had given birth to political systems whose essential features were remarkably similar both in themselves and also in the way they departed from the "simple" despotisms and tyrannies of the past. Those traditional dictatorships had been content with a monopoly of power in the political realm alone, but the new totalitarian regimes sought to establish complete control over every other aspect of life as well and they had proved themselves willing and able to murder as many millions as it took to achieve this dystopian objective. Morally, then, Communism, for all its rhetorically humanitarian trappings, was as much an example (in Hannah's own words) of "absolute evil" as Nazism. And it was also just as dangerous, having as its ultimate ambition (again in Hannah's words) "global conquest and total domination."

As a student at Columbia and Cambridge and then as a junior member of *Commentary*'s editorial staff, I had come to know a fair number of great figures in the intellectual world, and while always deferential, I usually managed to treat with them on a more or less equal footing. But so intimidated was I by the author of *The Origins of Totalitarianism* that I doubted I would have the courage to engage her comfortably in conversation. To my most happy surprise, however, talking to Hannah turned out to be very easy, and the vitality and warmth she always exuded made associating with her a great pleasure.

From a number of disparaging references in her posthumously published correspondence with Mary McCarthy, I have discovered that Hannah's feelings toward me in the early years of our relationship were not all that kindly nor her opinion of me all that high. Yet she certainly acted as though she liked me personally and thought well of my work. She would greet me with great cordiality whenever we met; she would solicit my views on whatever subject happened to be on her mind at the moment and then listen intently to what I had to say; she read and took the trouble to comment, usually appreciatively, on everything I wrote (I especially recall how intrigued she was by my article in *The New Leader* about the younger generation and the great interest she expressed in another piece I published around the same time in *The New Yorker* about Vladimir Dudintsev's *Not by Bread Alone*, the first big novel to emerge from the somewhat freer cultural climate that briefly followed upon Nikita Khrushchev's attack on Stalin in 1956);* after I became (to expressions of delight from her) editor-in-chief of *Commentary* in 1960, she gave me a chapter of her new book *On Revolution* to publish (even allowing me to edit the manuscript without complaint!);† and she consistently told me how "excellent" the magazine had become since I had taken it over.

We were also on friendly, if not intimate, social terms. Hannah readily accepted invitations to parties at my home, and as a mark of special favor she would sometimes invite me to small gatherings at hers. In addition, I was on the regular guest list for the one big party she gave every year on New Year's Eve—at which the Germans, arriving promptly at 9:30, would congregate in one room with the marzipan and the liqueurs while the Americans, filing in around midnight, would gather in another with the bourbon and the scotch. At one such party, in an attempt to desegregate the festivities, she dragged me into the German crowd to meet one of her oldest and best friends, an eminent scholar to whom she—never seeming more German herself, even through her merry grin—introduced me as follows: "Norman Podhoretz of *Commentary*, Hans Jonas of Gnosticism."

Why Hannah should have thus pretended to an affection and a respect for me that she did not actually (or perhaps not just fully) feel, I cannot explain. One possibility, which has been suggested by someone

---

*An infinitely more important product of that period was the publication of Aleksandr Solzhenitsyn's first novel, *One Day in the Life of Ivan Denisovich*, but it took a while before this unprecedented and earth-shattering account of life in the gulag made its way to the West.

†This was unusual not only in Hannah's case but with most of the German Jewish refugee intellectuals with whom I came to deal as an editor. Even though few of them ever really mastered English (one of the great exceptions being the eminent historian and journalist George Lichtheim), they always acted as though their prose was never in need of correction or improvement. My favorite example is the fight I had with the political theorist Hans J. Morgenthau, a regular contributor to *Commentary* in the early 1960s (who, as rumor had it, later became Hannah's lover). Shortly before he too became an ex-friend, he angrily accused me of tampering too freely with the manuscript of one of his pieces. "But Hans," I protested, "the sentence I changed was ungrammatical," to which he shot back (without a trace of humor or irony in his heavily accented voice), "How do *you* know?"

who knew us both at the time, is that the real pretense was not in how she acted toward but in how she talked about me to Mary McCarthy. There may be something to this. My relations with Mary had gotten off to a rocky start because of an article I wrote about her for *Commentary* in 1956 which was less than wholly enthusiastic. Later we moved onto friendly terms after being brought together by her former lover Philip Rahv ("I *told* you you would like him," he reported saying to her the next day). Nevertheless, I strongly suspected that she continued to harbor a grudge and that I remained a target of the malice "our leading bitch intellectual" famously directed at practically everyone she knew. If so, Hannah may well have wished to create the impression that she agreed with her friend about me. For her devotion to Mary was so great that it gave added point to the joke which circulated throughout the Family when Mary revealed in one of her autobiographical books that she had had a Jewish grandmother: from that point on, Hannah became "Mary McCarthy's Jewish grandmother" behind both their backs.

But even assuming that the disparaging references in Hannah's correspondence with Mary represented her true feelings, the apparent affection and respect with which she treated me in the early days of our friendship may have been a kind of reward for my enormous regard for her. A little later, similarly, she may have been repaying me for the fight I put up over her article on the crisis in Little Rock.

I myself, and everyone I knew, saw this crisis in the starkest moral terms. So little question was there that the Negroes (as they were then called) were morally and legally right, and that the whites were morally and legally wrong, that there seemed nothing to discuss except the timing and the amount of military force the federal government should use in escorting the black children through the mobs who were blocking the doors of Central High School against them. I was therefore fascinated to discover that Hannah not only had doubts about the wisdom of federal intervention but also took an utterly unconventional approach to the entire issue.

It went without saying that this unconventionality did not consist in the distribution of her sympathies as between the Negroes and the whites. As she would later feel constrained to say explicitly in a preface to the article when it was finally published: "Since what I wrote may shock good people and be misused by bad ones, I should like to make it clear that as a Jew I take my sympathy for the cause of the Negroes as for all oppressed or underprivileged peoples for granted and should appreciate it if the reader did likewise." Where she departed, and departed radically, from the conventional wisdom was in criticizing "the decision to force the issue of desegregation in the field of public education rather than in some other field in the campaign for Negro rights."

The analysis she offered in support of this criticism was based on a distinction (which she would later explore more deeply in her book *The Human Condition*) among the rights that properly belonged to the different realms of life (private, social, and political); and it was, of course, very brilliant. But what struck me most, and what to this day I remember most vividly about it, was not the abstract philosophical case she constructed but the moral indignation she expressed over the burden that was being placed on the children by the strategy of starting with the schools:

> The most startling part of the whole business was the federal decision to start integration in, of all places, the public schools. It certainly did not require too much imagination to see that this was to burden children, black and white, with the working out of a problem which adults for generations have confessed themselves unable to solve. I think no one will find it easy to forget the photograph reproduced in newspapers and magazines throughout the country, showing a Negro girl, accompanied by a white friend of her father, walking away from school, persecuted and followed into bodily proximity by a jeering and grimacing mob of youngsters. The girl, obviously, was asked to be a hero—that is, something neither her absent father nor the equally absent representatives of the NAACP felt called upon to be.... The picture looked to me like a fantastic caricature of progressive education which, by abolishing the authority of adults, implicitly denies their responsibility for the world into which they have borne their children and refuses the duty of guiding them into it.

As I already knew from *The Origins of Totalitarianism* and the many essays by her that I had also read, it was characteristic of Hannah to take off on her flights of metaphysical fancy from the ground of concrete human experience and then in the end to glide her way back down onto the same ground again. She herself once quoted the "great statement" of the Spanish painter Juan Gris: "If I am not in possession of the abstract, with what am I to control the concrete? If I am not in possession of the concrete, with what am I to control the abstract?" But I associated her unshakably solid footing in common everyday reality, which was one of the qualities I most admired in her work and most appreciated in her person, with her womanliness—and Hannah, though not physically attractive by conventional standards, was in every sense a very womanly woman indeed.

In this particular instance, even though I disagreed with her on the politics of the issue, I was enormously impressed by the originality of her position and the hidden corners and generally ignored complexities it brought to light. Hence, I felt sure that my colleagues would be as eager to publish the article as I was. But only one of them was (the one who had joined with me in asking her to write the piece) and even he later began moving to the other side.

As I saw it in those days, the purpose of an intellectual magazine like *Commentary* was not primarily to take political positions, and certainly not to restate the liberal clichés on everyone's lips, including our own. It was, rather, to do precisely what Hannah's article did—carry the discussion of important questions to a higher level and probe them more deeply than was being done elsewhere. Given the amount of experience I had had with my colleagues by then, I should not have been as surprised as I was to discover that their conception of the role of *Commentary* was much more narrowly political than mine. So far as most of them were concerned, the fact that Hannah was wrong about school desegregation nullified whatever value her supporting arguments and insights might have had. Beyond this, they feared (admittedly not without cause) that the publication of so politically heretical an article on so sensitive a subject might jeopardize the charter of editorial independence under which the magazine had always been allowed to operate by its sponsor, the American Jewish Committee.

In one heated editorial conference after another, I tried as hard as I could to persuade my colleagues that it would be a dereliction of our intellectual duty to reject this article. But the best I could get was a compromise proposal: they would agree to publish Hannah's piece on condition that she would agree to the appearance of a refutation in the same issue. The refutation would be written by Sidney Hook, who, as a philosopher himself, was especially well qualified to cope with Hannah's own basically philosophical approach. I myself disapproved of the idea, and I strongly doubted that Hannah would accept such a departure from the usual practice of running opposing viewpoints only in succeeding numbers of the magazine. But again I was mistaken. She said that she would go along provided she were accorded the opportunity to write a counter-rebuttal for the following issue. My colleagues were not at all happy with the idea of giving Hannah the last word, and neither was Sidney, who had at first been reluctant to undertake the assignment but then warmed to it once he read the galley proofs of Hannah's article. For the moment, however, the decision on how to proceed beyond the original debate was postponed, and everyone hunkered down for the storm that was soon to break.

Except that it never came. At an early point in the course of the negotiations going on in the office, about which I felt duty-bound to keep Hannah informed, she offered to withdraw the piece. But my own persistence, along with their anxiety over the scandal within the intellectual community that would be caused by *Commentary's* refusal to publish a major article by so eminent a writer (an anxiety which for the moment trumped their fear of how the American Jewish Committee would react), prevented my colleagues from jumping at this chance to get themselves off the hook. Then, about two months later, Hannah did them the great favor of writing to say that she had finally decided to submit the article for publication to another magazine.

Her reason for arriving at this decision became a matter of much dispute. In Sidney's version of the incident, Hannah, upon receiving the galley proofs of his rejoinder, was so shaken by the power of the case he had made against her that she lost her nerve and therefore changed her mind about simultaneous publication. In Hannah's version, as set forth in a letter to the editors of *Commentary*, the postponements to which publication of her article had been subjected had caused her considerable harm:

> I do not mind being attacked* and did not even object to the entirely unusual procedure of your commissioning an article for the sole purpose of attacking my article—instead of printing controversy as it arises from the circle of your readers. But I definitely mind being gossiped about. Ever since my article arrived in your offices, there has been a steady stream of gossip all over town. . . . This gossip, which was malicious in intent and sometimes bordering on slander, was possible only because you delayed publication, thus preventing people from reading and having their own opinion. By the same token, you were preventing me from any adequate defense.

And there was more:

> Since in the past few months all agreements between you and myself as well as all agreements at which you arrived between yourselves have been broken, I have no confidence that our agreement that I shall be given adequate space in time to reply to Mr. Hook's rejoinder will be kept. I have reasons to fear that when my reply arrives, another storm will break or be engineered in your offices which again will result in postponements or non-publication.

Although I did not then, and do not now, entirely discount Sidney's theory, Hannah did indeed have "reasons to fear" this outcome, having heard from me that my colleagues were coming closer and closer to the conclusion that the best solution would, after all, be to

---

*Lionel Trilling, putting it even more strongly, once told me that he "loved being attacked." But as we have seen, this was not in the least true of him, and as we shall shortly see when we come to her response to the reception of her book *Eichmann in Jerusalem*, it was not true of Hannah either. In my opinion, no one likes, let alone loves, being attacked—or, for that matter, even criticized. I have heard other writers insist that they are indifferent to what is said about them, but I never detected any such reaction in them when push came to shove. On the other hand, claims like these do evidently work to some extent as defenses against hurt and anger. (I only wish that they could for me.)

drop the whole thing. Instead of being angry with me for leaking this information to her, they were relieved when it resulted in her letter of withdrawal. Nor were most of them displeased when this incident, coming on top of several other such incidents (the worst involving the rejection of another controversial article I had commissioned—this one from the great English poet Robert Graves), had the further result of convincing me that I simply did not belong on the staff of such a magazine.

About a year later, "Reflections on Little Rock" finally appeared in, of all places, the socialist magazine *Dissent*, along with several rebuttals (though not the one by Hook, which, purged of all specific references to Hannah's still unpublished manuscript, had by then already come out in *The New Leader*). The editors of *Dissent* (putting, I thought, *Commentary* to shame) announced that they considered her views "entirely mistaken" but that they had decided to print the article anyway "because of Miss Arendt's intellectual stature" and "the importance of her topic."

Naturally, my resignation played well with Hannah, to whom loyalty was a supreme virtue, and shortly afterward she showed her appreciation by sending my wife a very expensive art book upon the birth of our third child. She also knew that, given my heavy responsibilities as a married man with three children, I was taking a risk in leaving *Commentary*. But she strongly endorsed my plan of trying to live on a part-time job in book publishing supplemented by an advance for a book of my own.*

A year or so earlier, in a letter to Mary McCarthy, whom I had not yet met, Hannah had described me patronizingly as "one of those bright youngsters with bright hopes for a nice career"—a judgment she probably now had to revise in light of the damage I was doing, at least partly for her sake, to those bright hopes. If, however, she did

---

*It was supposed to be a study of the postwar American novel, but I never got beyond the first two chapters. One of these chapters (on Norman Mailer) was published in *Partisan Review* in 1959 and was then included, along with the other one (on Saul Bellow), previously unpublished, in *Doings and Undoings*.

change her mind about me then, she undoubtedly reverted to her original judgment upon the appearance in 1967 of *Making It*, in which I scandalized the entire Family by defending precisely the kind of ambition for worldly success for which they professed contempt and whose (apparent) absence among them had so impressed Hannah upon her arrival in the United States. Besides, by the time *Making It* came out, our friendship had all but petered out, and I had no claim of loyalty on her such as might otherwise have kept her from joining in the general assault on that book.

The break between Hannah and me began with a series of articles she did in 1963 about the trial of Adolf Eichmann, which *The New Yorker* had sent her to Jerusalem to cover. Eichmann, the Nazi officer who had been responsible for rounding up the Jews of Europe and deporting them to the death camps, had escaped to Argentina after the war and had then been found and spirited off to Jerusalem by Israeli agents. The kidnapping caused an uproar all over the world, with Israel being accused of having violated international law both in forcibly removing Eichmann from Argentina and in then proposing to try him in an Israeli court rather than turning him over to an international tribunal. Among the outraged were a number of Jewish organizations, including the American Jewish Committee, which only a few months earlier had brought me back after the death of Elliot Cohen to succeed him as editor-in-chief of the magazine. Since *Commentary* still enjoyed complete editorial independence—and since, unlike my former colleagues, I was prepared to exploit this arrangement to the full—I felt free to take a position on the Eichmann affair that clashed with AJC's, and I did.*

In July 1960, introducing an article by Jacob Robinson, an expert on international law who made a convincing argument for Israel's

---

*I also helped a senior member of the AJC staff to head off a resolution condemning Israel that the Committee was preparing to issue and that would have done it great damage within the Jewish community.

legal claim to jurisdiction in the Eichmann case, I wrote an editorial defending the abduction and endorsing Prime Minister David Ben-Gurion's statement that "historic justice" demanded that the man who organized the mass murder of Jews be tried by the only sovereign power in world Jewry. Since Eichmann's job had specifically been concerned with murdering Jews, I declared, his crimes could more accurately be defined as crimes against the Jewish people than as crimes against the international community in general. To this I added that anyone who feared that by trying Eichmann Israel would be pretending to speak for Jews in other countries ought to consider that Israel did at least have the right to speak for those Jews who were the actual victims of Nazi persecution, some three hundred thousand survivors of which now lived in Israel.

This editorial was written before the trial began, and Hannah told me she liked it. I was therefore less startled than I might have been to read many years later in Young-Bruehl's book that she made exactly the same points in a letter to her old teacher Karl Jaspers (who was not Jewish but whose wife was). According to Young-Bruehl:

> Jaspers had felt that the Israelis should not try Eichmann but rather turn him over to an international tribunal. . . . He was concerned . . . about the Israelis' right to "speak for all Jews." . . . Arendt countered that Israel could speak for the Jews, "at least for the victims," if not in a legal sense then "in a political sense," and then reminded him that "a majority of the European Jews who had survived the Holocaust lived in Israel."

(If, however, this was what she thought—conceivably under the influence of my editorial—before the trial began, she would later reverse herself, attacking the Israelis in her book for *not* having turned Eichmann over to an international tribunal.)

To write about the trial for *Commentary* I chose Harold Rosenberg, who, though best known as an art critic, had also been trained as a lawyer and could find his way around contemporary history and politics as well as anyone in sight. The article he produced for the November 1961 issue of *Commentary* was a powerful and eloquent critique of the trial as a "form" for telling the story of the terrible fate that had befallen the Jewish people. Rosenberg was right to stress this particular inadequacy of the trial, for hard as it would be to believe in later years, when movies and television programs and museums and college courses devoted to the Holocaust would become commonplace, in 1960 such knowledge as was by then available had not yet, as he said, "entered the general consciousness or even that of many Jews." Rosenberg had hoped that the trial would shed more light than it did on "the evolution of the Nazi murder plan out of programs of discrimination and expulsion," and he deplored the fact that Eichmann "had to be allowed to compete with the survivors in their telling of the story of the Jews of Europe." The trial, he concluded, had "presented . . . an indispensable account of the tragedy of the Jews in this era, but it was an account marred in the telling and needing to be gone over and interpreted again and again."

Both as an editor and as a writer, then, I was already intensely involved in the issues surrounding the Eichmann case when the five articles that in revised form would make up Hannah Arendt's book on it started appearing serially in *The New Yorker* in February 1963. Although the tone I took in my editorial had been very cool, there was nothing cool about the feelings which had been unleashed in me by the debate over the Eichmann case, especially among Jews. On the contrary, I was very angry over the animus against Israel that came to the surface the minute Eichmann was captured and that remained in the air throughout the entire trial.

It was not, however, as a Zionist that I was aroused to all this anger. For contrary to the impression created in the minds of many people by my later writings on Israel, I had never been much of a Zionist. Not that I was ever an anti-Zionist either. Various Jewish factions had opposed the establishment of a Jewish state in Palestine: socialists because they saw it as a form of reactionary bourgeois nationalism; assimilationist Jews who feared that it would lead to charges of dual loyalty; Reform Jews because they saw it as a reversion to a primitive stage of tribalism; Orthodox Jews because they considered it a sin to restore Jewish sovereignty in the Holy Land before the advent of the

Messiah.* I did not agree with any of these positions. In my opinion, the Holocaust had demonstrated irrefutably and once and for all that a guaranteed refuge was needed for Jews fleeing persecution and murder. But neither did I agree with the "non-Zionists" and the "binationalists." These two groups accepted that a refuge was needed, but the non-Zionists thought it could and should be established in some mysterious way that did not involve Jewish political sovereignty, while the binationalists thought it could and should be done through a state in which political sovereignty was shared jointly by Jews and Arabs (even though under this arrangement Jews might well be a minority).† I, however, was with the Zionists in believing that the need for a refuge could be answered *only* by a state in which Jews were the majority and enjoyed full sovereignty on their own.

Yet I had no great love for the sovereign Jewish state that had actually come into being. After my first visit in 1951, I wrote a long letter to Lionel Trilling giving him "an honest account of my reactions." After about six weeks of covering "almost every inch of the country," I said,

> I finally went away . . . with a slightly bitter taste in my mouth and a sense of having been strangely dispossessed. I felt more at home in Athens! . . . They are, despite their really extraordinary achievements, a very unattractive people, the Israelis. They're gratuitously surly and boorish. . . . They suffer under the illusion that Jewish history becomes significant only from the First Zionist Congress onward. . . . On the

---

*In each of these groups, however, there were prominent exceptions: the Labor Zionists among the socialists; rabbis like Stephen Wise and Abba Hillel Silver in the Reform movement; and the Mizrachi party among the Orthodox. But to me, the most impressive of all the exceptions was Abraham Isaac Kook, the first Ashkenazi chief rabbi of mandatory Palestine, who once declared that he kissed the ground on which the Jewish pioneers (the *chalutzim*) set foot: despite the fact that they were all secularists and atheists, it was, he said, holy ground. "These fiery spirits," as he called them, were "people who do not have the slightest idea what an important role they play in the scheme of Divine Providence. They are called but do not know who is calling them."

†The term *Palestinians* had not yet come into existence to describe the Arab residents of mandatory Palestine. They were then known by everyone, including themselves, simply as Arabs. Conversely, the Jews living there were often called Palestinians. Thus, what is today *The Jerusalem Post* was in the pre-state era *The Palestine Post* and what later became the Israel Philharmonic Orchestra was then the Palestine Symphony.

other hand, they realize that their claim to status as a civilization rests on the past and that only the most intensive of efforts at establishing a living continuity with the past can overcome the artificial process by which the country was contrived. And on the other hand, they are too arrogant and too anxious to become a real honest-to-goodness New York of the East.*

I freely admitted to Trilling that these reactions were "uncharitable" and probably unfair, which they most assuredly were (and in retrospect I can only shake my head in wonder at the cocky certainties of which I was capable at the age of twenty-one). They were also surprising coming from someone who, having been subjected to a Jewish education that was very intensive by American standards, spoke Hebrew fluently and knew enough about Israel and its place in Jewish history to have answered his own complaints.

I also had a related problem with Jewish particularism. My parents, like many eastern-European immigrants who had been raised in strictly Orthodox homes but who wanted more freedom for themselves in America, were highly selective in their observance of the commandments. But Reform and Conservative synagogues seeming insufficiently Jewish to them, they still belonged to an Orthodox congregation. When I was five or six, they sent me to the congregational school (known as a *heder*) that was run by the rabbi every afternoon after "regular school" was out. I remained in this *heder* until the age of twelve, when my father persuaded me to continue my Jewish studies for three more years at a Hebrew high school (two nights a week and Sundays) and then to proceed to the Seminary College of Jewish Studies, the purely academic division of the Jewish Theological Seminary. There I spent another five years (again, two nights a week and Sundays) earning the degree of Bachelor of Hebrew Literature

---

*It was, incidentally, through this letter that I first came to the attention of *Commentary*. Trilling sent a copy to Elliot Cohen, surmising correctly that he (a former "non-Zionist" who had reconciled himself to Jewish statehood once it had become a reality but who, like his old ally in this, Hannah Arendt, remained suspicious and grudging in his support) would find my sentiments congenial. Cohen himself did not respond, but I soon received an invitation from his managing editor, Irving Kristol, inviting me to write for the magazine.

while I was simultaneously attending Columbia by day and getting my B.A. there.

For an American of my generation, this was an unusually sustained immersion in Jewish culture, and it certainly saved me from the cavalier and philistine attitude of many of my contemporaries toward Jewishness and Judaism, about which their ignorance knew no bounds and the vulgarity of their ideas knew no limits. Their attitude annoyed me sufficiently to challenge it whenever it came up, but the piety I felt toward Jewish tradition did not extend to belief in the Jewish religion or in the observance of its laws. By the time I was a senior in college I had developed doubts about the existence of God, I had given up being kosher, and I was paying no more than pro forma attention to the major Jewish holidays I had once (if not all that strictly) observed.

Nor did my piety toward the tradition result in a wish to preoccupy myself largely or primarily with things Jewish. When I was offered the editorship of *Commentary*, I hesitated and then finally accepted only on the understanding that I had a mandate to change it from a Jewish magazine that carried a certain amount of general material to a general magazine that carried a certain amount of Jewish material. *Commentary* would continue to have a special interest in Jewish affairs, but it would mainly be an intellectual American magazine addressing itself to the entire range of contemporary issues, just as I myself was doing in my own writing as a literary and social critic.

It would be going too far to say that the Eichmann case induced a radical change of heart in me both about Israel and about Jewish particularism. After all, while my sour personal feelings about Israel and Israelis had not changed much since my first visit nine years earlier, I had no residual reservations such as afflicted old non-Zionists like Elliot Cohen and Hannah Arendt about the need for a Jewish state. And just as the denigration of Jewish tradition by some of my friends always got my back up, so their reflexive bias against Israel always provoked me into sounding like a Zionist true believer.

In 1956, for example, on the occasion of the invasion of Egypt by a coalition—one that would become unthinkable in the years ahead—consisting of Israel, France, and Great Britain, I wrote an article for *Midstream*, a Zionist magazine, blasting the Jewish intellectuals of New York for refusing to recognize that as Jews they were inescapably implicated in the fate of Israel. I also attacked them for failing

> to support a movement whose essential purposes are to restore the Jews to an honorable status among the nations, to repair the ravages done to the Jewish personality by two thousand years of Diaspora, to insure that Jewish lives shall not be in constant jeopardy, and to save Jewish lives that are imminently threatened.

The Eichmann case, then, was not the first time I had ever leaped to the defense of Israel and of particularistic Jewish interests. But it was the first time I ever clearly understood the dangerous implications of the notion that Jews in general and the Jewish state in particular were required to be morally superior to everyone else. In the concluding paragraph of my *Commentary* editorial, I quoted Edmond Cahn, a professor at the NYU law school, who had recently written that

> if Eichmann should be convicted and put to death, we could only say that the Israelis had conducted themselves "like the nations." On the other hand, if the prosecutor should recommend or the court impose a sentence of life imprisonment, the whole world would respond with renewed faith and admiration.

To this I replied:

> I wonder why it is that Israel must always be asked to act more nobly than other nations. Isn't this demand a way of telling Jews that they must *justify* their existence instead of taking it for granted that they have a simple right to exist and therefore to be "merely" human, and "like the nations"?

In thus rejecting the assumption that Jews, alone among all the peoples of the earth, were asked to justify the space they took up on it, I was returning to a point I had also made in my *Midstream* article of 1957, where I declared that "no apologies are required for asserting one's right to existence . . . because this right is absolute." But the full realization that I had found a way around the much-vexed question of why Jews should go on existing as a distinct and separate people only came to me with the Eichmann case. I now began to see that the question itself was illegitimate: the Jews were there because they were there, and unless and until they themselves decided to disappear through conversion and assimilation, no one had the right to set special conditions for their continued existence.

Admittedly, I was not always consistent in holding on to this new understanding. Only three years after my editorial on Eichmann, I wrote an article for *Commentary* called "My Negro Problem—and Ours" which, in criticizing the then-sacred liberal goal of racial integration, caused a furor not unlike the one Hannah had stirred up with "Reflections on Little Rock." As I would later remark, there was something in "My Negro Problem" to offend everyone, and where the Jews were concerned, it was this passage:

> In thinking about the Jews I have often wondered whether their survival as a distinct group was worth one hair on the head of a single infant. Did the Jews have to survive so that six million innocent people should one day be burned in the ovens of Auschwitz? It is a terrible question, and no one, not God Himself, could ever answer it to my satisfaction.

Yet shortly afterward, in reading Hannah Arendt on Eichmann, it came to me that this "terrible question" was no different from the one I had already decided was illegitimate. More than anything else, it was because that very same question lay behind her book on the case that I felt compelled to take it on.

This was not an easy thing for me to do. The response to *Eichmann in Jerusalem: A Report on the Banality of Evil* within the Jewish community at large ranged from indignation to blind rage, and even within the Family the predominant reaction was violently negative. So intense was Family feeling over what Hannah had wrought that a public debate—which was actually a disguised protest meeting—was staged under the auspices of *Dissent* by its editor, Irving Howe. Hannah was invited but declined to attend, which spared her the sight of her attackers being cheered by the audience and her defenders loudly booed. I also vividly recall how the critic Lionel Abel, who had already written a very hostile article about the book for *Partisan Review*, started banging the table at which he was waiting his turn to speak when the historian Raul Hilberg, author of the scholarly landmark *The Destruction of the European Jews*, said that the victims could have done more to save themselves. The audience, following suit, nearly drowned Hilberg out with shouts of protest, and Abel then began his own presentation by expressing regret for having formerly admired Hilberg as a scholar.

This poisonous atmosphere infected most of the reviews of Hannah's book, as well as the denunciatory statements issued by a number of Jewish organizations. As I would make a point of stressing in the article I was eventually to write, many of the criticisms of Hannah were either wrong or unfair, sometimes to the extreme of outright defamation. In particular, she was repeatedly accused of exonerating Eichmann when she clearly stated that he was guilty of participation in mass murder and deserved to be hanged. So, too, she was accused of charging the Jewish victims of the Holocaust with going like sheep to the slaughter, when she herself had heaped scorn on the Israeli prosecutor Gideon Hausner for making that very charge in his interrogation of the survivors who testified at the trial. And because her book was sprinkled with derogatory references to Zionism and Zionists, she was often assumed to be writing out of a lifelong anti-Zionist bias, when she had actually once regarded herself as a Zionist and had been active in the movement both in Europe and America.

At the time, I had a vague impression of Hannah's involvement with Zionism, but I had no idea of the full extent of it, which is well documented by Young-Bruehl. As a young woman in Germany, Hannah had decided that she was a Zionist, and in Paris, where she found temporary refuge after fleeing from the Nazis who had taken over her homeland, she had worked for a Zionist organization (Youth Aliyah). Then in her early years in America, she often spoke before and cooperated with Zionist groups. At some point, however, she grew disillusioned with the mainstream Zionist leadership (largely, it seems, for compounding its failure to back a boycott against German goods in the 1930s with a refusal to insist on a Jewish army in World War II). Yet even then she joined forces with the non-Zionists rather than with the anti-Zionists. She also lent support to the binationalists, for whose leader Judah Magnes she had great respect.* Yet she was no more enthusiastic about a state in which Jews would share sovereignty with Arabs than she was about a state in which Jews would share sovereignty with no one. What exactly she wanted I have never been able to ascertain; mainly she seemed intent on showing that everyone else was wrong.

In any event, not even when the Zionist organizations were attacking her so ferociously over *Eichmann in Jerusalem* did she go over to the unambiguously anti-Zionist American Council for Judaism. Responding to the Council's offer of support, she wrote:

> You know that I was a Zionist and that my reason for breaking with the Zionist organization was very different from the anti-Zionist stand of the Council: I am not against Israel on principle. . . . I know, or believe I know, that should catastrophe overtake this Jewish state, for whatever reasons (even for reasons of its own foolishness), this would be the perhaps final catastrophe for the whole Jewish people, no matter what opinions every one of us might hold at the moment.

My sentiments exactly. The problem was that very few, if any, readers of *Eichmann in Jerusalem* could have guessed—and probably would have been bewildered to discover—that this was how Hannah felt.

As profoundly disturbed as I too was by her book, I felt very reluctant to jeopardize my relations with Hannah by associating myself with the attacks on her, especially as so many of them were hysterical and off the mark. I had heard via the Family grapevine that she was becoming more than a little paranoid about what she took to be a campaign against her organized and orchestrated by the Jewish establishment. There was a danger, then, that if I wrote a critical piece for

---

*Magnes, born in America, was a Reform rabbi who had helped found and had then become president of the Hebrew University in Jerusalem, which, in turn, became a hotbed of his movement, known in Hebrew as *Brit Shalom*.

Commentary, she not only would regard me as having committed the cardinal sin of disloyalty but would probably think I had acted under orders from the American Jewish Committee.

Nevertheless, I felt that I had no choice. Even if someone else were to write critically about the book for *Commentary*, I knew that Hannah would still hold me responsible, and so I might as well do the job myself. My hope was that if I did it the right way—that is, by accurately stating what she had actually said and then trying to refute it, in large part out of her own mouth—our friendship might still survive.

It did not occur to me then, but it does now in retrospect, that in writing "Hannah Arendt on Eichmann: A Study in the Perversity of Brilliance" I was reversing the stand I had taken six years earlier on her piece about Little Rock. In that controversy, I had fought for Hannah because of the originality of her arguments and the brilliance of her insights, whereas the attitude of my colleagues was that these qualities, by making the mistaken position they served seem more persuasive, also made her article all the more pernicious. *Eichmann in Jerusalem* was, if anything, even more original and more brilliant than "Reflections on Little Rock," but what I said about it came very close to what my colleagues had said about that article.

The originality here lay in Hannah's telling of the story of how the Nazis had succeeded in their genocidal plan against the Jews. In the generally accepted version, there was no moral ambiguity: the Nazis were evil murderers and the Jews were their hapless and helpless victims. But this was too simple a picture to satisfy Hannah. As I observed in my article, in place of the Jew as innocent martyr, she gave us the Jew as accomplice in evil; in place of the monstrous Nazi, she gave us the "banal" Nazi; and in place of the confrontation between guilt and innocence, she gave us the collaboration of criminal and victim.

According to Hannah, I went on, the Nazis needed the cooperation of the Jews themselves to carry out their genocidal plan against them, and they received it "to a truly extraordinary degree." In every European Jewish community, she wrote,

> Jewish officials could be trusted to compile the lists of persons and of
> their property, to secure money from the deportees to defray the ex-

penses of their deportation and extermination, to keep track of vacated apartments, to suppy police forces to help seize Jews and get them on trains, until, as a last gesture, they handed over the assets of the Jewish community in good order for final confiscation.

All this, I acknowledged, was true and had long been known. What was new was Hannah's assertion that if the Jews (or, rather, their leaders) had not cooperated in this fashion, "there would have been chaos and plenty of misery but the total number of victims would hardly have been between four and a half and six million people."*

In attacking this part of her version of the story, I began by showing that it contradicted some of the most important points she herself had made in *The Origins of Totalitarianism*. One such was that totalitarian regimes aimed at securing the complicity of their victims. From this it followed that the Nazis could have been expected to want Jewish cooperation not for any utilitarian or practical purpose but purely for its own sake. Yet now she suddenly decided that they sought Jewish help because without it there would have been "an impossibly severe drain on German manpower."

Enfolded within this disregard of one of her own central ideas was an even more startling contradiction of *The Origins of Totalitarianism*. For there, in demonstrating that nothing in the Nazi program had a higher priority than "cleansing" Europe of the Jews, she had underlined the fact that resources badly needed at the front in 1944 and early 1945 were tied up so that the ovens of Auschwitz could be kept working at full capacity. It was, I wrote, "ridiculous" by her own account to contend, as she was now doing, that the additional strain which would have been put on German resources in the absence of Jewish cooperation would have forced the Nazis to ease off or back away.

What was more, in characterizing as "truly extraordinary" the degree of cooperation given by the *Judenräte*, or Jewish Councils, to the

---

*This little detail—so casually questioning the accuracy of the figure of six million and feeding into the idea, beloved of anti-Semites and Holocaust "revisionists," that the Jews were exaggerating their losses—would have been enough all by itself to outrage many of her readers.

Nazis, she wildly overstated the case. For example, I said, when Jacob Gens, the notorious leader of the Vilna *Judenrat*, declared that "with a hundred victims I save a thousand people, with a thousand ten thousand," he was assuming that the Nazis were rational beings and that their aims must therefore be limited and subject to negotiation. In this, he was making exactly the same mistake about their literally incredible intentions toward his people that was made by all those European leaders of the 1930s who had believed that war could be averted if Hitler were "appeased" by being given at least some of what he was demanding. There was, in short, nothing "extraordinary" about Jewish cooperation: it was just another form of appeasement.

Attacking Hausner for the question he kept putting to survivors who testified at the trial ("Fifteen thousand people were standing there and hundreds of guards facing you—why didn't you revolt and charge and attack?"), she complained, quite rightly, that the question was "cruel and silly" because "no non-Jewish group or people had behaved differently." Yet she herself apparently thought that there was nothing cruel and silly in asking the same question about the cooperation of the Jewish leaders, even though no non-Jewish leaders had behaved differently—not before the war and still less under Nazi occupation.

As to her stress on the *Judenräte* as a factor in the number of victims claimed by the Final Solution, I countered it by drawing on the wealth of available historical evidence (either ignored or distorted by her) that clearly showed how pitifully insignificant a portion of the numbers killed could plausibly be traced to what the Jewish leaders themselves (as opposed to the surrounding population) did or failed to do. Refusing to enter once again into the endless debate over their behavior, I summed up my critique of this part of Hannah's version of the story with what was in effect a renunciation of my old belief in originality as a great intellectual virtue:

> They did what they did, they were what they were, and each was a different man. None of it mattered in the slightest to the final result. Murderers with the power to murder descended upon a defenseless people and murdered a large part of it. What else is there to say?

If, in Hannah's version of the story, carrying out the plan of geno-cide required Jewish cooperation, it did not require that the Nazis who carried it out be monsters or even Jew-haters. Since the murder of Jews was dictated by the law of the state, and since selfless loyalty to the law was regarded by the Germans under Hitler as the highest of virtues, it even called for a certain idealism to do what Eichmann and his cohorts had done. In this connection, Hannah quoted the famous remark attributed to Heinrich Himmler, who, as head of the SS, was the official most directly in charge of the death camps: "To have stuck it out and, apart from exceptions caused by human weakness, to have remained decent, that is what has made us hard."

In her view, then, Eichmann was telling the truth when he denied in his testimony at the trial that he was or ever had been an anti-Semite; he did his duty to the best of his ability, and he would have performed with equal zeal even if he had loved the Jews. Far from being the brute and the sadist and the fiend that Hausner portrayed in prosecuting him, Eichmann was, as Hannah saw him, a banal personality, a nonen-tity whose evil deeds flowed not from anything in his own character but, rather, from his position in the totalitarian Nazi system.

At this juncture in the narrative, having conveniently forgotten *The Origins of Totalitarianism* in her treatment of the Jews, Hannah just as con-veniently remembered it in dealing with Eichmann. Leaning heavily on that book, she produced a portrait of him as an ordinary man whose conscience was made to function "the other way around" by a system with enough power to wipe away commonsense reality and replace it with a new reality molded to the lineaments of the official ideology.

Just as I had acknowledged the originality of Hannah's interpreta-tion of the role of Jewish cooperation in the Final Solution, so I now ac-knowledged the brilliance of her portrait of Eichmann. And just as the moral and historical errors behind that interpretation taught me that originality was not so great an intellectual virtue as I had once thought, so I learned from Hannah's portrait of Eichmann that there was noth-ing admirable about brilliance in itself. Indeed, I wrote, "there could hardly be a more telling example than this section of her book of the in-tellectual perversity that can result from the pursuit of brilliance by a mind infatuated with its own agility and bent on generating dazzle."

It was perverse to deny that Eichmann was an anti-Semite: how could a man have joined the Nazi party, let alone the SS, without being an anti-Semite? It was perverse to see Eichmann as a man of conscience: how could a man of conscience have participated knowingly in mass murder? It was perverse to regard him as ordinary even unto banality: how could a banal individual have been entrusted with a large measure of administrative responsibility for a top-priority item in the Nazi program and done so hugely evil a job so well? If Eichmann had been living in the ideal Nazi future—a world long since totally sealed off from outside influences—the things Hannah said of him might conceivably have made sense. But he was living in the imperfect Nazi present, in a regime that was only about ten years old when he took charge of the rounding up and deportation of Jews to the death camps. This meant that he had to know he was being criminal by the standards under which he himself had been raised and that also still reigned supreme in the "decadent" culture of the West. And however great was what Hannah described as "the moral collapse the Nazis caused in respectable European society—not only in Germany but in almost all countries, not only among the persecutors but also among the victims"—Eichmann surely knew that not everyone looked upon the murdering of Jews as a fine and noble occupation.

Despite Hannah's praise of the editorial on Eichmann in which I had criticized the demand that the Jews act more nobly than other nations, her own book, I concluded, was yet another and even more egregious instance of the same inordinate demand "on the Jews to be better than other people, to be braver, wiser, nobler, more dignified—or be damned." This habit of judging the Jews by one standard and everyone else by another was, I freely conceded, a habit she shared even with those Jews who thought that the main defect of her version of the story was her failure to dwell on all the heroism and all the virtue that the six million displayed. But the truth, I insisted, was that the Jews under Hitler acted as people will act when they are set upon by murderers, no better and no worse: the Final Solution revealed nothing about the victims except that they were mortal beings and hopelessly vulnerable in their powerlessness. I ended my article with a plea to my fellow Jews:

"The Nazis destroyed a third of the Jewish people. In the name of all that is humane, will the remnant never let up on itself?"

―――――――――

In later years, especially following the Six Day War of 1967, the double standard would become the weapon of choice in the hands of Jews who thought that Israel only had a right to exist if it conformed to their leftist political views and of Arabs and their supporters throughout the world who thought that Israel had no right to exist at all. I would therefore find many occasions on which to return to the idea that had first occurred to me during the Suez crisis of 1956 and that the Eichmann case, and especially my contention over it with Hannah, had pushed to the very heart of my thinking about the Jewish people.

This idea was given greater salience and depth in an article in *Commentary* by the theologian Emil L. Fackenheim, who argued that a new commandment, the 614th, had been added by the experience of Auschwitz to the traditional 613. Positively the 614th commandment proclaimed that "there shall be Jews," and negatively it prohibited "posthumous victories for Hitler." To me this primarily meant that a Jew, simply by virtue of being a Jew who lived at a time when a determined effort was made to wipe the Jews off the face of the earth merely because they were Jews—not just Jews of this or that kind, religious or secular, assimilated or particularistic, Bundist or Zionist, rich or poor, but any and all Jews—was obligated to do everything in his power to make sure that no such effort would ever be allowed to succeed. And with a new one even now being made, with Israel as its target, I resolved, in taking upon myself the yoke of this commandment, to obey it by relentlessly championing the Jewish state against its political and ideological enemies, who, wittingly or not, were working to destroy it.

In my interpretation of it, the 614th commandment did not set special terms for its observance: it did not stipulate that the Jews had to be more than human in order to be or that the Jewish state had to operate under moral and political restrictions that no other state, either in the past or the present, had ever been forced to accept. The doctrine of the chosen people was not a suicide pact, let alone a license to impose conditions upon the Jewish state that would result in its vulnerability to murder.

On a lesser level, I also took it upon myself to stand up for Jewish interests in America whenever they were disregarded or threatened. In the past, in response to any important event, Jews had always asked the question "Is it good for the Jews?" Then, in what I would characterize as the Golden Age of Jewish Security that had dawned in America in the aftermath of the Holocaust, they had found it unnecessary and embarrassingly particularistic to go on asking it. But I would argue that with the emergence in the late 1960s of openly expressed anti-Semitic ideas on the radical Left and especially in the black community, Jews ought to start asking that question again and to begin acting politically on it. Under the aegis of this idea, *Commentary* would become more aggressive than it had ever been before in defending Jewish interests both at home and abroad, even as, with regard to the overall balance of subject matter, it would remain a general magazine with a special emphasis on issues of particular concern to Jews.

But all this was in the future; in the present, meanwhile, my contention with Hannah still had a way to go even after "Hannah Arendt on Eichmann: A Study in the Perversity of Brilliance" was published. I had been hoping against hope that this article (which was already drawing an enormous amount of mail, almost all of it favorable) would not cause her to break with me. I was therefore overjoyed when, instead of writing an angry letter declaring that she wanted nothing further to do with me (she had already written such letters to a few of our mutual friends), she called and invited me over to thrash out the differences between us. "I may be brilliant," she laughed, showing herself at her best, "but I am definitely not perverse."

Happy as I was for this chance to salvage our relations, I was also full of trepidation as I entered her gloomy apartment on Riverside Drive the next afternoon. I was about to be challenged by one of the most formidable minds in the world, and though I was confident enough about the soundness of my article to believe that I could hold my own, I was also nervous, because my effectiveness would be reduced by a great reluctance to repeat to her face the hurtful things I had already said in print.

It was about 2 P.M. when I arrived, and Hannah, greeting me less warmly than usual but not coldly either, got right down to business. In her hand she held the page proofs I had as a courtesy sent her in advance, and I could see at a glance that they were very heavily underlined and annotated. My heart sank at the prospect of having to defend every little detail of my article—which was exactly what she forced me to do. As I would later describe the scene in *Breaking Ranks*, for nearly five hours we sat there arguing while the room grew darker and darker, and I began wondering when she would switch on a light (for some reason she never did, and for some reason I never asked). The exchanges between us were for the most part polite, with an occasional burst of testiness coming from her. But to my great puzzlement, most of the points she raised were so weak that I had no trouble disposing of them and, with one exception, so trivial that I can no longer recall what they were.

The exception had to do with a passage in my article in which I said that Eichmann, and the Nazis in general, were madmen on the Jewish question. To explain what I meant by this, I cited the difference between the Germans and the Rumanians. The Rumanians were the worst anti-Semites in Europe and were delighted to join in the slaughtering of Jews, until they discovered that there was money to be made in saving Jews, whereupon they began saving Jews. This, I wrote, was pathological anti-Semitism bounded by rational limits. The Germans, by contrast, regarded the Jews, whom they had already rendered utterly helpless with the stroke of a pen, as dangerous enemies, and they were so convinced of the necessity to do away with these enemies that they were willing to let the war effort suffer rather than let up. That was pathological anti-Semitism bounded by no rational limits, and if there was any banality to be found in the Holocaust, it lay in this insanity and not in the pedestrian character of Adolf Eichmann.

"But Norman, my dear," Hannah remonstrated through the near darkness in a tone suggesting that she thought she really had me now, "I can assure you that the Nazis were not crazy at all." To this I retorted that I had said they were crazy not in general but only when it came to the Jews. Either lapsing into a rare fit of obtuseness or willfully refusing to grasp a distinction that would have robbed her of what she clearly considered a trump card, she repeated the same thing in exactly the same words, and then did it again yet a third time when I tried once more to clarify what I had been trying to say. At which point I gave up, and a little while later, at about 7 P.M., we decided to call it quits.

Hannah, however, was not quite through with me yet. In deciding to write the article, I had feared that she would think I had been put up to it by the AJC, and I was now to find out that my fear had been well founded. "Let me ask you a question before you go," she murmured in the near darkness as I rose to leave. "Why did you do it?" I answered that I had written my article reluctantly, out of a sense of duty. She shrugged and smiled a knowing, patronizing smile into which she put a combination of disbelief, disappointment, and resignation. It was a smile that said as clearly as words would have done, "You're lying, of course, but it was foolish of me to expect that you would be man enough to tell me the truth."

Hannah had behaved so much better than most writers (myself included) would have done in response to an attack by a friend that I let this unspoken insult pass. After all, she had a perfect right to feel that I had let her down, and blaming this—as I had no doubt she was doing—on the exigencies of my position as editor of *Commentary* could even be taken as a way of absolving me personally for siding with the enemy. Furthermore, when an admirer of hers, a professor at the University of Maryland, asked her if she would come down there to participate in a public discussion of her book, she replied that I was the only one of her critics with whom she would be willing to share the platform. When I heard this, I was at first flattered, until it occurred to me that maybe she thought I would be a pushover as compared with some of her other opponents.

Still, I agreed to participtate, even though the deck would be stacked against me by the inclusion of Dwight Macdonald, who was second in the Family only to Mary McCarthy as Hannah's friend and defender. Dwight was also a friend of mine and a fan of my writing (it was he who had called it to the attention of *The New Yorker*), and I in turn admired his lively, witty, and quirky prose, much of which I had been happy to publish in *Commentary*. I did not, however, admire his attitude toward the Jewish people. He had spent much of his life among Jews, but he could never see any point in the survival of the Jewish people as a distinct group; and while he had long since ceased being a Trotskyist, he still saw Zionism through the old Trotsykist spectacles as a form of reactionary bourgeois nationalism.* In relation to Hannah, his attitude was as close to reverential as so fundamentally irreverent a person could get. Besides, as a vigorous opponent of the concept of collective German guilt for the Holocaust (about which he had written a famous treatise), he rather liked the idea of piling some of the guilt onto the shoulders of the Jews themselves.

As it turned out, since the professor who had arranged this event and served as moderator was also clearly on Hannah's side, it was three and not two against one, with Dwight mainly intervening to agree with everything Hannah said. The audience, on the other hand, seemed to be split more evenly down the middle. The passions aroused by *Eichmann in Jerusalem* were such that not even the huge gymnasium in which our debate was held could accommodate the crowd that showed up on that Sunday afternoon in the spring of 1965; never before or since have I seen people literally, not metaphorically, hanging from the rafters. And in spite of the fact that we spent a goodly portion of our time on arcane philosophical matters, every remark each of us made brought forth cheers from one part of the audience or another. At one point, denying that Germany was as sealed off from outside influences as Hannah maintained, I said that she even exaggerated the extent to which the Nazi concentration camps—the "laboratories" of totalitarianism, as she had often called

---

*Trotsky, of course, was Jewish himself, his real name being Bronstein. Playing on this fact in commenting on the anti-Semitism of the Soviet regime, a rabbi in Russia once quipped that "the Trotskys make the revolutions and the Bronsteins pay the bill." But a few years ago history reached into Trotsky's grave to make *him* pay the bill for his anti-Zionism when a great-grandson of his not only emigrated to Israel but joined an ultra-Orthodox community on the West Bank. The young man thus turned the radical gene in his blood to uses that would undoubtedly have horrified the ancestor from whom he had inherited it.

them—succeeded in creating a fully realized totalitarian reality. For this I was treated to a prolonged ovation. But then she got at least as great a hand when she responded that my remark could only have been made by a person who had never been in a concentration camp or even "in the neighborhood of a concentration camp."

Here I bit my tongue, hard, because I instinctively sensed that if I let fly with the sarcastic riposte that was on the tip of it, Hannah would never forgive me. Along with many (or, rather, most) émigré German Jewish intellectuals, Hannah could never stop regarding America as culturally inferior to the land of her birth. Not even the fact that Germany had given rise to Nazism overrode this feeling. On the contrary, since Nazism in the view of these intellectuals (a view of which *The Origins of Totalitarianism* represented the most powerful expression) was a product of forces common to the modern world in general rather than (as other theories held) peculiar to Germany, it could even be interpreted in a weird sense as a mark of Germany's advanced cultural development. Not that any of them, and least of all Hannah, would ever have put it this way. But some such notion lurked beneath the surface, and it was this that emerged in her remark that day in Maryland.

What I wanted to say in response to that remark was something like this: "It is true that growing up in America, with its superficial culture, has deprived me of the great spiritual and intellectual advantages Miss Arendt derived from living in a society that produced concentration camps, but one does the best one can."* Instead, I remained silent, forfeiting a chance to deal her a crushing blow and thereby

---

*This persistent belief in the superiority of German culture, despite Nazism but also in a certain sense because of it, did not apply to America alone. One night Hannah came to our apartment for a small dinner party at which the only other guest was a fellow German Jewish intellectual who had found refuge in England and was now visiting New York from London. At a certain moment in the conversation, when the name of John Locke came up, Hannah turned to him and said, "Ach, these English, they think they have philosophers," and the two of them shared a chuckle of amusement at the thought. What, after all, was Locke compared with the likes of Heidegger? It did not seem to occur to either of them that there might be some relevance in the fact that Locke and his successors had laid the philosophical basis for a free society while Heidegger had found it consistent with his philosophy to support the Nazis.

proving to be a pushover after all. Judging by how pleased she seemed when we left (and how warmly she complimented me on my performance), she thought she had won the debate, and we parted that day on amiable terms. But things were never the same again. I would run into her once in a while, usually at some large gathering, where we might exchange a bit of casual conversation, and now and then I would even ask her to write something for *Commentary*, but she never did. By the time of her death in 1975, so great had the distance between us grown that I had not been in contact with her at all for a number of years.

If, however, this estrangement began with our differences over things Jewish, it was not over things Jewish that it widened and deepened. A new gap opened up between us after 1965 that had more to do with Communism than with Zionism and that focused on America rather than on Israel.

There were strange paradoxes here. As the author of *The Origins of Totalitarianism*, Hannah had perhaps done more than any single writer to establish the moral equivalence between Nazi Germany and Soviet Russia, thereby supplying the theoretical basis not only for hard anti-Communism but also for exactly the kind of resistance to Communist expansion the United States was mounting through the policy of containment. Furthermore, she held fast to this theory, first when Khrushchev's de-Stalinization policies seemed to contradict it and later when she was attacked by certain members of the academic Left for refusing to make a distinction between Communism, whose fault in their estimation lay in failing to live up to its noble ideals, and Nazism, whose fault supposedly lay in living up all too well to its evil ideals.

Nevertheless, in practice Hannah was curiously suspicious of anti-Communists, between whom and "former Communists" (like her husband) she always drew an obscurely invidious distinction. However, Whittaker Chambers, though also a former Communist, did not benefit from this distinction. In fact, she even went so far as to tell me once that Alger Hiss might well have been framed by the FBI, and when, amazed, I pointed to all the damning evidence against him, including the famous typewriter, she smiled: "But, my dear, don't you know that it's nothing for the secret police to forge a typewriter?"*

In line with this attitude—and understandably ever on the alert for signs of a turn toward fascism in her adopted country—Hannah came to associate herself closely with the "anti-anti-Communists," to whom the McCarthyism of the 1950s seemed a greater menace than Communism itself and who despised such hard anti-Communists within the Family as Sidney Hook and Diana Trilling. By the mid-1960s she had begun moving noticeably to the Left and stayed there for the remaining ten years of her life. In those years she did most of her writing for *The New York Review of Books,* in whose eyes America and not the Soviet Union was the great threat to the peace and freedom of the world. She dismissed the idea (which seemed self-evident to me even when I myself had joined the anti-war movement) that the American intervention in Vietnam had been undertaken as part of the fight against Communist expansionism. She even heaped praises on the disgracefully rosy and idealized portait of North Vietnam, one of the most rigidly Stalinist societies in the world, that Mary McCarthy drew in a series of articles for *The New York Review,* later collected into a book. ("This still and beautiful pastoral of yours. . . . [is] one of the very finest, most marvelous things you have ever done").†

---

*Her own account of this conversation in a letter to Mary McCarthy does not speak well for her accuracy in the reporting of details. "By the way, the Podhoretz kid, for a moment under the misapprehension that I wanted to do a piece on [Hiss's book *In the Court of Public Opinion*]: 'Oh, no, *Commentary* could never afford to take a controversial stand on the Hiss case.' Sic! This one sentence almost persuaded me to do something." What I actually said was not that *Commentary,* of which I was then still an associate editor, could not "afford" such a piece but that it would never publish it. At so early a stage in our relationship, I did not have the courage to add that in this case, unlike the fight over her article about Little Rock, I would have sided against her on the ground that her opinion seemed to me about as much in touch with American realities as the speech Trotsky had once made which began with the immortal salutation: "Workers and peasants of the Bronx!"

†Memories are short, and so I think it might be a good idea to quote a few phrases from Mary's report on North Vietnam. In "glaring contrast to Saigon," she wrote, "Hanoi is clean. . . . The sidewalks are swept, there is no refuse piled up, and a matinal sprinkler truck comes through, washing down the streets"—on which, again in glaring contrast to Saigon, she never observed any prostitutes. Nor did she ever come across "a child with a

Hannah also developed a soft spot for the student radicals of that period—perhaps made even softer by the fact that her Eichmann book was popular among them because its picture of Nazi Germany corresponded with their conception of "Amerika." Worse yet, she herself hovered on the brink of some such idea. At first she interpreted Watergate as "an attempt to abolish the Constitution and the institutions of liberty," and she not only compared the former CIA agent E. Howard Hunt, who had been involved in the affair, with Eichmann but drew an analogy between the men around Nixon and "the men who surrounded and helped Hitler and Stalin." Even after moderating this preposterous and offensive judgment, she continued to insist that "our form of government and the institutions of liberty" were in a severe crisis. Only about six months before her death in 1975, she spelled it all out at length in a piece for *The New York Review*, which, as Nathan Glazer put it in *Commentary*, was notable for echoing "the ordinary liberal or progressive opinion" on every issue of the day.

---

dirty face," and "wherever you go, you are met with smiles, cheers, hand clapping. Passers-by stop and wave to your car on the road." As for the countryside, there "you see the lyrical aspect of the struggle," and there too "children and young people were radiant with health; as far as I could judge, everybody under forty was in peak physical condition." She then went on to describe the murderous Prime Minister Pham Van Dong as "a man of magnetic allure, thin, with deep-set brilliant eyes, crisp short electric gray hair, full rueful lips drawn tight over the teeth. The passion and directness of his delivery matched something fiery, but also melancholy, in those coaly eyes. An emotional, impressionable man, I thought, and at the same time highly intellectual."

Even allowing for Hannah's opposition to the American role in Vietnam and her great devotion to Mary, I still find it hard to comprehend that the author of *The Origins of Totalitarianism* could have brought herself to describe as "marvelous" and "beautiful" sycophantic language that could easily have come from a professional propagandist in the service of this or any other totalitarian regime. Worse yet was her failure to call Mary on the ridicule she heaped on the American prisoners of war whom the North Vietnamese cleaned up and paraded out for her to meet. These men—who we later learned (and as she should have guessed) had been abused and tortured by their Communist captors and who would have been executed if they had so much as hinted at their true condition—seemed to Mary deplorably uncultured, especially as compared with the likes of Pham Van Dong. All they wanted to know from her, she complained, was stuff like how the Chicago Cubs were doing. About this singularly unpastoral part of Mary's disgusting book, Hannah, from her vast knowledge of how totalitarian regimes worked to conceal the truth about themselves (Potemkin villages in the Soviet Union, Theresienstadt among the Nazi camps), had not a word of suspicion to raise.

Meanwhile, as Hannah was moving to the Left, I was traveling in the other direction, even in relation to her own early work. As I have mentioned, after Khrushchev's de-Stalinization speech, I had been seized with doubts about the soundness of the section on the Soviet Union in *The Origins of Totalitarianism,* and I had then expressed them in my article on Hannah's Eichmann book. But as time went on, and as I learned more and more about what was actually still going on in the Soviet Union, these doubts evaporated.

So did the anti-anti-Communist position to which I had been attracted during my own sojourn on the Left from the late 1950s to the late 1960s. By 1970 I had reverted to the hard anti-Communism that Hannah's early work had done more than any other single intellectual influence to instill in me in my younger days, and I had now become a fierce opponent of the anti-Americanism that pervaded the Left and infected her own later writings. Under her tutelage, I had supported the cold war in its first phase as a struggle against Communist totalitarianism that was no less morally noble and no less politically exigent than the war against Nazism had been. Now, when the Soviet Union began taking advantage of the post-Vietnam demoralization of the United States to resume its expansionist thrust, I became a fierce advocate of renewed American resistance and an equally passionate defender of America against its ideological enemies both at home and abroad. As such, I thought that the things Hannah was saying during this period were perfectly described by a remark a friend of hers, the literary critic Erich Heller, had once made in another connection: "When Hannah Arendt put her very great intelligence into the service of an erroneous judgment . . . she was never simply wrong, she exploded into wrongness, with angry sparks flying about."

The irony is that, if other things had been equal, Hannah and I could in those years have found common ground again on the very issue that had first divided us. For while she had attacked Israel in 1956 over the Suez campaign, she acted in the Six Day War of 1967 and the Yom Kippur War of 1973 as though she were as much a believer in the 614th commandment as I was, rallying to Israel's side with anxiety over the dangers and enthusiasm over the victories.

But other things were not equal. Once upon a time I had admired her for being rooted in commonsense reality (the very dimension of life that totalitarianism in her account always tried to abolish). Yet it was precisely because she later lost her grip on that reality that she could fly off into so many erroneous judgments, just as it was because she remained so brilliant that she could seduce herself and others into thinking that these judgments were sound. Which only went to show once again how much I had once overrated the role in intellectual activity of brilliance in general and Hannah Arendt's in particular. But even taking Israel into account and leaving the issue of brilliance aside, we had grown too far apart on too many other important matters for us ever to become friends again. And so we never did.

CHAPTER FIVE

A FOUL-WEATHER FRIEND TO NORMAN MAILER

THE HIGHEST COMPLIMENT I WAS EVER PAID BY Norman Mailer was when he called me a "foul-weather friend." He grinned as he said it, pleased with himself for the wit and felicity of the formulation. I grinned back, both because I shared his own appreciation of the clever way he had put the compliment and because I knew that, having always stood more steadfastly by him in bad times than in good, I richly deserved it. Our friendship started in what was an especially rough period for him, and it slowly and gradually began to unravel when he was once again riding high. I, on the other hand, was in big trouble at that point, and he did not prove to be a foul-weather friend to me. But there was more—much more—to the story than that, and I would be false to the reality of it if I created the impression that the rise and fall of our friendship was, to borrow from Jay Gatsby, "merely personal."

By the time I first met him at Lillian Hellman's in the late 1950s, Mailer* had written three novels and a few sections of what would

---

*I more often called him that than Norman, feeling self-conscious about our shared first name. He had no such feeling and always called me Norman.

turn out to be an abortive fourth. The first, *The Naked and the Dead,* had been a sensation upon its publication in 1948, propelling him at age twenty-five into bestsellerdom and celebrityhood as the author of what the popular press took to be "the best and most definitive novel about World War II." Yet—and here is one large measure of how much things would change in the decades ahead—the very success of that book made Mailer as suspect in the eyes of the serious critical community as Lillian's plays had made her.*

From what I learned when I came to know him about ten years later, Mailer was shocked to discover that there was a literary world out there whose leading lights were at best dismissive and at worst contemptuous of best-selling books and the people who wrote them. A graduate of Harvard he may have been, but somehow he had managed to get through four years in Cambridge without really coming to understand that in the America of the late 1940s all culture was divided into three parts: highbrow, middlebrow, and lowbrow; that the highbrows more or less automatically dismissed any best-selling novel as middlebrow or lowbrow and therefore beneath notice; and that this tiny and obscure minority, powerless to command or disburse the worldly rewards of big money and national fame, nevertheless mysteriously enjoyed a virtual monopoly over the power to confer true literary status.

There were, to be sure, exceptions to the rule that commercial success debarred a writer from highbrow acceptance or acclaim, the main one being Mailer's god Ernest Hemingway, whose career had probably been responsible for misleading him on these matters. But even Hemingway was only a partial exception, since he had begun by publishing in what had once been called "little magazines" and had established himself as an important experimental writer (with an imprimatur from one of the cardinals of the avant-garde church, Gertrude Stein herself) by the time he broke through to commercial success. Mailer, by contrast, hit it big with no such prior credentials.

To make matters worse, he did so with a novel written straight out of the naturalist tradition against which the avant-garde and the

---

*Their own friendship began when she tried to adapt *The Naked and the Dead* to the stage. The project failed, but they remained on good terms.

highbrow critics who supported it had been setting their faces for some three decades. Even the few departures Mailer risked from traditional naturalism in *The Naked and the Dead* consisted of techniques borrowed from John Dos Passos, a novelist whose prestige among highbrows, very high though it had been when his magnum opus *U.S.A.* was completed in the 1930s, was already fading and who was soon to be relegated to almost complete critical obscurity. The fall of Dos Passos no doubt had more to do with his move from the radical Left to the libertarian Right than with the alleged decline of his later novels as works of art—not that anyone would admit this at a time when political considerations were not supposed to influence aesthetic judgment. Mailer, by sharp contrast, was emphatically on the Left, but from the point of view of the highbrows, his leftism, like Lillian's, was of the wrong—that is, Stalinist—variety (though unlike her, he was only a fellow-traveler).

In the essay about him on which I had been working when we first met,* here is how I described the politics behind *The Naked and the Dead:*

> In 1948 Mailer—who was shortly to become a leading figure in Henry Wallace's campaign for the Presidency—subscribed to the notion that our postwar difficulties with Russia were the sole responsibility of American capitalism. We had gone to war against Hitler not because the American ruling class was anti-fascist, but because Hitler had shown himself unwilling to play the capitalist game according to the rules, and the next step was to dispose of Russia, the only remaining obstacle on the road to total power. World War II, then, was the first phase of a more ambitious operation, while the army had been used as a laboratory of fascism, a preview of the kind of society that the American ruling class was preparing for the future.

To say it yet again, such blatantly Stalinist views had long been politically unacceptable in highbrow literary circles—just as unacceptable as the middlebrow literary genre through which Mailer put them forward. In fact, there were critics who saw middlebrowism itself as

---

*This was the same essay that would appear in *Partisan Review* in 1959 under the title "Norman Mailer: The Embattled Vision" and would then be reprinted in 1964 in *Doings and Undoings.*

one of the aesthetic faces of Stalinism. Thus, Robert Warshow, writing in *Commentary* a year before *The Naked and the Dead* appeared, drew a direct line between Stalinism and "the mass culture of the educated classes—the culture of the 'middlebrow.'" And without making the connection explicit, Dwight Macdonald, who would later become Mailer's friend and champion, first wrote a devastating exposé of Henry Wallace as a dupe of the Communists and then followed it up a few years later with an equally devastating assault on middlebrowism (or, as he renamed it, "midcult").

Oddly enough, not even in all the hundreds (or was it thousands?) of hours we spent talking after we became intimate friends did I ever ask Mailer when he first fully understood the importance of the highbrow literary community and, in particular, of *Partisan Review.* Nor did I ever find out whether the radical change he went through, both as a novelist and in his political orientation, in the three years between the publication of *The Naked and the Dead* and the appearance of his second novel, *Barbary Shore,* had anything to do with his newfound determination to win the highbrows over even, if necessary, at the expense of another popular success. There is good reason to believe that the influence over him of Jean Malaquais, a Trotskyist who became his French translator and close friend, played a serious part here. Yet my own guess is that in abandoning both the naturalism and the Stalinism of *The Naked and the Dead* and producing, in *Barbary Shore,* a Kafkaesque allegory in celebration of Trotskyism he was making a bid (whether conscious or half-conscious or unconscious I still cannot say) for highbrow approval.

But if that was what he was up to, he miscalculated badly. *Barbary Shore* was a flop both with the general public, for whom it was too obscure, and with the highbrow critics, who paid it very little attention. The highbrows ignored it partly because he had already been written off as just another middlebrow, and perhaps also because, even though he had lost (or abandoned) his popular touch, he still remained behind the high-culture curve. By 1951, the modernism of *Barbary Shore* was beginning to seem as dated as the naturalism of *The Naked and the Dead.* As for Mailer's politics, from the point of view of the highbrows, becoming a follower of Trotsky was certainly an improvement over being a Stalinist fellow-traveler, but Trotskyism too seemed old hat by 1951. (As my wife paraphrased the review William Barrett wrote for *Partisan Review* of *Barbary Shore,* "Oh, ho hum, now Mailer's taking up *this* stuff.") For this was a time when the highbrow literary world, with a few lonely exceptions, had grown disaffected with revolutionary socialism of whatever coloration. As such, it was in the process of laying a newly possessive claim to "our country and our culture," as the editors of *Partisan Review* entitled the symposium they ran in 1952, in which the changing attitude of their community toward these matters was most saliently registered.

On the other hand, the fact that Mailer was invited to participate in that very symposium meant that *Barbary Shore* had at least made him more of a figure to be reckoned with than before. William Phillips, the co-editor of *Partisan Review,* later admitted that Mailer's inclusion was "a political act" both on the magazine's part and on Mailer's, signifying that he had now become "part of our community"; and Mailer himself said, "In a funny way, the symposium was my coming out."

But being Norman Mailer, he came out swinging. In his contribution, he announced that he was shocked by the assumptions of the symposium, and he scolded the editors of *Partisan Review,* as well as many older novelists (he specifically mentioned Hemingway, Dos Passos, James T. Farrell, William Faulkner, and John Steinbeck) for having "traveled from alienation to varying degrees of acceptance, if not outright proselytizing, for the American Century." There was deliberate provocation, and even a touch of offensiveness, in Mailer's reference to the "the American Century," a term which the head of Time, Inc., Henry Luce, had coined a few years earlier in a famously triumphalist editorial in *Life* magazine. In using this term, Mailer was all but explicitly charging that the writers he named had at the very least associated themselves with, and at the very worst had sold out to, what he regarded as the true and most powerful enemy of everything they had traditionally stood for both in culture and in politics. But this stubborn stance of opposition to American society did not mean that Mailer was destined to remain a Trotskyist or any other kind of Marxist. On the contrary, having moved from Stalinism to Trotskyism, like the editors of *Partisan Review* long before him, he would soon go trailing after them again, this time into a repudiation of Marxism in particular and ideological thinking in general.

In taking this step, however, Mailer embarked on a very different road from the one the ex-Communists and former Trotskyists of *Partisan Review* were now on. So far as most of them were concerned, Marxism, in prophesying the doom of capitalism in the West and the ensuing triumph of a socialist revolution led by an aroused and mobilized working class, had shown itself to be a faulty guide to the future. For here we were in peacetime, when capitalism, which in the view of the Marxists had survived the Great Depression of the 1930s only through being placed on an artificial life-support system by the economic needs of the war, was finally supposed to experience its temporarily delayed collapse. Yet with the plug now pulled, this supposedly moribund system was showing even greater vitality than before. Meanwhile, Marx's revolutionary dreams had turned into a totalitarian nightmare in Russia, and the workers of America, the most advanced of the capitalist countries, were obdurately refusing to play their prescribed role in the Marxist scenario. Instead of rising up in revolt against their exploiters and oppressors, they were expressing great satisfaction with a system that was beginning to realize *their* dreams of prosperity and even of what the economist John Kenneth Galbraith would later famously denounce as "affluence."

This was very far from Mailer's take on the failure of the Marxist revolution, as he made clear in his notorious essay "The White Negro." Like Hannah Arendt's "Reflections on Little Rock," and just as improbably, it appeared in the socialist magazine *Dissent*, whose editor, Irving Howe (himself an ex-Trotskyist who still kept faith with elements of Marxist theory), had evidently decided on the basis of the *Partisan Review* symposium that Mailer could be a useful ally in the struggle to revive the waning influence of socialism among the intellectuals. But, if so, Howe, as he eventually discovered, had Mailer all wrong.* In "The White Negro," Mailer spoke of Marxist theory with respect, but he declared that it had failed "in application" because it

---

*Howe was, he later said, "delighted" to publish "The White Negro," but "after a while some of the editorial staff [of *Dissent*] began to sense that there was going to be a divergence. It wasn't yet totally clear, but the feeling was that what Norman was doing didn't have much political significance." The wonder is that this "divergence" was not already obvious to Howe and his colleagues in "The White Negro" itself.

had been "an expression of the scientific narcissism we inherited from the nineteenth century" and had been motivated by "the rational mania that consciousness could stifle instinct."

For Mailer the alternative was not some form of liberalism (as with Lionel Trilling) or democratic socialism (as with Irving Howe) or anarchism (as with Paul Goodman). It was "Hip," which Mailer rather pretentiously described as the American form of existentialism. In the rise of the hipster (who served in this new theory as a kind of substitute for Marx's proletariat), Mailer detected "the first wind of a second revolution in this century, moving not forward toward action and more rational equitable distribution, but backward toward being and the secrets of human energy."

This "second revolution" would not involve political action or the mobilization of masses; it would come about through the pursuit of immediate gratification that was the hipster's only *raison d'être* and that Mailer saw as the new wave of the future. Never mind that such a pursuit seemed trivial and was moreover disreputable in the eyes of virtually every moral philosopher from Aristotle to John Dewey: Mailer still cavalierly put himself through many intellectual contortions to ascribe a huge metaphysical significance to it. But the real proof of the theory was supposed to be furnished not by his essay but by his fiction, beginning with his Hollywood novel, *The Deer Park*, which appeared just before the "The White Negro" in 1956. *The Deer Park* was a better book than *Barbary Shore*, but it fell very far short indeed of the enormous claims Mailer made for it, and though it fared better than its immediate predecessor with both the critics and the public, he was left feeling frustrated and disappointed.

He then decided that something more daring and more ambitious was needed to fulfill his new vision, and he embarked on the production of "the proper book of an outlaw." So huge a project was this that it would, he thought, take him ten years to complete. Furthermore, resorting characteristically to a sports metaphor (though boxing rather than baseball was the sport he usually favored whenever he "got into the ring" with other novelists), he announced that it would represent "the longest ball ever to go up into the accelerated hurricane air of our American letters." This would be "a novel which Dostoyevsky and Marx; Joyce and Freud; Stendhal, Tolstoy, Proust and Spengler; Faulkner, and even old moldering Hemingway might come to read, for it would carry what they had to tell another part of the way."

All that ever came of this grandiose project, however, was two self-contained fragments. One of them, "The Time of Her Time," caused a furor because of its very graphic erotic passages (culminating in the achievement of the heroine's first orgasm, when she is forcibly buggered by the hero, with both the active and passive parts of this great event treated with tremendous portentousness by Mailer). The other, "Advertisements for Myself on the Way Out,"* fell almost completely flat in spite of the fact that it was accepted for publication by *Partisan Review* and might on that account alone have attracted more attention among the highbrows than it did.

It was shortly after the appearance of "Advertisements," and only a week or so before we first met, that I finished an early draft of my essay on Mailer. Having heard both Philip Rahv and William Phillips speak disparagingly of his work, I had been surprised by their willingness to run "Advertisements," and assuming that they had changed their minds about him, I thought they would now also be glad to publish my piece. But when I sent it to them some weeks later, they seemed reluctant to do so, and only agreed after chiding me for taking him too seriously. Phillips. "Rahv and I had reservations about Podhoretz's essay, but the situation was complicated by the fact that Rahv didn't like anybody praised too much. . . . We asked for changes, but we always asked for changes; the particular changes were necessary to mute his praise for Norman."†

Up to that point, Mailer had every reason to think of me as a

---

*Not to be confused with his autobiographical book *Advertisements for Myself* (1959), in which this "prologue" to the long novel-in-progress was reprinted.

†Except where otherwise indicated, the quotations in this chapter (including the one from Irving Howe in a footnote above) all come from Peter Manso's *Mailer: His Life and Times* (1985), a compilation of interviews with Mailer and practically everyone who ever knew or had anything to do with him, myself among them.

literary and ideological enemy. I had never reviewed or otherwise written about any of his novels before, but I had taken a very hard swipe in print at his celebration of the hipster ("The White Negro" of his title) and of what Mailer himself described as the hipster's psychopathic personality. Like many early readers of "The White Negro," I was fascinated by the sheer intellectual and moral brazenness it displayed, but I was also disturbed by it. I knew that Mailer was not connected either personally or in his literary style and manner with writers like Jack Kerouac and Allen Ginsberg, and yet in their "beatniks" and his hipsters I saw the same pernicious cultural and political implications, and I spelled them out in my attack on the Beats in "The Know-Nothing Bohemians."

In the concluding section of that piece, I quoted Mailer's suggestion about the "second revolution" that would move "backward toward being and the secrets of human energy." Without quite saying it in so many words, I in turn suggested that this kind of talk was reminiscent of fascism ("History, after all—and especially the history of modern times—teaches that there is a close connection between ideologies of primitive vitalism and a willingness to look upon cruelty and blood-letting with complacency, if not downright enthusiasm"). I then went on to charge flat out that the spirit of hipsterism was very close to that of the Beat Generation and that it was this same spirit which animated the "young savages in leather jackets" who had been running amok in recent years with their switchblades and zip guns.

What, I wondered, did Mailer think of those "wretched kids" who were responsible for a veritable epidemic of violent juvenile crime (or "delinquency" in the parlance of the social workers of the 1950s) that seemed to emerge out of sheer malignancy disconnected from the usual motives of robbery or revenge? What did he think of the gang that had stoned a nine-year-old boy to death in Central Park in broad daylight a few months earlier or the one that had set fire to an old man drowsing on a bench near the Brooklyn waterfront one summer's day or the one that had pounced on a crippled child and orgiastically stabbed him over and over again even after he was already dead? Was that what he meant by the liberation of instinct and the mysteries of being? There were, I said, grounds for thinking so, as the following passage from "The White Negro" demonstrated:

> It can of course be suggested that it takes little courage for two strong eighteen-year-old hoodlums, let us say, to beat in the brains of a candy-store keeper. . . . Still, courage of a sort is necessary, for one murders not only a weak fifty-year-old man but an institution as well, one violates private property, one enters into a new relation with the police and introduces a dangerous element into one's life. The hood-lum is therefore daring the unknown.

I called this one of the most "morally gruesome ideas" I had ever come across and a clear indication of where "the ideology of hipster-ism" could lead.

In spite of these powerful misgivings, "The White Negro" had aroused my curiosity about Mailer's novels, which I had (youthful highbrow snob that I was) never bothered reading before. Yet even if I had not been propelled by "The White Negro" into reading them now, I would have found it necessary to do so anyway: I had been toy-ing with the idea of undertaking a book about the postwar American novel that would go beyond John W. Aldridge's *After the Lost Generation* of 1951, and in any such book a consideration of Mailer's work would have to be included. And so I went carefully through the three he had so far published and astonished myself by concluding, as I would soon put it in my essay (intended as a chapter of the book I now was more than ever determined to write), that he was "a major novelist in the making."

Unaware of what I had in the works about him, Mailer eyed me with a leer that mixed menace with irony when we encountered each other in Lillian Hellman's living room, and he immediately assumed the boxer's crouch that I was to learn he loved to affect whenever an argument of any kind threatened to erupt. This was the first time he had ever seen me in the flesh, but I had seen him once before, when he was the fea-tured speaker at the rally in support of Henry Wallace's campaign for the presidency that was held on the Columbia campus in 1948; I was then eighteen and he was twenty-five. A newly minted celebrity and still inexperienced as a speaker, he did such a terrible job (as he would so often do even after a thousand performances on public platforms) that if not for the inclusion on the program of the veteran Communist folksinger Pete Seeger, the occasion would have been a total flop. Looking him over now, I noticed that the skinny young man of 1948 had in the ensuing years gained a fair amount of weight, along with a commensurate increase in self-assertiveness. All traces of the nervousness and the diffidence that had tied his tongue at the Wallace rally seemed to have been replaced by an insistent and dominating presence.

If I had not been armed with the secret of my forthcoming article, I would almost certainly have tried to steer clear of Mailer that evening. The reason was that at a very early stage in my career as a critic, and even before my night with Allen Ginsberg and Jack Kerouac, I had already discovered how unpleasant a face-to-face confrontation could be even with the friends of an author whose work I had panned, let alone with the author himself. Back in 1953, for instance, I had written (for *Commentary*) one of the few negative reviews of Saul Bellow's novel *The Adventures of Augie March,* and though I was lucky enough not to meet Bellow himself until many years later (by which point he had still not forgiven me, and never really would), I did have the misfortune shortly after the piece had appeared to run into the poet John Berryman, who was one of Bellow's most ardent boosters. Staggering drunkenly over to me at a big party in the apartment of William Phillips, he snarled, "We'll get you for that review if it takes ten years."*

In the case of Bernard Malamud, with a rather critical review of whose first novel, *The Natural,* I made my debut in *Commentary,* also in 1953, things turned out differently. When I met him a bit later, he was extremely cold, but as soon as he realized that I was a great ad-

---

*Not that Bellow himself remained silent. When my editor, Robert Warshow, who disagreed with my judgment of the book, sent a galley of the review to Bellow, he shot back a long letter, with copies to about a dozen people, denouncing "Your young Mr. P.," dismissing Warshow's avowal of admiration for the book, and ending with an admonition from Cromwell: "I beseech you in the bowels of Christ, think it possible you may be mistaken."

mirer of his short stories, he relented a bit; and when I subsequently expressed this admiration publicly in an article in *Partisan Review,* our relations became very cordial. (Until, that is, he too turned into an ex-friend when I broke ranks in the late 1960s with the Left. Malamud was no leftist himself and was less interested in ideological politics of any kind than any writer I knew, but he had a keen sense of *literary* politics and must have felt—accurately—that maintaining an association with me after I had become a *persona non grata* within the literary community would do his career no good.)

Yet even if I had tried to avoid Mailer that night at Lillian's, it would have availed me naught. Having figured out who I was even before we were introduced, he accosted me—skipping the social pleasantries and getting right down to business—with the inevitable charge of having misunderstood and misrepresented him. I have no clear memory of what I said in my own defense, but I do remember cutting the argument short by telling him that I was working on a long article about his whole body of work and that maybe he ought to hold his fire until he had had a chance to read it. He snorted something to the effect that there was no need for him to wait since he already had a pretty good idea of what a piece by me about him would say. "You wanna bet?" I grinned, resorting to the lingo of the Brooklyn streets from which we both came. "I'll bet you ten bucks."

Now, Brooklyn once was (and possibly still is) a real place with a distinctive culture of its own that left its mark on everyone who grew up there. Indeed, throughout my entire life, whenever I have found myself developing an instant rapport with someone I have just met, it usually turns out that he (or she) also stemmed from Brooklyn. So it was with Mailer. He was from Crown Heights, an economic step up from the Brownsville of my youth but governed by exactly the same street culture, and we had even attended the same high school. Like me, and practically every Brooklyn boy I had ever known, he was direct and pugnacious and immensely preoccupied with the issue of manly courage.

This "macho" obsession in Mailer has often been attributed to the influence of Hemingway, but it was much more the product of the Brooklyn boy's code of honor and his terror of being thought a "sissy." In Mailer's particular case, the "sissy" problem was aggravated by his reputation in adolescence as being coddled and overprotected by his mother. According to one of his childhood friends: "If you didn't play ball, you were done for. . . . [But] Norman wasn't allowed to play because his mother was afraid he'd be hurt." According to another boyhood friend:

> There was this feeling that he was more subject to doing what his parents said. None of us obeyed our parents; he did. . . . He seemed to be on a shorter leash, more obedient, kind of quiet. . . . In those days none of the kids had *any* manners. Norm had manners, and he was different from the rest of us, who were like hooligans, real terrors. . . . I never saw Norm in a fistfight, even though we'd fight among ourselves.

Mailer would spend the rest of his life overcoming the stigma of this reputation as a "nice Jewish boy" by doing as an adult all the hooliganish things he had failed to do in childhood and adolescence.

Be that as it may, Mailer was certainly recognizable as a Brooklynite at our first meeting that night. Accepting my offer of a bet, and treating it as a poker player's bluff, Mailer proceeded to speculate on the substance of my article, which, as I recall, took the form of a parody of the literary prissiness he associated with highbrow critics like me. But I refused to rise to the bait. "Just wait," I said, and drifted away to talk to someone else as his (second) wife, Adele, a dark and very sexy beauty who had been standing by silently during our conversation, flashed me a look that was challengingly flirtatious with a touch of contempt thrown in. "I'll make you a bet too," it said. "I'll bet you don't have the guts to take me on." (She was right, as would be definitively confirmed some years later when, after a particularly vicious spat with him, she would all but openly dare me to go to bed with her.)

Notwithstanding the tension between Mailer and me on that first meeting, we actually hit it off well, and when I left Lillian's party that night, I had the feeling that I would be hearing from him again. Sure enough, in the following weeks we saw each other several times, the initiative usually coming from him. Then, when I finally showed him the galleys of my essay, he was so pleased by it and so happy that it would be coming out in *Partisan Review* that it cemented a friendship already growing deep.

What Mailer liked most was arguing with me about ideas, especially his own ideas, which I continued to find wrongheaded and often foolish even after I had come to admire the power and boldness of his writing. To me this Harvard graduate seemed strangely uneducated (what on earth had they taught him there?), sounding like one of those autodidacts who used to roam around Greenwich Village spouting their big and usually conspiratorial theories. It was no secret to him that this was how I felt, but he never seemed bothered by it in the slightest: he just kept trying to persuade me that I was being too "establishment," too rigid and conventional, in my thinking.

Besides, for all my criticisms of his ideas, he knew that I regarded him as a man who had to go his own way and discover things for himself, and that this necessity was one of the engines of his talent as a novelist. I was someone who could learn from books or from the experience and mistakes of others, but not Mailer: if it did not register directly on his own pulses and in his own nervous system, it was not for him. He was absolutely determined to do everything for himself, to invent the world anew, and because I thought this admirable and courageous, I was careful not to judge him too quickly.

On the other hand, I could not abide his antics: the arm-wrestling contests to which he was always challenging everyone around him, the sudden putting on of accents (especially Irish or Southern) for no immmediately discernible reason, the readiness to get into fist fights. (A striking instance came at the famous masked ball Truman Capote threw at the Plaza Hotel in New York in 1965 to celebrate the great triumph he was then enjoying over his "non-fiction novel," *In Cold Blood.* I was sitting at a table with Lillian Hellman and McGeorge Bundy, the former Harvard dean who was now Lyndon Johnson's national security adviser, when Mailer, clearly in his cups, came by. I introduced him to Bundy, who was gracious in his patrician way, but within minutes Mailer invited him outside to settle their differences over Vietnam. When Bundy, declining this invitation to a fistfight, told him not to be so childish, Mailer spat back, "I paid you too much respect.")

Yet he was very careful never to lapse into this kind of thing when we were alone together, perhaps because he, nothing if not perceptive, realized that I would never tolerate it and that it might drive me away. Thanks in part to this self-restraint, our friendship was relaxed, not competitive.* We were drinking buddies, we exchanged intimate confidences, and we generally read each other's writings hot off the typewriter, sometimes aloud. Though I was not exactly the "intellectual conscience" to him that Edmund Wilson had been to F. Scott Fitzgerald in the 1920s, Mailer did pay close attention both to what I said in conversation and to my critical writings (the title he wanted me to give my first collection was *Hanging Judge* but I thought it the better part of prudence to use *Doings and Undoings* instead), and in this way I did occasionally serve as a brake on some of his more extreme flights of fancy.

Moreover, as the critic who had in effect brought him into the Family and given him the imprimatur of what the novelist Terry Southern memorably called the "quality lit biz,"† I felt a certain proprietary interest in Mailer—he was my tiger. Not only that, but I believed something larger was riding on his back. I once ventured the proposition that there was a sense in which the validity of a whole phase of American experience—the move in the 1950s away from "alienation" and toward self-acceptance as an American—was felt to hang on the question of whether or not Saul Bellow, who was in effect enacting that development in his work, would turn out to be a great

---

*For whatever it may be worth, Mailer's longtime secretary Ann Barry saw it differently: "There seemed to be a kind of jousting between them, intellectual jousting. Competitive. Little ripples. Posturing, rooster behavior. Not only intellectual, though, but mixed up with the personal. I knew the two Normans were very close, and they would do funny things together. . . . They'd get involved in little projects, and there'd be lots of telephone calls, arguments about someone misunderstanding or not having the right interpretation or not taking the correct line. . . . Podhoretz was considered a heavy hitter in those days, and I got the sense that Norman considered him in no way his inferior. My impression was that their relationship had to do with discussing the nature of what is a Jew, what is a radical, what is a political person, a writer, an artist."

†The cartoonist Jules Feiffer put the same point in somewhat less colorful terms: "Norman Podhoretz. . . . played a very important role for Mailer in terms of the literary community; he legitimized him, made him okay to the *Partisan Review* crowd because Mailer was the outlaw. Podhoretz had his credentials as a Trillingite, and then, of course, he wrote about Mailer and was one of the first to do so."

novelist. In this same sense, Mailer was the anti-Bellow, and the viability of the new radicalism, which he was testing out in *his* work, might conversely depend on whether *he* would turn out to be a great novelist.

Mailer's antics apart, there were two other problems between us. One was his entourage. Like many famous people, Mailer liked to surround himself with a crowd of courtiers, many of whom had nothing to recommend them that I could see other than their worshipful attitude toward him. A few of them I grew to like well enough—Roger Donoghue, an ex-boxer turned beer salesman; Mickey Knox, a blacklisted minor actor; Bernard Farbar, a magazine editor and aspiring writer. But even in the company of these, Mailer was always at his worst, and with the other hangers-on, who came and went and sometimes stayed, he could be positively intolerable—posing, showing off, bumping heads (another of his favorite sports), bullying, ordering about, and, underneath it all, flattering.

The flattering was especially in evidence with women, not only or even primarily as a means of seduction but mainly as a way of romanticizing and thereby inflating the significance of everything that came into his life. He would inform some perfectly ordinary and uninteresting girl that she could have been a great madam running the best whorehouse in town or that she had it in her to be a brilliant dominatrix, and once the initial shock wore off, she would be delighted. Or he might with similar effect tell some equally vacuous young man that he was a general at heart or a bullfighter or that he had the evil makings of a corporate president.

Mailer's wives especially got this kind of treatment. For example, he decided that Adele (who was born in Cuba and had Peruvian roots but came to Brooklyn at a very young age and grew up there) was a primitive Indian with passions to match, and he encouraged—or, rather, forced—her to live up to that image. One of her close friends described it well:

> [Norman] creates a person, and if the person subjects himself, if the person is vulnerable to that, he or she accepts it. . . . The idea that

Latin people are any more passionate or sexual than Jews is not so, of course, but, still, it was like he was doing an investigation of this kind of passion, something that he was going to practice—practice the hundred ways in which he and Adele could have a fight.

I think I must have witnessed at least a dozen or two of these "hundred ways" both with Adele and several of the wives who followed her, and it was very hard to stomach. Almost as hard to take was the spectacle of Mailer surrounded by his mostly raunchy court, and I tried as best I could to avoid seeing him in those circumstances and to meet him alone instead.

The other big problem was drugs. As I have already made clear in connection with Allen Ginsberg, I was a heavy drinker in those days, but I had no use for drugs. I was, quite simply, frightened by hard drugs like heroin, and even marijuana seemed dangerous to me. As an adolescent with an older friend who was connected to the jazz world on Fifty-second Street, I had tried pot and disliked it. I was also put off by the mystique that came to surround it in the 1950s and which Mailer totally bought. In later years, marijuana would become so common that the kind of talk then circulating about its powers to expand consciousness and introduce the mind into new realms of being would seem overheated. So too would the solemnity surrounding its use.

Mailer was always trying to turn me on to pot—for my own good, of course—and one night at a party in the Greenwich Village apartment he and Adele had recently rented, I gave in. The scene in retrospect looks even more ridiculous than it struck me at the time, with a dozen or so people sitting in a circle, passing a joint around, and inhaling it by turns with the reverence of devout Catholic communicants taking the Eucharist. In contrast to the loosening of tongues that drinking customarily caused, everyone in this circle communed only with himself and no one spoke (leading me to remark later that if pot were ever legalized it would never replace liquor at weddings and *bar mitzvahs*). Suddenly, the girlfriend of a well-known actor (who happened to be starring around that time in a play by Jack Gelber celebrating the glories of heroin) started to throw up all over the place. Yet not even this party-pooping accident disrupted the religious tone of the gathering. Everyone continued to sit in place privately listening—or maybe just pretending to listen—to the music of the spheres through the invisible headphones with which a puff or two had miraculously equipped them. As for me, there was no music of the spheres. All I got was a slight buzz in the head and an unpleasant feeling in the stomach. The next day Mailer scolded me for resisting and thereby allowing the "establishment" side of my character to beat down the radical in me. Very likely he was right. Subsequently, I made two other conscientious but equally unsuccessful attempts to overcome my resistance, and that was that for marijuana and me.

The only other experiment I would try with drugs was on Fire Island in the 1960s, when one of Mailer's courtiers (he himself was not present) persuaded me to sniff an amphetamine capsule. The buzz in my head this time was not at all slight, and the dizziness it brought with it did not live up to its advance billing as an extraordinarily pleasant sensation. I seem to remember Mailer teasing me when I told him about this, though he was not a great partisan of amphetamines or hard drugs in general. Down deep I think he was almost as afraid of them as I was. He gave me the impression that he felt obligated to try peyote and perhaps acid, but so far as I know he never used heroin or cocaine.

Then there was sex. If I was put off by Mailer's constant proselytizing for marijuana, I had an entirely different reaction to his even more obsessive preoccupation with sex. Here there was a complication. On the one hand, I thought Mailer made far too much of sex in his writing. By no means did I think sex was unimportant; on the contrary, in some ways I was just as obsessed with it as he was. But not as an *issue*. There was a part of me that resonated to the crack made by a critic (I believe it was Henri Peyre) that French literature was entirely devoted to something that ought to interest a serious person only ten minutes a week. If this criticism could be leveled at any American writer, it was Mailer (though he would later get a lot of competitition from Philip Roth and John Updike). Much as I admired the virtuosic workings of his prose, and much as I was fascinated by the wildly unconventional

workings of his mind, I was embarrassed on his behalf by the apoca-
lyptic significance he attributed to sex in general and to kinky or per-
verted sex in particular. It struck me as callow of him to treat oral sex
as such a big deal in *The Deer Park* or to attribute a veritably metaphysical significance to the act of heterosexual anal penetration in "The
Time of Her Time."

All this on the one hand. On the other hand, if he wrote and even
talked like someone of such limited sexual experience that he lacked
all perspective on it, he was certainly creating a false impression so far
as the experience itself was concerned. By which I mean simply that he
was wildly promiscuous, both in and between marriages (of which he
was to have six). One might describe him as a pioneer of the sexual
revolution to come, except for the fact that, unlike the counterculture
radicals of the 1960s to whom casual sex was the norm, he did not
take sex in action any more lightly than he did on paper. No matter
how many women he might bed, he rarely went in for one-night
stands or anonymous couplings. When Mailer slept with a girl, she
was probably in for more than a physical encounter. Before being sent
on her way, she could expect a lecture, or a scolding, or a dose of advice on how to become better than she thought she was; and, as often
as not, he would arrange to see her again, and then again, and then
again. Combining the skill of a professional juggler with the talents of
a White House scheduler, he could keep a number of affairs going simultaneously for years, some of them even overlapping with his successive marriages. Where he found the energy and the time for all this
while still turning out many pages a day always baffled me. Evidently,
living that way fed rather than drained him.

Although I disdained his ideas about sex, I could not help envying
his practice of it. Here too there was a complication. For while I was
just as much "a nice Jewish boy from Brooklyn" as Mailer was, and an
even more serious student in school, I also had a secret double life (secret from my parents, that is) as a bad street kid. I liked hanging
around with the boys who were, usually with good reason, regarded as
bums by the adults in the neighborhood; I frequented poolrooms
where older bums, hustlers, and petty criminals held court; I got into
fistfights (though never willingly, and only when my terror of being

considered chicken overrode my fear of getting beaten up); and I gambled, betting what little money I had on sports events and often shooting craps on street corners, which occasionally led to a brush with the cops. But what was most important in this context was that I had also been much more sexually precocious than Mailer, having started earlier and having enjoyed an amount of success with girls that was unusual for those days, when "getting laid" as an adolescent really was the big deal Mailer would make of it as an adult (when it no longer was).

I had, however, said goodbye to all that by the time I first met him. At the age of (nearly) twenty-eight, I had been married only for about a year, and I believed strongly in marital fidelity. This belief derived not only from high-minded moral ideas about marriage but also from an ideology rooted in an earlier stage of the sexual revolution of the twentieth century. According to this doctrine, sex was good and also necessary to the health of men and women alike, but promiscuity was not the way to achieve true sexual fulfillment. To be promiscuous was to be stuck in an "infantile" or "immature" stage of development, deprived of the depths of erotic experience that could only be plumbed by marital or monogamous sex.

This was not, as people like the Beats and Mailer himself would later assume, the creed of the "square": it was the reflection of a highly sophisticated sense of life preached in various modalities by thinkers and writers from Sigmund Freud to D. H. Lawrence. Admittedly, it involved its own type of solemnity, its own exaggerations, and its own failures of perspective in relating sex to the rest of life. But those of us who held to it prided ourselves on being more serious about what Lawrence had called "the hard business of human relationships." We were convinced that our kind of sex was more profound and even more exciting (leading, not to put too fine a point on it, to better orgasms) than the superficial bohemian variety that Lawrence had also denounced as "sex in the head."

But of course I was young and the blood was hot and the temptations ever present. Resisting them was at least as hard as the "hard business" of building a good and lasting marriage, and my friendship with Mailer made it even harder. He subverted me by explaining that his own marriage to Adele had "in a funny way" (one of his favorite locutions) been strengthened, not weakened, by his infidelities, allowing him to rid himself of the resentment that he would otherwise have felt at being stifled and imprisoned by her. This was no sophistical trick: Mailer was very fond of my wife, he had great respect for her, and he had no wish to damage our marriage. Nevertheless, he thought that fidelity was yet another element of the "establishment" side of my character that would have to be overcome before I could realize my ambition for greatness, which, as I often told him, was just as burning as his.

I would eventually learn that I was wrong about this: my ambition was not remotely a match for his. But Mailer's ambition for greatness, and the naked frankness with which he expressed and pursued it without worrying about looking bad or actually making a fool of himself, was one of the main sources of my attraction to him. In my essay on him, I had quoted a statement he had made to an interviewer about his own intention to explore, as he put it,

> the possibility that the novel, along with many other art forms, may be growing into something larger rather than something smaller, and the sickness of our times for me has been just this damn thing that everything has been getting smaller and smaller and less and less important. . . . We're all getting so mean and small and petty and ridiculous, and we all live under the threat of extermination.

At this distance it is difficult for me to recapture the thrill I felt at the prospect that the arts and the life they reflected would grow "larger," and the conviction I developed that the road to this happy eventuality could be opened up only by breaking through the constrictions and the limits defined by traditional moral and cultural categories. At the same time, I was convinced that this could only be done by working one's way *through* those categories: merely dismissing them contemptuously, as the intellectually philistine Beat writers were doing, could lead into nothing but sterility and nihilism. If a new moral and cultural radicalism was to be born, it would have to be generated in the world of theory by the likes of Norman O. Brown. In his book *Life Against Death* (whose fame I had helped to spread by introducing it to Lionel Trilling), Brown issued a powerful challenge to Freud's doctrine that human possibilities were inherently and insurmountably limited. But he did so not by arguing, as earlier critics like Karen Horney and Erich Fromm had done, that the master's theories had been valid only, or mainly, for the particular kind of society in which he himself had lived. Disdaining the cheap relativism of such tactics, Brown set out to show that Freud's pessimistic sense of human possibility did not necessarily follow from his analysis of human nature, an analysis Brown accepted as sound in all essential respects. The brilliance of *Life Against Death* lay in the amazingly convincing case Brown was able to build for the consistency of that analysis with his own vision of a life of "polymorphous perversity," a life of play and of complete instinctual and sexual freedom.

Brown's vision, of course, jibed perfectly with Mailer's much less rigorous notion about the implications of the hipster's pursuit of immediate gratification, and it scared me just as much. Even so, it gave a highly respectable theoretical justification to the sexual restlessness I could not help feeling and that Mailer was bent—again for my own good!—on encouraging me to act upon. He was especially keen on getting me to participate in an orgy (this exotic species of sexual experience having become a central element of his new philosophy), and I finally did, though without his help or knowledge.

Under the rationalization that going to an orgy was not, strictly speaking, a form of infidelity, I got entrée into one that consisted entirely of people I had never met before. But I was simply not up to it, and it turned out to be a total and humiliating disaster for me. Yet instead of feeling that Mailer had misled me, I decided that I was simply not good enough to break through my own sorry limitations. Naturally, I told him about it, and he shook his head in amazement. That was not, he said, what he had been talking about. What I had gone to was "a concentration-camp orgy," and I was lucky to have gotten out of there alive.

Some weeks later he invited me to spend an evening with him and one of his longtime girlfriends, who lived in another city and was in town for a few days. She turned out to be a beautiful woman who had actually read and liked my stuff, and the three of us had a very good time together over dinner in a restaurant. Afterward, we repaired to her hotel room for a nightcap. The atmosphere was sexually charged, and I began wondering, with a mouth getting dry, what Mailer was up to when he suddenly excused himself and went into the bathroom. A few minutes later he returned stark naked and directed a very serious look straight into the eyes of his girlfriend. It was as if he had decided to make up for having inadvertently misled me by demonstrating what a proper orgy was like. But his girlfriend, totally unprepared for this turn of events, was not having any of it, and she laughed him off with a witty apology to me.

I must admit that I was more disappointed than relieved. But this was not yet the end of the story. About ten years later, she showed up in New York again, and this time the three of us had lunch rather than dinner together. When it was over, she shooed away Mailer (who took this with so little complaint that I suspected it had been prearranged) and asked me to come up to her hotel room for a drink (by which she of course meant, in the parlance of the period, a "matinée"). Alas, her generous effort to make up for having disappointed me the first time around had come too late, and now it was my turn to say no. Not, God knows, in retaliation but because I had by the early 1970s decided that the radical ideas in the sexual realm with which I had been playing around were no less pernicious than their counterparts in the world of politics and I had now returned for good to my old set of beliefs in marital fidelity and everything that went with it.

But it was not only over drugs and his ideas about sex that Mailer and I had our differences and difficulties. There was also the issue of loyalty. As a "foul-weather friend," I stood up for him when, in the course of a violent fight with Adele toward the end of the big party at which Allen Ginsberg had yelled at me and that I had already left a few hours before, he stabbed her with a penknife, coming within an inch of killing her. They were then living on West Ninety-fourth Street, and we were just a dozen blocks away in a second-floor apartment that faced onto West 106th Street. After the stabbing, Mailer beat it out of his house and rushed up to mine. It was about 4 A.M.

when he stood there under our windows calling out to me, but I was so fast asleep that I never heard him. He then left, and waited until later in the day to telephone and ask me to meet him downtown in a coffee shop near the hospital to which Adele had been taken. Still hiding from the police, he refused to tell me exactly what had happened: if he did, I might have to lie and would then get into trouble myself. But what he mainly wanted was to extract a promise from me that I would do everything in my power to keep them from committing him to an asylum. He would rather go to jail than be institutionalized, he said, because if he were deemed insane his work would never be taken seriously again.

My impression of Mailer's mental condition differed from that of some of our mutual friends, including Diana Trilling, who thought he "needed psychiatric help," and Lillian Hellman, who (at least according to Diana) thought that it was now unsafe to be alone with him.* Unlike them, I did not believe that he was clinically insane, and my opinion was shared by Lionel Trilling, who, Diana later reported, "insisted that it wasn't a clinical situation but a conscious bad act; . . . [that] Norman was testing the limits of evil in himself, that his stabbing of Adele was, so to speak, a Dostoyevskian ploy on Norman's part, to see how far he could go." I also agreed with Mailer that institutionalization would make it easier for people to take his work less seriously. And since, finally, I felt that he should be allowed the right to choose jail over an asylum, and that this acceptance of responsibility was more morally honorable than pleading insanity, I promised to help as much as I could.

There was a strategy session by the Mailer family that Sunday evening at which I was among the few outsiders and where I made the case Mailer had persuaded me to make. Then I met him again the next day in the same downtown coffee shop. There he asked me to accompany him to the hospital, where, after visiting Adele, he would surrender to the police. I too went in to see Adele, who, although

---

*Lillian told me, and also Diana, that Mailer had once tried to break down her bedroom door, which may account for her response to the stabbing. But whether this event, if it actually occurred, took place before the stabbing or after, I cannot recall.

lying there frightened and crying, told me that she had decided not to press charges. Then the police who had been keeping watch over her room arrested him. Probably because he was a celebrity, they were very polite and even allowed me to go along with them all to the station house on 100th Street, where he was booked.*

They then sent him to Bellevue for psychiatric observation, and eventually a deal was struck, whose terms I never learned, that set him free after a couple of weeks. The day he was released he came to our house for lunch. As my wife would later describe the scene:

> He was absolutely himself, very calm, and definitely not tranquilized.
> . . . Norman had always had a "court," and when he got out [of Belle-
> vue] he turned up with the doctor who'd been examining him. . . . The
> doctor had been converted into another courtier.

I have often asked myself whether I did the right thing in acceding to Mailer's request; in a similar situation today, I would almost certainly push for psychiatric help. But in the early 1960s, when electroshock therapy (of which I had a great horror) was the main treatment used, I feared for the effects on Mailer's mind. I was well aware of the streak of craziness in him, but it did not seem to go very deep and for the most part it was under control. I had noticed that Adele had been ragging him all night and that the mood between them was getting very ugly—so much so that the novelist Barbara Probst Solomon, another mutual friend who was there, recalls my telling her that I "didn't like the look of things." Her recollection was accurate. Having been witness to more than my share of nasty scenes between Mailer and Adele, I decided to leave before another one exploded. In any event, my conviction that he was not clinically insane was reinforced by the very fact that he did not blame her for provoking him

---

*Mailer was very good with children (he had three of his own then and would eventually have another six), and mine, who adored him, steadfastly refused to believe that he had stabbed Adele. One of my daughters, then about ten, assured me that she knew who had really done it. "Who?" I asked. "Leonard Lyons," she answered, referring to the gossip columnist of the *New York Post* who had been writing of nothing else for days now. "Leonard Lyons?! What on earth makes you think that?" "Well," she said, "if he didn't do it, how come he knows so much about it?"

into the stabbing, that he took responsibility for it, and that he was ready to go to jail. Which was why I felt so uneasy over his escape from punishment and over my secret fear that he might have dishonored himself by allowing money to change hands to get him off. Still, there was no evidence whatever for this suspicion, and I bent over backward in trying to dismiss it as unworthy. Over the next few months I consistently defended Mailer against most of my Family friends, who did not need him to be institutionalized in order to use the stabbing as a good reason for persisting in their refusal to take his work seriously.

Our friendship accordingly deepened and we saw each other even more often than before. By now I had become the editor of *Commentary*, and I was working very hard in trying to drag the magazine out of the cold-war liberalism in which it had been stuck under Elliot Cohen and to pull it in the leftward direction I myself had already been moving as a critic for the past three years or so.

By mutual agreeement, Mailer did not at first figure in this project. For one thing, we both recognized that he was too wild for a magazine sponsored by the most establishmentarian of all Jewish organizations, the American Jewish Committee. As the editor, I enjoyed complete independence, and I was making such full use of it in articles about both foreign and domestic policy that I was already being subjected by the Trillings and other Family friends to accusations of having become too soft on Communism and too hard on America. But I was simultaneously being careful not to jeopardize the institution for which I was now responsible or my position in it by moving too far too fast in a culturally radical direction. This meant, at a minimum, no four-letter words or overly explicit sexual material whether in stories or in essays.

Confirmation that such prudence was necessary came when, even after I had already been running *Commentary* for nearly five years and after it had been well established as a main intellectual center of the new radicalism, I published an article by the psychoanalyst Leslie H. Farber called "'I'm Sorry, Dear.'" This was perhaps the first serious critique of the sexologists Masters and Johnson, and the moral assumptions behind it were actually quite traditional. Yet because it contained a frank discussion of the female orgasm and a description of a film Masters and Johnson had made in which women were shown masturbating, it caused a great deal of trouble for me with the AJC. One prominent member of my board resigned in protest, and a campaign was launched to get me fired.

But if Mailer at first agreed that it was advisable for him to stay out of *Commentary*, he soon began growing a little resentful about it, as I could tell from the remarks he kept making about how tame the magazine was. Then, all of a sudden, he came to me with a proposal. In Martin Buber's *Tales of the Hasidim*, he had decided that there was, as he would soon write, something in Judaism that called out to him—"a rudimentary sense of clan across the centuries." Mailer had grown up in a "modestly Orthodox, then Conservative" family, had gone to a Hebrew school, and had "passed through the existential rite of a *bar mitzvah*." But none of it had stuck. "I would never say I was not a Jew, but I looked to take no strength from the fact. . . . I left what part of me belonged to Brooklyn and the Jews on the streets of Crown Heights."

Indeed he had. In wiping out every trace in himself of the "nice Jewish boy from Brooklyn," he had done such a good job on the Jewish part that not even I—to whom the "Jidas touch" had once been attributed ("Everything you touch turns to Jewish")—could detect any lingering odor of it in his personality or his behavior. This man, who saw himself as a fearless spiritual adventurer, was apparently fearful of exploring his own spiritual roots, preferring instead the pretense of being an "existential hero" with no ties to the past.*

But now, perhaps proving that I really did have the Jidas touch, Mailer, of all people, came up with a plan to write a monthly column in which he would reprint stories from Buber and then provide his own personal commentaries on them. If this was his way of overcoming my increasingly irksome resistance to his appearance in *Commentary*, it was certainly very cunning. What idea could be more suitable than this for *Commentary*, one of whose purposes from the very beginning had been to arouse the interest of disaffected Jewish writers and

---

*I suspected then, and I am still inclined to think, that this fear had much to do with Mailer's failure to realize his full potential as a novelist.

intellectuals in their own origins? And what could be more quintessentially Jewish than a commentary appended to a text?

Nevertheless, I had grave doubts about whether I wanted such a column. *Commentary* was, after all, a magazine which prided itself on the maintenance of serious intellectual and scholarly standards, and Mailer's ignorance of the material he proposed to elucidate was vast. How could I, the editor of a magazine in whose pages Buber himself and Gershom Scholem, the greatest living scholarly authority on Hasidism, sometimes held forth on the subject, allow what they would rightly have called a total *am-haaretz* (illiterate ignoramus) to poach on their territory?

As we sat drinking together in a bar, I tried saying these things tactfully to Mailer, but it was no soap. For the first time in our relationship, he showed real anger toward me, calling me a "delicate bureaucrat," denouncing my disloyalty, and attributing it to the establishmentarian timidity that would in the end do me in altogether as a writer. With these charges, to which I was very sensitive, he beat me down (which was what I thought he really wanted to do even more than he wanted to write the column). But I salvaged what self-respect I could by insisting successfully against his initially furious refusal that it be a bimonthly feature instead of appearing every single month.

As part of his preparation for launching the column, he wanted to see some Hasidim in the flesh. He therefore asked me to take him to the Yom Kippur eve service at the synagogue of the Lubavitch sect, which, as it happened, was located in Crown Heights, right around the corner from where he himself had grown up. I was a little edgy about this, knowing that something very unpleasant might occur if Mailer failed to behave himself. So before yielding to his request, I made him promise that he would get himself a hat, put on a proper suit, remove any jingling coins or keys from his pockets, and carefully avoid doing anything that might offend the congregation. With a docility unusual for him, he accepted these conditions, and sure enough he arrived at the appointed time (well before sundown, so as not to risk being caught violating the prohibition against travel on the holy day) with a brand-new fedora on his head and all dressed up in a blue suit and white shirt and tie.

The synagogue was located in the basement of the building that served as the headquarters of the Lubavitch movement, and (in the manner of many Orthodox *shtiblach*, or small houses of prayer) it was very unprepossessing. The room was bare except for very heavy wooden benches, and since the holiday had not yet begun, young *yeshiva* students were standing around smoking and dropping their cigarette butts on the floor. To my great relief, nobody paid much attention to us when we came in (the Lubavitcher, unlike other Hasidic sects, were accustomed to being visited by curious fallen-away Jews), and soon the room grew as crowded as the subway at rush hour. Then, without any advance warning, someone shouted in Yiddish that the *rebbe* was coming, and miraculously, like the Red Sea for the Israelites fleeing from Egypt, the crowd immediately parted and the two of us were nearly decapitated as the benches were hoisted up with unbelievable swiftness to make a path for the *rebbe* through the mob.* The services then started without any further ado, but as soon as the opening prayer of *Kol Nidre* was over, Mailer whispered that he had seen enough, and asked if we could leave. Once outside, he pronounced himself delighted by how "mean and tough" the Hasidim were. Their attitude, he said (with considerable shrewdness), was "Out of my way, motherfucker," and he was all for it.

"Responses & Reactions," as we called the column, turned out to be something of an anticlimax, neither creating great curiosity nor provoking a scandal. After six installments, Mailer lost interest, and the column was quietly dropped. Yet even though he had won his point against me, the whole episode left a bad taste in both our mouths—in mine because I had given in to his bullying, in his because I had been less than fully loyal to him.

_____

Soon enough, however, I was to commit what was in Mailer's eyes a much more serious act of disloyalty, and one for which he never ever

_____

*This was the same Menachem Mendel Schneerson who many of his followers would come to believe was the Messiah.

forgave me. Mailer had become obsessed with the Kennedys, and had written a couple of famous pieces for *Esquire* about them. The first, "Superman Comes to the Supermarket," had pleased John F. Kennedy by representing him as a true existential hero (the greatest accolade Mailer could bestow on anyone). But the second, "An Evening with Jackie Kennedy," had offended her deeply (not that that was so hard to do). This bothered Mailer, who wanted very much to be inside the circles of power (though always on his own terms), and I had the impression that he was on the lookout for some way to square things with her.

Some months after the assassination of her husband, Jackie moved to New York, and one Sunday afternoon, as I was sitting around my apartment not doing much of anything, an unexpected call came. It was from my friend Richard Goodwin, who had worked in various capacities for President Kennedy and had somehow managed the trick of staying on in the White House with Lyndon Johnson without being branded as a traitor by the Kennedys (in whose government-in-exile he figured as a leading courtier). Goodwin said that he was in town with someone who wanted to meet me, and asked if they could drop by for a drink. Within minutes, he showed up at my door with a jeans-clad Jackie Kennedy in tow.

She and I had never met before, but we seemed to strike an instant rapport, and at her initiative I soon began seeing her on a fairly regular basis. We often had tea alone together in her apartment on Fifth Avenue, where I would give her the lowdown on the literary world and the New York intellectual community—who was good, who was overrated, who was amusing, who was really brilliant—and she would reciprocate with the dirt about Washington society. She was not in Mary McCarthy's league as a bitchy gossip (who was?), but she did very well in her own seemingly soft style. I enjoyed these exchanges, and she (an extremely good listener) seemed to get a kick out of them too.

After a while, she invited me (along with my wife, whom she generally treated as an invisible presence) to a few of the dinner parties she had started to give. At the first of these which my wife and I attended, I arrived from the West Side in what Jackie considered improper attire, and as she ran her big eyes up and down from my head to my toes, she smiled sweetly and said, "Oh, so you scooted across the park in your little brown suit and your big brown shoes." To which the Brooklyn boy still alive in me replied, "Fuck you, Jackie." She liked that so much that I realized how tired she was of the sycophancy with which everyone treated her and how hungry she had become for people who would stand up to her even though she was the most famous and admired woman in the world. And so we became even faster friends than we already were.

Jackie's dinner parties were always star studded, but they rarely included literary types. Obviously, almost anyone she wished to summon was certain to accept, and yet she was oddly reluctant to invite people she had not already met. The upshot was that she asked Dick Goodwin to ask me to arrange a party in my apartment at which I would introduce her to some of the writers and literary intellectuals I had been telling her about. But Jackie herself then told me that I was not to include Norman Mailer, at whom she was still angry for the article he had done about her. If, however, I knew William Styron, whose novels she admired and whom she had already met, it would be nice to see him again. And so I invited the Styrons, along with about a dozen equally eminent writers whom she had never encountered before.

Nearly twenty years later—in accounting for having joined the general assault that had been launched against *Making It* when he wrote a review article about it for *Partisan Review* after assuring me in private that he had liked the book very much—Mailer would refer back to his "bruised feelings" at not having been invited to this party:

> Norman P. . . . had had these high hopes that my review was going to turn the day, and so it was a bitter disappointment for him, maybe even crueler than all the others. From his point of view I had betrayed him. And from my own point of view I did betray him to a degree. Yet I also felt, This is fair—he betrayed me with the Jackie Kennedy party. Because not only had he not invited me, he invited Bill Styron, who was then my dire rival. Betraying Podhoretz, therefore, wasn't the world's worst thing to me. Maybe it was my way of saying, "Fuck you back."

. . . Deep in me I could've been saying, "All right, now we get you for that Jackie Kennedy party. . . . So it could have been a double cross.

No foul-weather friend, he, that was for sure.*

Still, neither of us was ready or willing to allow his betrayal of me to cause a complete rupture between us. We got together and talked. I was more hurt and bewildered than angry—my own "bruised feelings" easily being a match for the ones he had suffered over the party—and he was more uncomfortable than I had ever seen him before. He simply claimed that he had reread the book, changed his mind about it, and then had to say what he really thought. He would now have to live with the consequences, though he slyly hinted that he had written the piece in the hope of showing me how and why I had "injured a promising book."

Among the consequences he would have to live with was a new idea about him that began taking shape in my head. We were now in a period when radicalism was coming to enjoy even deeper influence and greater power than it had achieved at its most recent high point in the 1930s, and under these circumstances Mailer once again came into his own. Indeed, he was a much bigger figure at that point than he had been as the *wunderkind* author of *The Naked and the Dead*. Most of the novelists of his own generation thought of him as (in his own parlance) the one to beat, and almost all the younger writers looked up to him as the Master. Occasionally his bad-boy antics would still get him into trouble—as when the curtain was rung down on him at the Ninety-second Street Y when he insisted on using obscene language during a reading, or when he had another, though minor, brush with the police (in Provincetown, where he owned a summer home). But the times they were a-changing, and the more outrageously Mailer behaved, the more admiration he brought upon himself from the spreading radical culture of the 1960s.

His writing too was more and more admired. In 1968, inspired perhaps by *In Cold Blood*, Mailer produced *The Armies of the Night*, which

---

*Incidentally, Jackie Kennedy was also so offended by *Making It* that she became an exfriend herself, and later she and Mailer had some sort of reconciliation.

he subtitled (presumably to distinguish it from Capote's "non-fiction novel") "History as a Novel—The Novel as History." *The Armies of the Night* was about an antiwar demonstration in which he had participated, and it won both the Pulitzer Prize and the National Book Award.

It also won my admiration, even though I had already begun the process of breaking ranks with the political perspective from which it was written. Most of it was originally published in *Harper's*, which could pay him far more than I could, but he let me have a section for *Commentary* anyway. I considered the whole book a dazzling literary performance, his best work in any genre since *Advertisements for Myself*, which I had called "one of the great confessional autobiographies of our time." (Since this extravagant judgment appeared in *Making It*, Mailer's attack on that book showed either that he was so incorruptible that not even so gratifying an estimate could buy him off or that his lust for revenge—"a dish," as he had once said, "best eaten cold"—was greater than his appetite for praise. Uncharitably, I incline toward the latter explanation.)

But if I admired *The Armies of the Night*, the fiction Mailer was turning out gave less and less warrant to my old estimate of him as "a major novelist in the making." As far back as 1964, when I was still counting on him to fulfill his early promise, I had been very disappointed in *An American Dream*, and though *Why Are We in Vietnam?* (which came out three years later and was actually about hunting in Alaska and had nothing to do directly with Vietnam) was filled with extraordinarily evocative passages of description, I was disappointed in it as well. Then in 1983, long after it was all over between us, came *Tough Guys Don't Dance*, a mystery set in Provincetown which struck me as positively silly. So, in that same year, did his hugely ambitious novel about ancient Egypt *(Ancient Evenings)*, into which he poured all his obsessions about buggery. This was followed in 1991 by the equally ambitious but perhaps even sillier *Harlot's Ghost*, the novel in which all his wildly romantic paranoia about the CIA was given full play. Both of these books had their wonderful moments, and they both testified to the aging Mailer's continued possession of large reservoirs of creative energy and talent. But so foolish were the ideas behind them that I simply could not take them seriously. And so embarrassed was I by the whole concept of *The Gospel According to the Son* (1997), in which he rewrote the New Testament versions as he imagined Jesus would have told the story, that I could not bring myself even to read it.

The steady stream of nonfictional works that were interpersed between these novels also bore witness to the tremendous stores of literary energy that Mailer still had in reserve. Yet none that followed *The Armies of the Night* lived up to the literary standard of that book. *Miami and the Siege of Chicago* and *St. George and the Godfather* (about the presidential nominating conventions of 1968 and 1972) were well enough written, but they left no lasting impression. As for *A Fire on the Moon* (1970), about the astronauts, it was one of the few actually boring books Mailer ever wrote, and *The Prisoner of Sex* (1971) seemed to me a craven effort to appease the ever more powerful women's movement, whose sensibilities he had offended in so many of his earlier pronouncements about sex, while simultaneously pretending to go against it. He redeemed himself somewhat in 1979 with *The Executioner's Song*, his much-acclaimed nonfiction novel about the murderer Gary Gilmore (for which he won yet another Pulitzer Prize), but I thought it still represented a severe falling-off from *The Armies of the Night*.

The same silliness that wrecked most of Mailer's later novels also showed up in much of his nonfiction of the 1970s and 1980s. In his book on Marilyn Monroe, for example, he uninhibitedly indulged his inveterate weakness for confusing great success or power with intrinsic merit, and in the one he did on the "art" of graffiti he reverted to his old confusion between criminality and creativity.* By the mid-1990s my expectations of getting anything worthwhile out of him had grown so weak I could no more bring myself to read the nonfiction books he produced on Picasso and Lee Harvey Oswald in 1996 than I could bear even to look at his version of the Gospel story, which was published about a year later.

---

*He then acted out the same confusion more dangerously by helping to free a convict writer named Jack Abbott who, no sooner out of jail, went on to commit a murder.

I have searched my soul to find out whether these adverse reactions, which presented themselves to me as disinterested aesthetic judgments, were in reality driven primarily by ideological considerations. Was I, that is, concluding that Mailer had not turned out to be a major novelist only because I had simultaneously been losing my faith in the cultural revolution whose viability I had once thought his work was supposed to confirm? While I cannot dismiss the possibility out of hand, neither can I dismiss the converse possibility: namely, that the weaknesses of his later books actually should be placed in evidence—the special kind of evidence that literature, properly understood and interpreted, provides—against the view of life out of which they emerged and were written to serve.

But whatever may be case about that issue, I am reasonably sure, after conscientiously probing the region surrounding the lowest depths of critical integrity, that not even a minor contribution has been made to my harsh judgment of his later work by a lingering resentment over his article on *Making It.* Nor, to give credit where it is richly due, did Mailer ever stoop to making such an accusation against me. Indeed, though our trust in each other would never quite recover from the blows it had suffered from *Making It,* our friendship remained surprisingly strong for nearly another ten years.

Not, to be sure, as strong as it had been before, when, among many other personal involvements, I had even seen him through the next two wives he married after he and Adele finally divorced. First came Lady Jeanne Campbell, the granddaughter of the great British newspaper publisher Lord Beaverbrook and the daughter of the Duke of Argyle. As if her lineage were not enough to arouse the sexual conquistador in Mailer, the fact that in winning her he would be appropriating the former mistress of the head of Time, Inc. himself, Henry Luce, made her completely irresistible (Allen Ginsberg had written, "I'm obsessed with Time magazine," but in this he had nothing on Mailer, who, if anything, was even more impressed with its power). Unlike Adele before the stabbing, Jeanne was afraid of Mailer: once in our apartment, when he started to snarl at her, she ran out of the living room, hid under the covers of our bed, and pleaded with us to let her spend the night there.

The marriage to Jeanne lasted just long enough to produce a child, and then came Beverly. Like Adele (but unlike Jeanne, whose attraction lay more in her lineage than in her looks), Beverly was a great beauty, though blond and Southern rather than dark and "Spanish." I was even still around when, after splitting up with Beverly, he married one of his girlfriends, Carole Stevens, to legitimize their child and immediately divorced her to marry Norris Church (to whom, as of 1998, he was still married after about twenty years). By the time Norris entered the picture, however, Mailer and I had already been drifting further and further apart. There were three reasons.

First of all, I could never do with Mailer what I had done with Lillian Hellman, whose writings I had once pretended to like in order to keep our friendship going. He continued to care about my opinion of his work, he insisted that I be candid about it, and he took my criticisms with extraordinarily good grace (if not always in good temper). He also insisted on dragging me to see the shooting of the incredibly amateurish movies he began making in the late 1960s, and he never really tried to bully me into saying anything good about them. He was also considerate and tactful enough not to pressure me into supporting him when he ran quixotically for mayor of New York on a platform that included, among other original ideas, a proposal that all disputes between juvenile delinquents be settled by jousting tournaments in Central Park. For all that, however, not even Mailer was entirely exempt from the law that genuine friendship (or perhaps any kind of friendship at all) is impossible with a writer whose work one does not admire. He behaved very well on this particular score, but the resentment inevitably built up in him even as I, feeling that I had fallen into a false position in my relations with him, grew more and more uncomfortable in his company.

Secondly, my patience with his marital storms had been wearing thinner and thinner. Unlike Jeanne, Beverly was not in the least afraid of Mailer: she taunted him constantly and stood up to him when they fought. Several of these fights were staged in my presence, and they were at least as ugly as the ones I had witnessed with Adele (though, thankfully, they never came to real violence). The worst, featuring Beverly seizing a dish of mushrooms Mailer had cooked and hurling it at him while screaming that he was "evil," erupted during a weekend my wife and I were spending with them in Provincetown. When we left, I told her that I had just about had it with Mailer and his wives.

Then, of course, there was politics. At first Mailer could hardly believe that I was serious when I began showing signs of breaking with the orthodoxies of the Left. How could I possibly mean it when I said that America, far from being the "totalitarian" country he had always believed it to be (and more so than ever since the Vietnam War), was the only hope of defeating the real totalitarianism that was being spread by the power and influence of the Soviet Union? How could I possibly mean it when I said that, far from being in the grip of the "military-industrial complex" he so hated and feared, we were in fact falling dangerously behind in our military strength and needed an arms buildup to counter Soviet power? Mailer loved to argue and had never in all the years I had known him avoided a political fight with me. Yet once, in the 1970s while having dinner in my apartment, he got so upset by my incomprehensible new ideas about politics that he announced he was unable to continue the discussion and actually stood up and left the room so that he could pull himself together before going on. Even then, when he returned, he suggested that we change the subject.

Ultimately, however (as with Diana Trilling), it was *Breaking Ranks* that put paid to our twenty years of friendship. By coincidence, I finished writing that book just as Mailer was also finishing *The Executioner's Song*, and he invited us to dinner with Norris for a kind of celebration in his house in Brooklyn Heights. He told me that he thought I would like *The Executioner's Song*, and I told him that he probably would dislike what I had written about him in *Breaking Ranks*. "Well," he said, "you owe me one," and I laughed and replied, "Yes, I do, but we'll see if you still feel that way when you've read the book." It was, my wife remarked to me afterward, a very pleasant evening, and I agreed—adding, however, that Mailer would never forgive me for *Breaking Ranks*.

In telling the story there of how I came to break with the Left, I had to devote a certain amount of space to the reception of *Making It*, which had been a turning point in my relation to the radicalism of the 1960s. Obviously, the part Mailer had played was an important element in this account, I pulled no punches in laying out the facts and analyzing them. I described carrying the galleys to Provincetown because, having heard so much about the scandal the book had already caused, he was eager to see for himself what the fuss was all about. I then related that when he had read through the galleys, he told me how good a book it was and how unfair and even incomprehensible he found the malicious talk about it which had been going the rounds. I went on to summarize the article he later produced in which the kindest thing he could bring himself to say about *Making It* was that it was "a not altogether compelling memoir" and in which he now blamed the ferocity of the response to it on its own faults and failures, And, finally, I recounted the conversation we had in which his only explanation for what I had every reason to regard as a betrayal by my "old dear great and good friend," as he described himself in the piece, was that he had read the book again and simply changed his mind.

I had eventually come up with a different explanation and I now set it forth in *Breaking Ranks*. I said that the first time Mailer read the book, he had not realized (any more than I myself did until much later) how subversive it was of the radical party line of the day both in its relatively benign view of middle-class American values and, even more seriously, in its denial that the intellectuals—and the educated class in general—represented a truly superior alternative. But then he made a close study of the reaction to *Making It* in preparing for his piece, and it convinced him that the book had overstepped the line into outright apostasy. To defend it was a more dangerous business than he had counted on, and in the face of that danger, I said, he "simply lost his nerve."

True, as the bad boy of American letters—itself an honorific status in the climate of the 1960s—Mailer still held a license to provoke, and he rarely hesitated to use it, even if it sometimes meant making a fool of himself in the eyes of his own admirers. But there were, I said, limits he instinctively knew how to observe; and he observed them. He might excoriate his fellow radicals on a particular matter; he might discomfit them with unexpected sympathies (for right-wing politicians, say, or National Guardsmen on the other side of an antiwar demonstration); he might even on occasion describe himself as (dread word) a conservative. But always in the end came the reassuring gesture, the wink of complicity, the subtle signing of the radical loyalty oath.

Making It (as even Lionel Trilling had complained) contained no such gesture, no such wink, and for Mailer to defend it was, I went on, to risk "his newly solidified popularity." However, to attack me for having been too bold carried the equally unacceptable risk of looking like a coward, and so what he did instead was attack me for ruining what he characterized as "a potentially marvelous book" *not* by having gone too far but by having failed to go far enough in exposing the Left, which he himself acknowledged had become the new establishment.

This, I admitted, was a clever tactic. It enabled him to pretend to the courage of even greater acts of treason against the cultural ruling class than I had been convicted of committing while, by ratifying the sentence it had passed on me, he was actually submitting with the usual wink of complicity to the now frightening power of the new establishment. The very fact that even Mailer, one of the founding fathers of the radical culture, had been cowed into submission (like, *mutatis mutandis,* an old Bolshevik fearful of being denounced as a traitor by his own Stalinist comrades) was a measure of just how powerful that culture had become. It also signified that he "was not perhaps so brave as he thought he was."

I of course recognized that there was nothing—*nothing*—that would offend Norman Mailer more than to be accused of lacking in courage, which was why I was so sure he would never forgive me. And indeed about fifteen years passed before he spoke to me again. Indirectly, through third parties, I received reports of how angry he was, and some years later he tried to turn the tables on me:

> What I find most distressing is that [Podhoretz] never asks himself whether *he* didn't lose his nerve living out on the Left during the 60's. Think of all those ongoing years of alienation, all those simmering fears of the ultimate wrath of the authority.

He, who had once affectionately called me a "hanging judge," now thought that I had become too "judgmental and narrow":

> He was merrier in the old days. He talks too much now of how he took care of me in those old days. I also took care of him. How many people I argued with saying, "No, no, Norman Podhoretz is not really as middle-class as he seems. He's really a great guy, and stand-up." Today he couldn't stand up without having his arms around a missile. He's just as brave and tough as all those other military-industrials.

Well, he too had come a long way from the "old days." Once during the late 1950s, when the two of us were about to go against Arthur Schlesinger, Jr., and Mary McCarthy in a debate about the 1930s, he warned me that he intended to appear on the platform in a work shirt and jeans because he would feel uncomfortable in a suit and tie. But now, if I had wound up with my arms around a missile, he had wound up practically living in a tuxedo. So attired, he would appear at least once a week in the society page photographs, and when I would occasionally bump into him at some party or other, it would invariably be a black-tie event.

By the 1990s he had also mellowed toward me. The first time we met at one of these events, he immediately started chatting. What was I doing here? Did I realize that our hostess was a social lion-hunter and that she was paying me a great compliment by having me over? (This was a mistake she was never to make again.) Clearly, he was feeling out the possibility of a rapprochement, but while polite, I kept my distance from him. And that was how it went whenever I ran into him: he would be cordial and I would be cool, he would wish to talk and I would wish to get away.

Thus, at a small dinner party to which we had both been invited by an unwitting hostess, he tried to engage me in an argument over the Soviet Union, where he had just spent several months researching his book about Lee Harvey Oswald. Now that the Soviet Union had collapsed, was I ready to admit that I had been wrong about its power during the cold war? "In a funny way," I was relieved to see that living in a dinner jacket had not prevented him from sticking faithfully to the left-wing party line, which on this issue held that our victory in the cold war had resulted from the Soviet Union's internal weaknesses and that Ronald Reagan's policies had had nothing to do with it. But I just smiled back, refusing to be provoked, and then I answered with a "Well, maybe" when he parted by saying that he would like to discuss all this with me some day.

By 1998, when he reached his seventy-fifth birthday, Mailer was not exactly falling back on hard times, but neither did he any longer occupy the special position he had enjoyed in the 1960s. His books, while still commanding huge advances, were not enthusiastically received, and neither did they sell very well. True, he remained a highly respected and even revered figure in certain literary circles—to the point where the fiftieth anniversary of the appearance of *The Naked and the Dead* could be celebrated with the publication of a 1,200-page anthology of his work, entitled *The Time of Our Time*, and a huge party to which the tickets were hot. But—to his great chagrin, I feel sure— they were not remotely so hot as the invitations had been to Truman Capote's black-and-white ball in 1965, and the party itself made hardly a splash. Nor did *The Time of Our Time* get much more than a polite nod from reviewers, and from some of them not even that. One of the unkinder cuts that came his way upon the appearance of the anthology was inflicted by a Columbia professor named James Shapiro writing in *The New York Times Book Review*. There was much praise for Mailer's early works there, but it was radically undermined by the attribution of his decline after 1980 to the "deep conventionality" of the views "about the family, homosexuality and, most of all, the relations between the sexes" that lurked "beneath his surface outrageousness." To this professor, in other words, Mailer was still the nice Jewish boy from Brooklyn he had spent his entire life striving not to be.

It was not easy to imagine anything worse from Mailer's point of view, and I felt for him. I also winced to hear him described as "a laughingstock" by a group of much younger literary intellectuals who sneered even at his early work and wondered how I could ever have thought he was "a major novelist in the making." I had trouble defending myself against this challenge, given that I had never reread the books in which I had found so much promise when Mailer and I were both young (because I did not have the heart to look at them in the light of what came after both for him and for me).

Considering how things were going with his literary career, I suspected that Mailer might again have been able to use the kind of foul-weather friend I had once been to him. This suspicion was intensified when, shortly before the big party, he telephoned me for the first time in about twenty years. Hearing from him was surprising enough, but the reason for the call was even more surprising. It seemed that one of Mailer's sons, whose mother had been a Gentile and who therefore was not Jewish in the eyes of rabbinic law, had fallen in love with an Orthodox Jewish woman and wanted to convert. Could I recommend a suitable rabbi? I could and I did. But I also expressed my astonishment and offered my mock condolences at this unexpected turn of events. It reminded me, I told Mailer, of how a direct descendant of Trotsky had wound up living in Israel as the kind of extremist Orthodox Jew known as a *haredi*, and I imagined that he himself was no less distressed than the old anti-Zionist revolutionary would surely have been. No, Mailer said, for him it was not like that at all. He did not in the least mind or object to what his son was doing. Indeed, as the father of nine children, he found it fascinating to watch them go their separate and different ways. "Well," I responded, thinking of his own lifelong flight from Judaism and Jewishness, "my own take on this, to quote from a different part of the book you recently tried to rewrite, is that 'God is not mocked.'" There was a pause. "Where did I say that?" he asked. "*You* didn't," I laughed, "the New Testament did," and he laughed back.

A few days later, I received an invitation to the forthcoming party, and after a long debate with myself I decided not to go. If it was true that Mailer again needed me as a foul-weather friend, there was not the slightest possibility that I could satisfy that need. In our phone conversation, I had felt bound to say, exactly as I had done so many years earlier at his house when *Breaking Ranks* was on the verge of being published, that I had just written something about him (meaning this chapter) that he would not like. Back then he had replied, "Well, you owe me one," and on this occasion his response was that he would not of course have expected anything else from me at this stage of our lives. Nor, he went on pleasantly, would it bother him, so long as it was written "with a clean heart." Yet even having been granted this preemptive pardon (and even assuming that he would stick to it, which he had of course failed to do in the analogous case of *Breaking Ranks*), I had no wish to put myself in the false position of participating in the celebration of a career that had so bitterly disappointed my literary expectations. Besides, having spent the last thirty years and more trying to make up for and undo the damage I did in cooperation with Mailer and so many other of my ex-friends, both living and dead, I simply could see no way back to him, or to them, ever again.

REQUIEM FOR A
LOST WORLD

AND YET . . . AND YET, I CANNOT TELL A LIE: AS I admitted at the outset, and as I am constrained to confess again in approaching the end of this story with even greater feelings of ambivalence than I had when I started it, I regret the loss of the literary-intellectual world in which I used to live.

Today *Partisan Review* and *Commentary* still exist, but they no longer constitute an intellectual center in the way they once did. In the early 1960s, *The New York Review of Books* was founded and looked for a while as though it might evolve into just such a center, but it did just the opposite. It turned itself not into a venue of the most serious intellectual activity going on around it but, rather, into a spokesman for the radical movement of the 1960s. It thereby helped drive some of us into deeper and deeper opposition. Of course, other forces already at work in American culture were eroding the bonds that had kept the Family together. The most important of these was the opening up of new and wider audiences for its writings, which (as I described the process in the introduction) made the Family's members less and less dependent on one another to get published, to get read, to get understood, to get worthy opponents on whom to exercise their polemical talents. *The New York Review* did not by itself or all alone create the splits in the political sphere that I have been talking about throughout this book, but it did make a very large contribution to them; and this, in combination with the factors that were steadily dissolving the Family's cultural ties, gradually finished it off as an intellectual community.

Yet not only did *The New York Review* fail to create a new intellectual community to take the place of the one it had helped to destroy; it also never managed to create a new community in the same social sense as the older magazines had once done. Conceivably, there are lively parties today to which I am not invited that are similar to the ones I used to go to and give. At the old Family parties the guests vied with one another in making brilliant arguments for this and against that (while also managing to indulge freely in their second-greatest passion by gossiping with the wittiest possible malice about anyone who had the misfortune not to be present or to be out of earshot in another part of the room). But if similar parties are being held today, I think rumors of them would have reached me, and so I can only conclude that they are as much a thing of the past as the intellectual life out of which they originally emerged.

In spite of everything that I have said against my ex-friends here, I believe that the absence today of a community like the Family constitutes a great loss for our culture. We now have "policy wonks" by the thousand, but we have only a handful of thinkers who are willing and able to examine and critically debate either the assumptions these legislatively oriented minds do not even realize they are making or the intellectual foundations on which they stand. (The best thing John Maynard Keynes ever said was, "Practical men, who believe themselves to be quite exempt from any intellectual influences, are usually the slaves of some defunct economist.") True, this great imbalance is powerfully reminiscent of the situation that first brought the Family into being. But conditions today are so different in other respects that no such community as was born out of the cultural and political circumstances of the past has been able to reconstitute itself in New York, or anywhere else. The result is a diminution in the serious discussion of serious ideas.

I recognize that many people may think that the discussions

which went on within the Family were not so much serious as aridly sectarian. But as I hope I have demonstrated by now, nothing could be further from the truth. To the examples I have already given, I want to add a few more by way of trying to summarize what followed in the larger world from the issues that the Family spent so much time and energy raising, exploring, and fighting over almost literally to the death. In the course of doing this, I also want to venture an assessment of how well or badly the Family came out of its struggles over these issues.

For a start, it turned out to matter enormously whether or not the opposition to Stalinism shared by everyone in the Family (though not, of course, by all the ex-friends on whom I have concentrated in this book) necessarily entailed support of the American side in the cold war. On this issue (at least from the late 1930s until the anti-Vietnam movement heated up after 1965, at which point everything began to change), the Family for the most part covered itself with honor. In rallying to the cause of the West in the years immediately following World War II (even Dwight Macdonald did so at first), it used its special ideological skills—skills not all that common in the political culture of pragmatic America—to build the powerful moral and political case for our side in the cold war that grew out of its equally special understanding of the nature of totalitarianism.

This was a perspective that, on the one side, went beyond the narrowly political arguments of realpolitik and the dry considerations of national interest invoked by official Washington and that, on the other side, was more persuasive than the cruder and often ill-informed anti-Communism of the Right. As time wore on, it gradually filtered down and spread. In my opinion, if this had not happened, the long struggle to defeat Communist totalitarianism, with the sacrifices in blood and treasure it entailed, would not have enlisted as much popular support as it did. I have been accused in the past of making exaggerated claims in suggesting that the election of a strong proponent of the same view like Ronald Reagan would not have been possible if that view had not been given new life in the post-Vietnam years by the neoconservatives who came out of the Family. But I am more than ever convinced that this is true.

To repeat what I said in talking about Diana Trilling at the end of her life, it is a great irony that even those few of my ex-friends who were still strongly anti-Communist (especially Diana herself) should have been so hostile to the very president whose election and whose policies in office owed so much to the ideas that they themselves in their turn had done so much to nurture. In this connection, it is instructive to remind ourselves that Reagan—who was entirely at one with the pre-Vietnam Family in stressing the moral aspects of the cold war over considerations of realpolitik, and who as president was willing to suffer the opprobrium that he knew would follow his denunciation of the Soviet empire as "evil"—began his political life on the Left. In fact, it was as a result of his struggle with the Communists in the Screen Actors Guild, of which he became president long before becoming president of the United States, that he began moving to the Right. This meant that he differed in several crucial respects from many of the new political friends and allies he encountered there.

It went without saying that Reagan's new friends on the Old Right were all anti-Communists. Yet, as Richard Gid Powers demonstrates in *Not Without Honor*, his richly detailed and nuanced history of American anti-Communism, the Old Right tended to worry less about aggression from outside than about the threat of internal subversion. And in tracking down the sources of that threat, they were not always able to tell the difference between a liberal, a socialist, and a Communist. (Admittedly, they were aided and abetted in their confusion when the Communists represented themselves as "liberals in a hurry" or when certain self-described liberals always seemed to act as apologists for the Communists or when other self-described liberals kept pushing social and economic policies which looked pretty much like socialism to the naked eye.) Still less were they able to distinguish among the more arcane factions of the radical Left.*

There was also a problem with the business community and the

---

*The classic example of that confusion is the cop in the joke who when told by someone whose head he is about to smash with his nightstick in breaking up a Communist rally, "But officer, I'm an *anti*-Communist" responds by yelling, "I don't care what kind of Communist you are," and then flails away with a will.

"country-club Republicans" in particular. They made all the right (in both senses from a conservative point of view) noises about taxes and government regulation. Moreover, they could usually be counted upon to support conservative politicians who deployed anti-Communist rhetoric over those of their rivals who thought that such rhetoric was probably more dangerous than Communism itself. Yet few of these country-club Republicans had ever actually spoken to a Communist or read any Communist literature. Some of them seemed to conceive of the Soviet Union as one huge regulatory agency, a sort of gigantic Federal Trade Commission armed with nuclear weapons (which was about as close as they could come to an image of absolute evil).

Others among these country club Republicans, American to the core, were so temperamentally remote from and unfamiliar with the phenomenon of ideological fervor that they thought the Soviets could in effect be bribed out of Communism by the right business deals. This was why they warmly endorsed the policy of détente with the Soviet Union and the opening to Communist China under Richard Nixon and Gerald Ford in the 1960s and 1970s (just as they would go on in the 1990s to lobby against using China's human rights violations as a reason for setting any restrictions on trade with that country). It was also why, during Reagan's first term, the bankers were so eager to help the Communist regime in Poland out of its economic crisis by rolling over the loans which had come due and in this way simultaneously help it to overcome the challenge then being posed by Solidarity. In the pungent observation of the columnist George Will, they loved commerce more than they loathed Communism.

Not Reagan. True, being a politician, he was less than fully consistent.* On one day he could sound like the Hannah Arendt of *The Origins of Totalitarianism* in denouncing the Soviet empire as evil, and on the

---

*There is a joke that applies here as well, this one a Jewish joke. A man, having grown rich, buys a big yacht and dresses himself up as its captain. When his mother asks him why he is out in such a uniform, he says, "Because, Mama, I'm a captain now," to which she replies, "Well, by you you're a captain, but by me you're a captain, but by a captain you're no captain." Compared with most politicians, very few of whom believe in anything very strongly, Reagan was a principled ideologue, but to an ideologue he was no ideologue.

next he could accept a policy toward Poland designed by the bankers to hold that empire together. But the difference between Reagan and the bankers was that he had spent too many years on the Left to entertain the illusions about the situation that they did when, out of strictly political considerations, he threw them this—to him—unsavory bone. He himself made the same point to an adviser who told him during his second term that some people thought he was becoming too trusting of Mikhail Gorbachev. (I was among these people, as I made abundantly clear in an article, called "The Reagan Road to Détente," that I wrote for *Foreign Affairs* in 1985, just as his second term was beginning.) "Oh, don't worry about that," Reagan replied. "I still have the scars on my back that I got from fighting the Communists back in Hollywood."

It is fascinating to see how close this language was to words that, according to a (possibly apocryphal) story I heard while living in England, had been used in 1945 by the British foreign secretary Ernest Bevin. Like Reagan, Bevin was a former trade union leader, and like Reagan in Hollywood, he had fought the Communists for control in the British labor movement. Almost immediately upon being appointed foreign secretary by the newly elected prime minister, Clement Attlee, Bevin accompanied his boss to the summit conference with Stalin at Potsdam. Upon returning, the inexperienced foreign minister was asked whether he had found it difficult to negotiate with the Soviet delegation. "No," answered Bevin, "I know those Russians; they're just like the Communists."

It it also interesting to note that early in his first term Reagan said much the same thing me about his understanding of Communism as he would say in his second to the adviser who worried about his softness toward Gorbachev. In 1982, provoked by his failure to hang tough over Poland, and by a few other incidents that also suggested he was not living up to his anti-Communist convictions, I published a long article in the *New York Times Magazine* to which the editors gave the ungainly but accurate title "The Neo-Conservative Anguish Over Reagan's Foreign Policy." Though I had met him a few times, and though he had written a blurb for my little book *The Present Danger* just before becoming president, I was still taken aback when Reagan telephoned a few days after my *Times* article appeared to defend himself against it. Naturally, I was also flattered. But my mind was by no means set at ease when he told me that the Soviets were in such terrible economic straits that many of them were reduced to eating dog food and when he then hinted that he might be able to defeat them through economic pressures alone (that is, with precisely the weapon which his failure to use in Poland had riled me in the first place).

In all fairness, however, I have to add that the military buildup on which he was already embarked, and later his campaign to develop an antimissile system, both of which I unreservedly backed, turned out to be the functional equivalent of economic pressure in the sense that trying to match him put an intolerable strain on Soviet resources. I do not agree with those who believe that this was the whole story—that is, that Reagan in effect bankrupted the Soviets into submission. But I cannot deny that this was one of the key elements of his success.

Far more important, though, was his firmness in holding out against those of his own advisers who urged him to cut back on military spending (in order to keep the deficit under control). Just as he resisted these pressures from the inside, so too did he refuse to yield to others coming from the outside. In particular, he would not bow to the demands of the movement to "freeze" the number of nuclear weapons at their present level even when it seemed to be sweeping the country. Equally or perhaps more important was his decision to go ahead with the deployment of intermediate-range missiles in Europe. Wisely, as I believed, this move had been planned even before Reagan's election to counter what the Soviets had done on their side of the line with the same category of missiles in the 1970s (and with the additional purpose—this one unwise in my judgment—of creating "bargaining chips" for future arms-control negotiations).

As the time drew near for deployment, rallies involving many millions of protesters were held everywhere to prevent it from going forward whereas supporting voices were few and far between. So few and far between were they that when a television debate on the issue was scheduled in The Hague to coincide with one such demonstration, the producers were evidently unable to find any nongovernmental official in the whole of Europe who was willing to argue on the air for deployment. Desperate—and having read *The Present Danger*, whose German and French editions had been festooned with Reagan's blurb and advertised as his "bedside book"—the producer called me in New York and offered to fly me over on the Concorde that very day if I would agree to appear on the program. Reluctantly (because, frankly, I was afraid that I might let the side down by not holding up my end sufficiently well) I accepted.

The debate went on for about five (or was it six?) hours, and just as I had expected, it turned out to be me against representatives of five European countries. What made things even more difficult for me was the staging of the broadcast in a room with a glass wall overlooking the square toward which more than a million people from all over Europe kept converging all day. As far as the eye could see, the streets were packed solid with people (many of them young women with babies in their arms), and they were yelling and singing and chanting and waving signs. Never have I felt—or, rather, actually been—so alone and isolated. Even though I knew it to be untrue, my eyes and ears told me that not a single other person in the world was in favor of the policy I was doing my best to defend. But standing one's ground in a debate was not the same thing as doing so in action. And I must confess that I began wondering whether, under the kind of circumstances I was witnessing at first hand, Reagan would actually have the stomach to go ahead with deployment.

But he did. And when he did, he not only compensated for his weak response to the Polish crisis but showed once again how consequential were the kinds of arguments the Family had been having for so long over what foreign policies should follow from opposition to Communist totalitarianism.

There was another Family argument—this one impinging on the realm of domestic rather than foreign affairs—that sometimes seemed sectarian and arid but that also turned out to matter enormously in the world out there and in the lives of countless people who had never even heard of it and would almost certainly have found it incomprehensible if they had. It was an argument over the question of whether

Stalinism represented a betrayal of the socialist dreams of the Russian Revolution or their logical fulfillment.

On this point the Family (myself included for a while, I fear) did not on the whole cover itself with honor. Here, its ideological skills were mainly deployed in defending the viability and desirability of socialism in one form or another. Unable to overcome its ancestral antipathy to capitalism, the Family helped keep the false promises of socialism alive, and out of this, as I eventually came to see, emerged many of the social programs that did more harm to the poor (and to the country as a whole) than good.

It was only with the unexpected appearance in the mid-1960s of the fallen-away neoconservative branch of the Family that a new intellectual case was gradually developed in favor of capitalism as a species of freedom in itself and as the necessary condition for both the creation and the wider distribution of wealth. (In nothing were the neoconservatives so heretical with respect to Family tradition as in this.) Of course, such a case had long since already been made by Friedrich Hayek and Milton Friedman, among others. But the recent defectors from socialism who became "the new defenders of capitalism" (as I called them in an article I wrote under that title for the *Harvard Business Review*) gave a much-needed boost to arguments that had by then been ignored or forgotten. In the process they also contributed to a revival of interest in the works of Hayek and Friedman.

Obviously, the issue mattered even more to the countries living under Communism than it did to the United States or the West generally. Again, I could see this with my own eyes and hear it with my own ears. During my trip to Prague in 1988 to meet with Vaclav Havel and other dissidents, I discovered that some of them were secretly translating Hayek and Friedman and circulating them in *samizdat*. They were also doing the same with those new defenders of capitalism about whom I myself had written and many of whose articles I was publishing in *Commentary*—Irving Kristol, Michael Novak, Peter Berger, William Barrett, and others.

Even in the Soviet Union, the heart of darkness itself, the same issue was burning bright, though there it was casting shadows as well as light. This I also discovered at first hand when at the height of Gorbachev's *glasnost* policy a group of which I was a member went to Moscow at the invitation of his government to deliver a series of lectures to various gatherings of academics and intellectuals. When, in the first two of the three lectures I gave, I declared that Stalin bore complete responsibility for the outbreak of the cold war, I was enthusiastically applauded. The applause was just as loud when I argued that the totalitarian system he had built was the mirror image of the one built by Hitler in Germany.* But when, speaking at the University of Moscow, I said in the third lecture that I was fully in accord with Aleksandr Solzhenitsyn's belief that Stalin, in doing these things, was being true to the logic of Lenin's principles and programs, there was very little applause and the questions from the floor were mostly angry.

For at that point in the evolution of their thinking, most (though not all) Soviet intellectuals, together with Gorbachev himself, were still trying desperately to hold on to the idea that there was a noble Communist tradition inaugurated and represented by Lenin to which they could find their way back. In the end, when the system collapsed, however, statues of Lenin were hauled down from their pedestals throughout the Soviet empire and smashed to bits, and in Russia the city of Leningrad was given back its old name of St. Petersburg.

If the Family (returning now to it) did not cover itself with honor on the issue of capitalism versus socialism, neither did it exactly come out with laurels in the fight over the counterculture. Just as it was unable to see beyond its archaic hostility to capitalism, so it seemed incapable of transcending its correlative hatred of the bourgeoisie or of

---

*Long, scrupulously accurate, and implicitly approving reports on these lectures appeared in all the major Soviet papers. The authors of these reports had to be careful even in the period of *glasnost,* and so they protected themselves by announcing at the beginning that an American intellectual known for his fanatical hostility to the Soviet Union was speaking in Moscow and that this presented a good opportunity for them to acquaint their readers with the thinking of their worst enemies in the West. There were also reports in *The New York Times* and *The Washington Post,* but they were as short and hostile as those in *Pravda, Izvestia,* and other Soviet newspapers were long and friendly. As I remarked to David Remnick, then the *Post* correspondent in Moscow, who would have thought we would live to see the day when an American anti-Communist like me would be treated better by the Soviet press than by the American?

perceiving the connection between middle-class values and the health and cohesion of a democratic society.

Even in the arts—again with a few exceptions, the most energetic being Hilton Kramer—the Family, which had been the great proponent of the modernist tradition and the great enemy of kitsch, offered precious little resistance to the erasure by the counterculture of the 1960s of any and all distinctions between high and low. Worse yet, some found highly sophisticated arguments to justify this erasure and even stood by while the idea was enshrined in the universities that no real difference in quality existed between Shakespeare and Jackie Collins. Here, too, the job of contending with a bizarre development that violated everything the Family had once stood for had to await the rise of the neoconservatives, who in this area (if not on the issues of capitalism and middle-class values) were the true heirs of the original Family tradition.

The record, in short, is decidedly mixed. On balance, however, I remain convinced that it is good for a country's culture to have an intellectual community like the Family, even if it promotes bad ideas as often as it does good ones. Without such a community, we lack a center around which we can gather and in which, whether through collaboration or competition, agreement or dissension, we can deepen and refine our thinking.

But the disappearance of such an intellectual community is not only a loss to our culture; it is a great loss to me personally as well. Which is to say that I miss my ex-friends, the dead as well as the living. Even the passing of Allen Ginsberg, who was never a friend in the way the others were, has left a gap: who else will ever contend so passionately with me in his fantasies and visions? Conversely, the death of Lionel Trilling, who never really became an ex-friend, as Diana did in her widowhood, has left me bereft of intimate personal contact with a supremely intelligent interlocutor and an elder who, even when things were at their worst between us, always cared about me, as I never ceased caring about him. At moments I miss Diana too, impossible though she made it for me in the last years of her life to maintain any sort of relationship with her. She was a great pain in the neck even when we were friends, but at the same time, she was so quirky in her take on things that being involved with her invariably made life more complicated and therefore more interesting. I miss Lillian Hellman, an incomparable playmate with whom I had so much fun—more perhaps than I had with any of my other ex-friends—that I was able for what now seems an amazingly long time to overlook the flaws in her writing and to forget about the evils of her politics. I miss Hannah Arendt, whose great brilliance I came less and less to value but breaking with whom diminished the amount of warmth and vitality and mother wit that once surrounded me whenever I was in her company (even if her warmth toward me in particular may have been an act). And I miss Norman Mailer, the only one of the ex-friends on whom I have concentrated in this book who is still with us (and may he, in the words of the old Jewish blessing, live to be 120). As a friend he took up so much space in my life and was so insistently and relentlessly demanding a presence that his departure created a vast vacuum which has never been filled.

With all these people, as well as the other ex-friends whose names I have dropped in this book and many who have gone unmentioned (most of them part of the Family but some only tangentially, if at all, related to it), I shared in some of the best and most scintillating talk I have ever had with anyone at any time or anywhere. I do not wish to exaggerate. I have been fortunate enough to meet people who were not members of the Family in any sense and with whom I have had equally scintillating conversations, people who, like Falstaff, were not only witty in themselves but the cause that wit was in other men.

Still, what made the Family special in general was the high concentration it contained of writers and intellectuals who not only had superior minds (even, to say it once more, but now for the last time, if they too often put them to bad use) but whose major passion in life was ideas and the arts, and who could get just as wrought up in an argument over the work of a novelist or painter as they could about political ideologies. And what made the Family special for me in particular was the regular contact I had with it.

From these contacts I learned a lot, some of which I had to spend years of effort unlearning, or (where Hannah Arendt's *The Origins of Totalitarianism* and the work of Lionel Trilling in general were concerned) relearning. Which means that even as ex-friends they retained an important place in my consciousness. Indeed, if as the 1960s wore on they had not begun saying and doing things that I found, at first to my own surprise, repugnant and dangerous, I might never have been forced into discovering what in the depths of my soul I really believed, and I might have been struck forever dumb by the falsity of my own position.

For saving me from this fate, and for refreshing my sense of what I am still fighting against whenever I read or think about them, I owe my ex-friends a perverse debt. I was who I was in some part because of my friendship with them, and I am who I am in larger part because we ceased being friends. In all truth, I much prefer who I am to who I was. Nevertheless, I cannot help feeling nostalgic about the "old days" when I was, in Norman Mailer's authoritative estimation, so much "merrier" than I am now, and I cannot help missing the people I admired, liked, enjoyed, and even (in a few cases) loved when I was young and they, though not so young, were all at their best and still in their prime.

ACKNOWLEDGMENTS

A briefer and somewhat different version of Chapter One originally appeared in *Commentary* under the title "My War with Allen Ginsberg." All the rest is new, though a few bits and pieces were adapted from some of my previously published writings.

I also happily welcome this opportunity to acknowledge with the deepest gratitude the support I have received from the Lynde and Harry Bradley Foundation, the Carthage Foundation, and the John M. Olin Foundation. It is through their great generosity that—since retiring as editor-in-chief of *Commentary*—I have found a perch as a senior fellow at the Hudson Institute and have thereby also been provided with the time and the resources I needed to write this book. Among those resources has been the complete freedom to say whatever I wished to say in the way I wished to say it, which of course means that I alone am responsible for the views expressed in this book—views that may or may not be shared or endorsed by the Hudson Institute or by any of the foundations listed above.

INDEX